# The Economics of Leisure and Sport

Recent years have seen an unprecedented growth in demand for and supply of leisure goods and services in the UK and worldwide. This trend has given rise to an increase in courses which focus on the administrative and scientific sides of leisure.

This text provides an excellent insight into the key principles of economic analysis. Using a clearly laid out step-by-step approach, central points of economic theory and analysis are identified and examined using examples from the sport and leisure industries. Key topics include demand and supply, elasticity and pricing, production and costs, business objectives, and privatisation issues within the leisure industry. The final chapter explores the degree to which leisure can be influenced by changes in government policy.

Providing a useful insight into a rapidly growing field, *The Economics of Leisure and Sport* will be excellent for students of leisure and recreation at an introductory level. The provision of 'questions for discussion' at the end of each chapter makes this book an ideal resource, and a glossary of economics terms will aid learning.

**Andrew Cooke** is Senior Lecturer in Economics at Nottingham Trent University.

# The Economics of Leisure and Sport

Andrew Cooke

INTERNATIONAL THOMSON BUSINESS PRESS
I ⓣ P An International Thomson Publishing Company

London • Bonn • Boston • Johannesburg • Madrid • Melbourne • Mexico City • New York • Paris
Singapore • Tokyo • Toronto • Albany, NY • Belmont, CA • Cincinnati, OH • Detroit, MI

**The Economics of Leisure and Sport**

**Copyright ©1994 Andrew Cooke**

I(T)P · A division of International Thomson Publishing Inc.
The ITP logo is a trademark under licence

*British Library Cataloguing-in-Publication Data*
A catalogue record for this book is available from the British Library

**First published by Routledge 1994**
**Simultaneously published in the USA and Canada by Routledge**
**Reprinted by International Thomson Business Press 1996 and 1999**

Typeset in Times by Solidus (Bristol) Ltd
Printed in the Croatia by Zrinski d.d.

**ISBN 1-86152-499-4**

International Thomson Business Press
Berkshire House
168–173 High Holborn
London WC1V 7AA
UK

http://www.thomson.com/itbp.html

*To Vivien and Rebecca*

# Contents

# Figures

# Tables

# Preface

Since the mid 1960s, there has been an unprecedented increase in the demand for and supply of leisure goods and services within the UK. Not surprisingly, this growth has been the catalyst for greater academic interest to be shown in all leisure-related subjects ranging from the applied sciences through to the social sciences. There are now many courses which can be taken by students interested in studying leisure and sport as an academic discipline, usually emphasising its scientific and administrative background. Although many such courses include at least one economics-based module, many students have had no previous exposure to the subject. The aim of this text is to provide a sympathetic insight into the key principles of economic analysis using relevant examples taken from the leisure industry.

Speaking generally, there are two approaches which can be taken when writing such a book. The first is to select a number of relevant topics from the leisure industry and to wrap appropriate economics around each one. The main problem with this approach is that many readers are not given sufficient exposure to the economics *per se* thereby making it unlikely that they would be able to apply key principles to different situations. Given the constraints of many degree programmes, not all students will have the time or opportunity to consult more general texts in order to supplement the deficiencies in their knowledge and understanding of the subject. This text aims to circumvent this problem through adopting an alternative approach. Specifically, it uses economics as its starting point and uses examples from the leisure industry as a means of illustrating each concept. Using this approach, students should not only be able to comprehend the principles which underpin the economist's approach but also gain an insight into some of the main issues which are of interest to economists interested in the leisure industry. Much of the analysis is microeconomic in flavour, in other words, concerned with the analysis of individuals, households and firms in terms of their desire to demand and supply leisure-related goods and services. However, space is also set aside to consider leisure in its wider context, as an industry affected by changes in government policy and international performance.

Given the anticipation that most readers will be new to the subject of economics, Chapter 1 will be used to lay down the main parameters as to what distinguishes economics from other academic disciplines and hence the approach economists use when applying their subject to the analysis of everyday situations. Chapter 1 is also used as a focal point for an overview of the main sources of data which economists use to analyse the leisure sector. Indeed, it is these sources which are used in many of the examples used in subsequent chapters.

Chapter 2 is written from the point of view of the individual as a consumer of leisure and highlights the approaches economists use to gain an insight into demand. This provides a framework for the analysis contained in Chapter 3 which looks at the problems economists face when attemping to estimate demand empirically and how the demands of consumers interact with the desires of suppliers to form a market for leisure goods and services. Within these two chapters consideration will be given, amongst other things, to the analysis of demand for leisure time, the valuation of unpriced leisure activities, such as countryside recreation, and the characteristics of the market for golf facilities.

The setting for Chapter 4 is the possibility that unregulated markets may generate undesirable outcomes with respect to the price that is charged or the quantities which are demanded and supplied. Sport and leisure is a classic area where governments at national and local level have seen the need to intervene in the market so as to encourage the consumption of leisure and the supply of appropriate facilities. In this respect, the analysis considers the economic rationale for the rapid growth in the construction of municipal leisure centres, public subsidy of the arts and the encouragement given by goverment to private sector sponsors of sport, leisure and the arts. However, this has not been the only response to what economists term 'market failure'. Chapter 4 also considers the reasons for the emergence of a voluntary leisure sector alongside private and public suppliers.

The analysis contained in Chapter 5 provides a link between the theory of Chapters 2 and 3 and economists' concerns about market failure identified in Chapter 4. In particular, it considers how economists measure the responsiveness of demand and supply to changes in any of the key variables which can affect it. Particular emphasis is given to why it may be advantageous for suppliers to charge different consumers different prices for what is essentially the same product. The analysis will focus upon the pricing policies used at sports centres in order to encourage visitors to use the facilities which are available.

Chapters 6 and 7, although remaining microeconomic in flavour, focus upon the firm as a supplier of goods and services. In Chapter 6, emphasis is given to how economists analayse the costs incurred by firms when they supply goods and services to the market. It will be seen that there is a clear distinction between costs in the short run and costs in the long run. Two differing examples will be used during the analysis. First, whether it is possible to define the relationship between the inputs and outputs of cricket teams and, second, the relationship between 'output' and average cost in the case of leisure centres. Chapter 7 on the other hand considers the objectives which owners and managers may employ with respect to the day-to-day running of firms. Traditionally, economics has assumed that the primary objective is to maximise profit. However it will be seen that this need not be the case and that researchers inside and outside the leisure sector have encountered examples where profit maximisation is not necessarily the norm.

The final chapter is organised to illustrate the degree to which leisure can be influenced by changes in government policy. In particular, it seeks to provide students with an insight into the processes which have prompted the present government's economic strategy, with its emphasis upon the control of inflation and public spending and the reduction of state intervention in markets. This discussion will provide a backdrop for a discussion of the implications of compulsory competitve tendering as it affects the provision of public sector leisure.

To assist students with their understanding of the subject, each chapter concludes with two questions which can form the basis of a class discussion or written essay work. Furthermore, there is a glossary which highlights some of the most important terms students are likely to encounter while studying economics.

# Acknowledgements

The decision to write a book condemns authors to undergo long periods of frustration, punctuated by moments of inspiration. Thus, few books are completed without the help and support of others. This exercise has been no exception and I am indebted to my family, my friends and my colleagues at work, without whom my sanity would have been long gone. In particular, I should like to thank my wife and daughter who have put up with my long working hours, my parents, Barry Harrison for his unerring encouragement (and endless supply of terrible jokes), and everyone with whom I have lifted a glass of ale during an evening. It would be wrong of me to let this moment pass without registering my gratitude to Brian Elgie who inspired me to pick up my first economics book.

At this point it is also customary to offer thanks to the organisations which have allowed the author to reproduce tables in whole or part form which provide a statistical insight into the leisure industry. The following tables are Crown Copyright and are reproduced with permission from the Controller of Her Majesty's Stationery Office: 1.7, 2.1, 2.2, 2.3, 4.2, 8.1. Other statistical tables, located in Chapter 1, are reproduced with permission from the Sports Council/Henley Centre for Forecasting: 1.2, 1.3, 1.4 and 1.5.

# Chapter 1

# Economics and the leisure environment

## WHAT IS ECONOMICS?

Whenever we watch the television or pick up a newspaper, we are made aware of economic change which is affecting our daily lives. However, if asked in the street as part of an interview or survey, few people would be able to explain lucidly what economics actually *is*. This should be of no surprise. Even practitioners of the subject are yet to identify a definition to which they would all subscribe. Most explanations highlight the fundamental problem for economists in terms of *scarcity and choice*. That is, while almost all resources are scarce, human desires are infinite and therefore force people to make choices. Such decisions confront us every day of our lives, ranging from how much income to spend on individual goods and services to how much time to allocate between different activities inside and outside the workplace.

Economics usually assumes that such choices are made in a *rational* way. This means that faced with an array of affordable alternatives, an individual will buy the combination of goods and services which offers greater potential benefit than any alternative combination. People on low incomes, such as many pensioners, are forced to prioritise their spending towards the basic necessities of life: food, shelter, clothing and warmth. In contrast, individuals with relatively large budgets are more likely to be able to satisfy these basic requirements for survival and also have money left over to finance non-essential expenditure as well, for example on leisure activities. This scarcity and choice problem is not confined to individuals and households. They confront economic agents at every level of the economy. Firms have to allocate their resources between different departments and different projects while at a more aggregated level governments have to make choices between spending their revenue on a whole range of goods and services ranging from hospitals and roads through to law and order, social security and military equipment. Thus, whether we are analysing a single individual, a multinational company or a national government, the problem of resource allocation is a fundamental one.

Conventionally, economic issues are addressed under two basic headings, *microeconomics* and *macroeconomics* and as these names suggest, much rests upon the level of aggregation of the analysis. Microeconomics is concerned with economic issues affecting individual decision-making units, for example the factors influencing consumption and the labour supply decisions of individual persons or households. Microeconomics is also concerned with the rationale underlying choices made by firms such as how much output to produce, what means of production to use, and how much to invest in advertising and research and development. In contrast, macroeconomics relates to broader aggregates, relating to economic activity within a whole country, for example changes in the money supply, total consumer expenditure, the balance of payments and the level of unemployment. The scope of this book falls predominantly under the heading of microeconomics, focusing upon the analysis of individuals as consumers of sport and leisure and firms as producers of sport and leisure commodities. However, this does not mean that macroeconomic issues will be ignored. Many decisions made by consumers and firms are in response to changes in the economic environment within which they exist. For example, a downswing in world economic activity may increase unemployment and therefore generate more time for affected people to enjoy leisure activities. At the same time however, unemployment will reduce the financial resources these consumers have to exploit the leisure time they now have available. In other words, microeconomics and macroeconomics are inextricably linked.

## THE APPLICATION OF ECONOMICS TO THE REAL WORLD

One of the objectives of a science, whether a natural science such as physics or a social science such as economics, is to systematically observe and identify the phenomena which determine the relationship between variables influencing everyday events. Thus for economists, the intended result of this process is to establish a body of principles which offer an insight into the behaviour of economic agents or into how an economy operates in the way it does. Based upon this knowledge, it should then be possible to predict how an economy might react to a change in its circumstances.

The main problem for the economist is that it is not possible to test a hypothesis under controlled laboratory conditions. Although it is possible to collect data relating to a whole range of economic phenomena, each will be influenced by factors which are outside the control of the observer. Indeed, in extreme circumstances, it may be found that a particular hypothesis may be rejected using survey evidence from one data set yet accepted by another researcher conducting a separate survey. Other problems arise because the data are inaccurate, even within official publications. For example, estimates of a country's balance of payments are calculated from information supplied by every importer and exporter. However, it may be of advantage to the firms involved to conceal some of their transactions so as to avoid paying tax. Thus, even the information used to derive the national accounts of a country will not be completely accurate.

Nevertheless, despite the limitations which may be inherent in a data set, economists use a scientific approach to test their theories. Often, this will involve the building of a *model* which sets out a set of assumptions and the relationship between the variables believed to be influencing a particular event. The reliability of the model can then be tested by comparing its predicted outcome against what actually happens in the real world. Sometimes, a model may only include the relationship between a small number of variables. However, many economic relationships are complex, generating a need for the economist to try and identify the variables deemed to be most important and to omit the rest. Nevertheless, economic models can be large: the model used by the Treasury for its macroeconomic forecasts contains over 700 equations and 1275 variables!

Within economics, the distinction is often made between *positive* and *normative* statements. Positive statements relate to 'what was', 'what is' or 'what will be'. For example, the statement 'an increase in income will lead to an increase in consumer spending on leisure goods' is a positive statement. Such statements can be tested using appropriate data relating to income and consumer expenditure. In contrast, normative statements cannot be tested in this way. Instead, they are concerned with 'what ought to be' and therefore can be the subject of disagreement. Thus, a normative statement might be 'firms should require their employees undertake an hour's exercise each day'. Although it is possible to set up some sort of scientific experiment to establish the benefits to the firm of having a fitter workforce (for example increased output, less time lost due to illness, etc.), the idea of forcing employees to undertake a programme of exercise would generate widespread disagreement.

## ECONOMICS AND THE LEISURE INDUSTRY

For the economist, the leisure industry provides an unbounded source of examples. This reflects the fact that everyone, almost without exception, engages in some sort of leisure activity, even if it only amounts to reading a newspaper, going for a drink at a local pub or watching the television at home. Leisure pursuits can be enjoyed at all ages, across all income bands and all social groups and therefore their diversity reflects the fact that society has a complex set of tastes and preferences which themselves change over a lifetime. However, the growth and development of the post-war leisure industry could not have taken place without four interlinked trends. First, the general growth in the real income available for the consumption of leisure goods. In particular, this has enabled young adults to emerge as a distinctive market for leisure commodities. Directly linked to this rise in income has been the growth in the number of private vehicles on the road and hence the increase in mobility of large sections of the population. Third, an increase in the amount of leisure time available due to changes in employment patterns and the increased availability of labour-saving devices. Finally, we must add the increased recognition by government, at national and local level, that sport and leisure confers benefits throughout society as well as directly to the individual. This has been reflected in the increased funding available to promote sport and recreation for elite atheletes as well as generally in the community. Obviously, it would be inappropriate to argue that these changes have affected everyone equally. Some people, for example those on very low incomes, may have very little chance to take advantage of the increased leisure opportunities which do exist. Nevertheless, the lifestyle of many people has changed since the end of the Second World War, albeit to different degrees, and this will be reflected in the content of this book.

## SOURCES OF INFORMATION FOR THE LEISURE ECONOMIST

Sport and leisure is an increasingly important research area for the economics profession. The industry is extremely diverse in the nature of its 'output', encompassing the supply of facilities in which to enjoy the arts, to consume food and drink, to participate and to spectate, as well as the manufacture and distribution of a seemingly infinite range of commodities. Not surprisingly, such activities can make therefore an important contribution to the prosperity of local and international economies. Furthermore, sport and leisure is not the preserve of the commercial sector. It is also an established area of activity for public and voluntary bodies.

To gain an insight into the changing economic circumstances of any area of economic activity, commentators need access to accurate data. This may prompt the production of data which meets their specific requirements. Alternatively or in addition, analysts have recourse to information intended to identify broader economic trends. Researchers concerned with sport and recreation issues have often registered concern that the most accessible statistics, particularly those produced by central government, are poorly defined and unsuitable for accurate analyses. To some extent this may still be true. Nevertheless, the diversity of information which is now available has improved considerably in comparison with what was obtainable during the 1960s and 1970s, a period when the leisure sector of the economy was undergoing considerable change. Nevertheless, economists often find themselves having to make do and compromise. Two such approaches are known as the *deductive* and *inductive* methods.[1] The deductive method relies upon 'global' estimates of economic activity, from which the economist then would try to isolate the leisure-related activity. In contrast, the inductive method uses information gathered from a representative sample and then uses this information to predict a more aggregated relationship. However, it should be understood from the outset that the usefulness of a data set will in part depend upon whether it is being used for similar purposes to which it was originally intended.

A discussion of the relative merits of the leisure statistics available to researchers, including economists, can be organised in two ways. The first is to base a list upon the origin of each data set. This would, for example, point to central government sources (such as the national income accounts), reports on the sport and leisure sector produced by commercial consultantancy firms (for example, Mintel) and information disseminated by such leisure-driven organisations as the Sports Council or the Countryside Commission. An alternative approach is to evaluate different sources of information in terms of the type of analysis which the researcher intends to undertake. For example, a list of data sources required for a study evaluating the contribution of the leisure industry to the national economy will be different from that needed to gain an insight into the conditions influencing the demand for a local swimming pool. Since readers are likely to find both approaches will offer important insights for their own studies of economics, the aim of the following analysis is to provide both. Each overview is not intended to be exhaustive. Nevertheless, they are intended to highlight the diversity of statistical sources which are available and the types of economic analysis to which they can be addressed. The final two elements of this section of the chapter will focus upon two more general issues. First, the distinction between cross-sectional data and time-series data and secondly, the problems associated with data interpretation in an inflationary economic environment.

### Alternative sources of leisure-based data

Table 1.1 identifies 12 potential sources of information about sport and leisure. Their accessibility will vary according to the facilities which the reader has at his or her disposal. For each category at least one indicative example is provided. Six of the most useful and easily obtainable sources of information are then discussed in more detail below.

### The National Income Accounts

Evidence appertaining to the economic importance of leisure to the United Kingdom economy can be found in the national accounts, frequently referred to as the 'Blue Book'. Some of the categories used in accounting tables fit neatly into everyday definitions of leisure. For example, the heading 'Recreation, Entertainment and Education' includes spending on such things as sports goods, betting and gaming, books, radio and television. However, not all categories are neatly defined from the point of view of the leisure economist. For example, expenditure on travel falls into the more general categories of air travel, sea travel and land travel. It is difficult therefore to extrapolate the exact amount of money being spent on these categories as leisure activities and how much is being spent on other types of journey, such as business travel. This is a classic example of a publication which is produced for a general readership and therefore, for more detailed information, the leisure economist is usually forced to seek more specialised insights elsewhere. Nevertheless, the Blue Book is an invaluable starting point for any study.

### The Employment Gazette

An insight into the number of people employed in leisure-related industries can be gleaned from the *Employment Gazette*, published monthly by the Department of Employment. Each issue is made up of

*Table 1.1* Potential sources of information for the leisure economist

| Source | Example |
| --- | --- |
| Government | *National Income Statistics* *General Household Survey* *Family Expenditure Survey* *Employment Gazette* |
| Public bodies | Arts Council Countryside Commission Monopolies and Merger Commission reports Sports Council |
| Local government | Spending plans Annual reports |
| Local sports centres | Usage figures |
| Statistical compendia | *Social Trends* (HMSO) *Digest of Sports Statistics* (Sports Council) |
| Commercial organisations | Mintel Key Note Henley Centre for Forecasting |
| Academic journals | *Leisure Studies* *Regional Studies* *Applied Economics* |
| Academic working papers | Used to report work in progress in academic institutions. Often not found in libraries but can be obtained direct for a small fee |
| Professional bodies | The Chartered Institute of Public Finance Accountants (CIPFA) statistical information service |
| Published accounts of firms | For example, the Rank Organisation or Allied-Lyons |
| Newspapers and popular magazines | Sports pages and leisure/lifestyle sections in newspapers; specialist magazines such as *Trout Monthly* |
| Trade publications | *Journal of Leisure Management* |

two distinct sections. First a series of articles written by industrial and labour market specialists which sometimes focus upon leisure-related economic activity. For example, the May 1991 issue contains an article by Baty and Richards reporting on the Leisure Day Visits Survey (to which we will refer at a later stage of this chapter). Second, each issue of the *Gazette* contains a 70-page set of official labour market statistics. Of course, not all these statistics are constructed in a manner which is immediately suited to an economic analysis of the leisure industry and, as with the Blue Book, the level of detail offered to the leisure economist is often insufficient. For example, in the new 1992 Standard Industrial Classification (SIC) system,[2] by which industrial activities will be classified from 1995, such headings as 'Recreational, Cultural and Sporting Activities' (Category 92) is fairly self explicit. However Category 52, which covers a wide range of retail activities whose sub-headings include the selling of leisure commodities, will not be published in general publications at the level of disaggregation which would be of immediate use to the leisure economist. The *Gazette* also includes specific data on employment in local authorities (from which we can determine numbers engaged in providing leisure services) and a comprehensive set of tourism data. Inflation rates, as they affect different types of commodities, including separate headings for 'leisure goods' and 'leisure services' are also included. Less explicitly directed towards leisure but nevertheless useful from the point of view of gaining an insight into the factors which will influence the demand for leisure are national and local unemployment statistics.

*The General Household Survey*

*The General Household Survey* (GHS) is administered by the Office of Population Censuses and Surveys (OPCS)[3] and has been undertaken since 1971. It is based upon a detailed survey of a sample of households resident in the UK and monitors a wide range of socio-economic variables. The GHS has included questions on sports participation, such as swimming, playing golf, keepfit/yoga, fishing and walking, in a separate section on leisure activity periodically since 1973.[4] Questions on more general leisure activities, such as watching television, reading books and gardening, have been included since 1977. In the past, criticisms were directed at the GHS because questions required respondents to recall their sport/leisure activities in the four weeks prior to interview. Thus, people who engaged regularly in a particular activity, but less than once every four weeks, were likely to be ignored in the overall findings. Since 1987, interviewees have been questioned about their participation in the previous 12 months.[5] This will enable the GHS to provide a more complete insight into the levels of participation for different sport and leisure activities.

*Social Trends*

*Social Trends* is produced annually by the government's Central Statistical Office and provides up-to-date statistical insights into a wide variety of socio-economic topics. The most useful chapters for people concerned with the economics of leisure and sport include 'Population', 'Expenditure and Resources', 'Transport and the Environment' and, most importantly, 'Leisure' though relevant information can be found in other chapters too. The publication draws together information from a wide variety of sources, not only cutting across government departments but also utilising non-government statistics from home and abroad. In many respects, this publication can be viewed as the first port of call for anyone wishing to obtain an up-to-date insight into the trends which influence sport and leisure activity in the UK, particularly from a demand point of view. Information about income and spending within a more localised perspective can be found in a sister publication *Regional Trends*. Unfortunately, *Regional Trends* does not have a specific chapter on leisure.

*Consultancy reports*

Specifically geared towards practitioners who want to gain a detailed up-to-date insight into many aspects of the leisure industry are specialist reports produced by commercial data-gathering and forecasting organisations, for example Key Note and Mintel. These publications are forward-looking by nature and provide the reader with indicators as to which variables have been and are most likely to exert an influence on specific parts of the industry. For example, Mintel's *Leisure Intelligence* is published annually in four volumes and provides a detailed insight into a wide range of leisure-based activities, ranging from swimming to DIY, keep-fit to camping and caravanning. The leisure activities which are examined each year do vary and therefore the reader should be prepared to check previous years' volumes as well as the most recent ones.

*The Chartered Institute of Public Finance and Accountancy*

Readers who require fairly detailed information about public-sector leisure provision often find it useful to refer to publications produced by the statistical information service of the Chartered Institute of Public Finance and Accountancy (CIPFA). CIPFA is one of six institutes which oversees the British accountancy profession. Their data are drawn from the majority of local authorities in England and Wales (for 1992–3, figures are drawn from 337 out of the 450 authorities) and embrace a variety of parameters including: net per capita expenditure on indoor and outdoor sport and the arts, the population of each local authority area, the general type of facilities each authority provides (this is highly aggregated) and the prices charged by each council. The two main publications to consult are *Leisure and Recreation Statistics Estimates* and *Charges for Leisure Services Statistics*. Both are published annually. CIPFA also produce a journal, *Public Finance* (previously, *Public Finance and Accountancy*), which periodically contains articles which are of direct relevance to an up-to-date understanding of leisure and recreation in the public sector.

**Data requirements by type of analysis**

At some point readers may find themselves carrying out their own analysis of a sport or leisure-related issue from an economist's perspective. Of course, it is difficult to predict the exact nature of this task. Thus, three typical areas of study will be highlighted to serve as examples. The first is concerned with an analysis of the factors influencing the demand for some sort of leisure facility, such as a squash court. The second will focus upon the supply of leisure goods and services by the commercial and non-commercial sectors, while the third will address the more general question of how much sport and leisure contributes to the national economy. Since the first two subject areas will provide examples for much of the economic analysis discussed in this book, we shall only use this section to pin-point potential data sources. In contrast, the consideration of the wider economic importance of sport and leisure will be less truncated and will be used as an opportunity to outline the findings of an extremely important Sports Council study which focuses on this very issue.

*The demand for a leisure facility*

Although the very nature of such an exercise implies the need to obtain localised data, it is possible to gain a general insight into some of the factors which influence the demand for a facility from relatively accessible sources. As already noted, a useful starting point is *Social Trends* since it provides data, albeit aggregated, across a range of appropriate headings. This can be supplemented from the primary sources used by *Social Trends*, such as the *GHS* or *Family Expenditure Survey*. More explicitly focused towards sport and leisure participation is the Sports Council's *A Digest of Sports Statistics for the UK* (1991). This publication not only identifies the socio-economic profile of consumers of an almost exhaustive range of sport and leisure activities, but also trends in the membership and number of clubs affiliated to each activity's controlling body. Information is also supplied covering contact addresses for each sport and information on the circulation of relevant journals and magazines.

If the facility in question is run by a local authority, then consideration should be given to Sports Council policy regarding the promotion of physical activity across all sections of the community. In this respect, the documents *Sport in the Community: The Next Ten Years* (1982) and *Sport in the Community: Into the 1990s* (1988) should be consulted. General information about the level and distribution of prices between different local authorities with respect to sports facility provision can be derived from CIPFA's *Charges for Leisure Services*; attendance figures can be obtained from CIPFA's *Leisure Usage Statistics*; while information about the population size of each local authority area, together with the types of facilities which are provided by each council, can be found in CIPFA's *Leisure and Recreation Statistics Estimates*. Insights into the demand issues relating to the arts (such as galleries, libraries, opera, drama, dance and music) can be gleaned from *Cultural Trends*, a publication produced by the Policy Studies Institute. As noted at the outset, however, if the analysis is to target a specific facility, then there is a need to obtain more localised data. This may necessitate the use of a questionnaire to identify the socio-economic characteristics of a catchment population, together with information relating to other factors which can influence demand, such as the availability of public transport or consumer awareness of the facility. This evidence may then be compared with evidence gathered from more general sources.

### The supply of leisure goods and services

If emphasis is to be given to the supply of leisure goods and services, rather than the demand for them, then the data requirements can be somewhat different. Again, the informational needs will vary according to whether the focus is to be upon the commercial, public or voluntary sectors. If the emphasis is upon the public-sector sports provision, the previously cited Sports Council documents should be consulted since it is possible to gain an insight into the rate of growth of local authority facilities from the early 1970s with reference to the Sports Council's commitment to 'Sport for All' (a concept discussed in later chapters of this book) and the growth in the number of clubs associated with many leisure activities. Information produced by CIPFA may again prove useful since it can be used to identify what facilities are provided within different council areas as well as the level of net expenditure per head of local population.

Leisure provision by the commercial sector embraces an almost endless variety of leisure activities including the manufacture of leisure goods (such as televisions) and the provision of indoor and outdoor facilities. By referring to the annual reports of the major operators within the leisure sector, one can gain an insight into a wide variety of leisure markets. For example, one of the activities of Allied Lyons is the production and distribution of alcohol through its brewing interests (Tetley and Ansells) and network of pubs and off-licences (Victoria Wine). We may highlight other branches of the leisure industry. The Granada Group plc is a major supplier of rented television and video equipment as well as a network of bingo clubs, social clubs and night clubs. Some people may not realise that the Ladbrooke Group plc has a chain of do-it-yourself stores (Texas) as well as its more obvious interests in bookmaking, while Bass plc owns a string of hotels (Holiday Inns), bookmaking outlets (Coral) and snooker clubs alongside its brewing activities and network of public houses. Annual reports of these and other companies can often be obtained from libraries or the career information services at most colleges and universities. It should also be noted that *Cultural Trends* (see above) provides a background to the nature of a variety of arts-based leisure activities. By definition, this will encompass areas of interaction between commercial and public sectors of the leisure industry.

## *The contribution of sport and leisure to the national economy*

The third type of analysis to be considered involves that needed to gain an insight into the leisure industry within its wider macroeconomic context. The first explicit attempt to carry out such an exercise, entitled *The Economic Impact and Importance of Sport in the UK* was undertaken for the Sports Council by the consultancy organisation the Henley Centre for Forecasting (subsequently referred to as the Henley Centre) for the year 1985. The information in this publication has now been superseded by a more streamlined document produced by the same organisation, *The Economic Impact of Sport in the United Kingdom in*

*1990* (published July 1992). Three things should be noted at this point. First, the updated analysis is in part complementary to the original one. In particular, some methodological issues are addressed in more detail in the first report than in the second, mainly to avoid unnecessary duplication. Although this will not pose a problem in most cases, some readers may find it helpful to have both documents to hand if they wish to gain an insight into the full complexities of the investigation. The second point to note is that both publications are focused primarily upon the economic importance of 'sport' rather than the economic importance of 'leisure' *per se*. Although the distinction between the two can be blurred at the best of times, it should be understood from the outset that the figures which are derived subsequently are based upon a much narrower remit than is adopted elsewhere in this text. Nevertheless we are left in little doubt of the contribution of sport (and leisure) to the national economy. Finally, data sets used in economics can have very short 'sell-by dates'. Thus, assuming that the lead time between a future third edition and the present second edition of the Henley Centre report is to be the same as that between the first and second editions, some readers may find the need to look elsewhere for more up-to-date figures as the second edition reaches the end of its lifespan.

One source of information identified in the Henley Centre report is the national accounts. For students specialising in economics, the difficulties which arise from calculating such figures is an important element in an introductory semester's course in macroeconomics. However, many readers of this book will be studying economics within a more broadly based programme, perhaps embracing both scientific and administrative aspects of sport and leisure, such that there is only a limited opportunity to consider these problems. Readers wishing to gain more knowledge of national income accounting should consult an introductory economics text.

Basing our analysis upon the evidence contained in the Henley Centre report, we can highlight briefly three main variables to illustrate the degree to which sport contributes to the UK economy: aggregate consumer expenditure on sport-related goods, aggregate employment in sport-related activities and the value of sport-related output. Table 1.2 provides an opportunity to compare the level of consumer expenditure on sport-related goods with that spent on other items.

In 1990, the total value of consumer expenditure in the UK amounted to £349 billion. This suggests that sport-related expenditure is not a particularly important area of expenditure for households, which, if we take the highest figure of £9.75 billion, amounts to less than 3 per cent

*Table 1.2* Selected categories of UK consumers' expenditure in 1990 prices (£million)

| Category | Expenditure (£million) |
| --- | --- |
| Motor vehicles | 17,384 |
| Beer | 11,742 |
| Womenswear | 11,439 |
| **Sport (incl. gambling)** | **9,753** |
| Cigarettes | 7,771 |
| **Sport (excl. gambling)** | **6,909** |
| Furniture and floor coverings | 6,285 |
| Electricity | 6,193 |
| Bread and cereals | 5,958 |
| Menswear | 5,718 |
| Spirits | 5,007 |
| Wines and ciders | 4,980 |
| Gas | 4,869 |
| DIY goods | 4,743 |
| **Sport (excl. gambling and exceptional items\*)** | **4,230** |
| Newspapers and magazines | 3,195 |
| Pets | 2,246 |
| Recorded music | 1,738 |
| Books | 1,382 |
| Bingo admissions | 264 |
| Cinema | 219 |

*Source*: Sports Council/Henley Centre for Forecasting (1992, table 3.10, p. 30)
*Note*: *Excluding gambling, boats, footwear, TV rental, public school fees.

of the total. Nevertheless, even excluding gambling expenditure, spending is on a par with such major items as furniture and floor coverings and electricity. Furthermore, the survey focuses specifically upon sport-related, rather than leisure-related expenditure. Many of the categories identified in table 1.2 can be seen to fall into a more general definition of leisure.

A more detailed breakdown of the expenditure items which make up each of the highlighted sports-based categories is provided in table 1.3. It is strongly recommended that readers of this text consult Appendix Two of the Henley Centre report since it shows, in an extremely lucid way, the diversity of sources utilised to obtain data for each category of sports-based expenditure.

Let us now turn our attention to the number of jobs which can be attributed to the provision of sport-related activities. As with the

Table 1.3 Consumers' expenditure on sport-related goods and services (£million)

| Goods and services | Expenditure (£million) |
|---|---|
| Admissions | 233 |
| Sports goods | 595 |
| Bicycles | 47 |
| Boats | 1,417 |
| Participant sports, subscriptions and ad hoc admissions | 1,214 |
| Clothing and footwear: | |
| clothing | 804 |
| footwear | 1,171 |
| Repairs and laundry | 35 |
| Travel | 384 |
| Books and magazines | 115 |
| Newspapers | 339 |
| Video (purchase and rental) | 14 |
| BBC licence | 59 |
| TV rental | 61 |
| Skiing holidays | 391 |
| Public schools | 30 |
| Sub-total | 6,909 |
| | |
| Gambling: | |
| football pools | 519 |
| horse racing | 2,096 |
| raffles and gaming | 229 |
| | |
| Total consumer expenditure | 9,753 |

Source: Sports Council/Henley Centre for Forecasting (1992, table A2.5, p. 63)

informational requirements of the expenditure-based survey, there was a need not only to make use of official government statistics but also of alternative sources of information, in particular, insights derived from questionnaires. Table 1.4 shows sport to be a major employer of individuals, of similar magnitude to printing/paper/publishing and postal services/telecommunications. The total of 467,000 represents a 24 per cent increase when compared with the figure generated in the 1985 study.

The final method of measuring the economic importance of sport-related activities is to consider the value of sport-related output. This

*Table 1.4* Employment in the UK in selected sectors, 1990 ('000s)

| Sector | No. employed ('000) |
|---|---|
| Mechanical engineering | 765 |
| Banking and finance | 634 |
| Food, drink and tobacco | 557 |
| Printing, paper and publishing | 496 |
| **All sport-related economic activity** | **467** |
| Postal services and telecommunications | 441 |
| Chemical industry | 329 |
| Agriculture, forestry and fishing | 305 |
| Footwear and clothing | 301 |
| Timber and wooden industries | 254 |
| Textiles | 214 |

*Source*: Sports Council/Henley Centre for Forecasting (1992, table 3.8, p. 28)

*Table 1.5* Value of output in sport-related economic activity in selected categories of manufacturing output in the UK in 1990 (£billion)

| Category | Value (£billion) |
|---|---|
| Electrical and instrument engineering | 14.02 |
| Mechanical engineering | 12.73 |
| Paper, printing and packaging | 11.66 |
| Chemicals and man-made fibres | 11.40 |
| Food | 9.49 |
| **Sport-related economic activity**[a] | **8.27** |
| Motor vehicles and parts | 6.37 |
| Metal manufacturing | 4.09 |
| Drink and tobacco | 3.54 |
| Clothing, footwear and leather | 3.30 |
| **Sport-related economic activity**[b] | **3.28** |
| Textiles | 2.83 |

*Source*: Henley Centre for Forecasting (1992, table 3.4, p. 21)
*Notes*: [a]Including commercial non-sport sector.
[b]Excluding commercial non-sport sector.

exercise did encounter specific problems which arose because there are some categories of manufacturing which are not explicitly sport-related in themselves but include some element of sport-related activity, for example clothing, footwear and leather. Thus a distinction is made between *core* sports output and the *commercial non-sport sector*.

It can be seen from table 1.5 that if we use the 'purest' definition of sport-related production, then output is on a par with such activities as 'textiles', 'clothing, footwear and leather' and 'drink and tobacco'. If the commercial non-sport sector is included then the value of output exceeds that of 'motor vehicles and parts' but is below that of 'food'. The distribution of this output is such that 21 per cent of activity is in the commercial sport sector, 8 per cent in local government and 10 per cent in the voluntary sector. The remainder is commercial non-sport activity.

A report which provides an alternative insight into the contribution leisure activity can make to the national economy, this time from the perspective of a specific activity, is the Leisure Day Visits Survey. This exercise was most recently conducted between 1988–9 by the OPCS on behalf of the Department of Employment, British Tourist Authority and English Tourist Board. A summary of the findings of the survey has since been undertaken by Baty and Richards (1991) as an article in the May edition of the *Employment Gazette*. One of the problems which is encountered in such an exercise is the definition of what a leisure day visit actually is. Although the survey uses a number of disclaimers, for example that the trip must last three hours or more and that it must not include tasks associated with the workplace or home, there remains a 'grey area' of what should or should not be included. Nevertheless, it was found that spending on day trips by UK residents between April 1988 and March 1989[6] amounted to £5,212 million or approximately one-fifth of all tourism spending in the UK for that year. To this figure, we may add expenditure of £10,900 million by UK residents spending at least one night away from home. Expenditure by UK residents was found to account for almost two-thirds of all UK tourism spending in 1988–9. The remainder arising from overseas visitors to the UK. Using the Survey, we may also identify the main purpose (in broad terms) of day visits in 1988–9 and the level of expenditure directed towards each activity listed. This information is set out in table 1.6.

Alternatively, if we focus on the breakdown of expenditure on the goods and services consumed during day trips by UK residents, it is found that just under one-third of spending is food and drink related (£1,575 million). Of the other three specific categories identified, travel accounts for 25 per cent of expenditure (£1,213 million), gifts and shopping (non-essential) absorbs a further 17 per cent (£882 million) and admission charges, 10 per cent (£537 million). The remaining 19 per cent of expenditure (£1,005 million) is unclassified.

*Table 1.6* Leisure day visits, 1988–9

| Activity | Visits (millions) | Proportion (%) | Expenditure (£million) | Proportion (%) |
|---|---|---|---|---|
| Outdoor activities | 174 | 28 | 1001 | 19 |
| Visits to friends and relatives | 144 | 23 | 582 | 11 |
| Visiting attractions | 82 | 13 | 598 | 11 |
| Shopping (non-scheduled) | 64 | 10 | 1498 | 28 |
| Other activities | 182 | 25 | 1574 | 30 |

*Source*: Baty and Richards (1991, p. 260)

## Cross-section and time-series data

A particular feature of both reports highlighted in the previous section is that they provide a snap-shot of leisure-related economic activity during a particular period of time. In the case of the Henley Centre report, the year is 1990, whereas the Leisure Day Visits Survey covers April 1988 to March 1989. These reports, and such publications as the *General Household Survey* and the *Family Expenditure Survey*, are known as *cross-sectional* studies. In contrast, some publications not only provide cross-sectional data but also past values of a particular set of variables, dating back months or even years. Such observations are known as *time-series* data. Time-series data allows us to identify specific trends in a particular variable so that it is possible to determine whether it has been increasing, decreasing or remaining constant over a period of time. Examples of time-series data can be found in the national accounts since observations are not only given for a particular year, but also for previous years. This allows judgements to be made in terms of how well the economy is performing now relative to previous years. One of the problems which can arise when using time-series data which incorporate prices is that inflation can cloud our understanding of the information before us. Thus, there is a need to find some mechanism which allows meaningful comparisons between years to take place.

### Interpreting statistics in the presence of inflation

The presence of inflation means that price levels are rising. If it is an ongoing phenomenon then a fixed sum of money will buy progressively fewer goods and services over time. The prevailing rate of inflation is calculated by monitoring the price increases affecting a representative weighted 'basket of goods' bought by an average family. Thus, the degree to which individual households are affected by inflation in terms of the official rate will depend upon the degree to which their spending pattern conforms with the 'official' one. Some of the reasons why inflation seems to be an ever-present feature of our daily lives, and how governments have tried to control it, will be considered in more detail in Chapter 8. For the moment, we shall simply be concerned with its effects as it relates to the interpretation of time-series data. The problem emerges when prices are used as a basis for a particular statistical trend. For example, as we have already seen, one set of figures found in the national accounts is that documenting changes in the value of output over recent years. If this value is calculated using prices prevailing in each successive year, then even the value of identical levels of output will grow over time. A similar problem will arise in the case of household incomes measured over time, such that it may appear that incomes are rising when in reality householders are becoming worse off in terms of what goods and services they can buy. To take account of this problem and therefore gain an insight into the *real* changes taking place over time, economists base their calculations on a fixed set of prices, regardless of the year actually being analysed. To illustrate, let us consider some leisure expenditure figures from the 1992 edition of the *National Accounts* for the years 1981 and 1991. These are set out in table 1.7.

It can be seen that there are four columns of figures. The first two come under the general heading of 'nominal prices' while columns three and four come under the heading of '1985 prices'. 'Nominal prices' simply means that we use the prices for each good or service which prevailed in that particular year. Thus in the case of table 1.7, we are referring to prices prevailing in 1981 and 1991. Alternatively, we can base estimates upon the prices prevailing in a particular year, which in this example is 1985. This allows us to obtain a more accurate picture of how the level of consumer spending has changed between the two years. The actual base year which is used for this insight is, when all is said and done, arbitrary. Official statistics tend to change this base year in five-year intervals. Thus, past figures will have used 1980 prices whereas future *National Accounts* will incorporate base prices from the year 1990. However, there is no reason why readers should not come across figures from alternative sources which use different base years. In economics, it is standard practice to use the terms *nominal* or *money* as a prefix if we are basing our estimates upon the prices as they prevailed

*Table 1.7* Expenditure on selected leisure goods and services in 1981 and 1991 (current and 1985 prices, £million)

| Goods/services | Nominal prices | | 1985 prices | |
|---|---|---|---|---|
| | *1981* | *1991* | *1981* | *1991* |
| Alcohol | | | | |
| beer | 5971 | 12775 | 8561 | 8211 |
| spirits | 2908 | 5354 | 3693 | 3681 |
| wine/cider | 2273 | 5426 | 2692 | 3935 |
| DIY | 1800 | 4598 | 2240 | 3263 |
| Recreation goods/services | | | | |
| TV, radio and other durable goods | 1769 | 4347 | 1668 | 5126 |
| TV and videotape charges, licence fees and repairs | 1732 | 3363 | 1995 | 2606 |
| sports goods, toys, games and camping equipment | 1339 | 3557 | 1510 | 2897 |
| other recreation goods | 2441 | 6668 | 2917 | 5493 |
| betting and gaming | 1626 | 3134 | 2102 | 2196 |
| other recreation and entertainment services | 1778 | 5033 | 2351 | 2847 |
| books | 531 | 1502 | 909 | 1023 |
| newspapers and magazines | 1686 | 3303 | 2451 | 2288 |
| catering (meals and accommodation) | 8820 | 31049 | 12261 | 20028 |
| household expenditure abroad | 3131 | 8978 | 4277 | 6523 |

*Source*: UK National Accounts ('Blue Book'), London: Central Statistical Office, 1992, adapted from tables 4.7 and 4.8, pp. 40–3

in each year of consideration. For example, economists may refer to nominal expenditure or money income. If, on the other hand, we are applying a constant set of prices, in this case those of 1985, then the term *real* is used as a prefix, for example real income. Thus, it should now be clear that it is important, when reading published reports, to establish whether the author is using nominal or real figures as a basis for his or her calculations.

Let us focus upon the first line of figures in table 1.7, that appertaining to expenditure on beer consumption. It can be seen that using the prices which were actually prevailing in 1981 and 1991, the respective levels of expenditure were £5,971 million and £12,775 million. At first sight it would therefore appear that beer consumption has increased considerably over the ten-year period. However, let us see what happens when 1985 prices are used by consulting the figures in columns three and four of the table. By using only one set of prices (1985), we may now infer that the amount of expenditure directed towards beer consumption had actually fallen, from £8,561 million to £8,211 million. From the information we have in the table in front of us, we cannot provide a definitive reason why this reduction in expenditure has occurred. A detailed economic analysis of beer consumption would be required. This would not only involve considering changes in the actual numbers of beer drinkers and the amounts they actually drink but also the levels of expenditure directed towards other products, both leisure and non-leisure. For example, people may be spending less money on beer because they are spending more money on wine and cider (the figures do suggest that this may be part of the reason), or they may be drinking less beer because more money needs to be directed towards the consumption of more essential items of expenditure, for example mortgages, food, clothing or heating. This inter-relationship between our demands for different products will be considered more fully later on in this book.

## QUESTIONS FOR DISCUSSION

1    Why is the leisure industry of interest to economists?
2    What statistical sources should be used to demonstrate the importance of leisure as an economic activity?

# Chapter 2

# The demand for leisure

## INTRODUCTION

This chapter focuses upon what economists mean by the term *demand*. Most writers are united in defining demand in terms of the *willingness* and *ability* of an individual, or group of individuals, to buy a good or service at a given price within a particular period of time. Stressing the point that the consumer is willing to engage in a transaction implies that there is no coercion and that the product in question must possess one or more desirable attributes. It would be illogical to buy a product if it does not have some desirable qualities. Even if the individual later discovers that he or she was wrong in terms of the qualities that could be derived from the product, it was nevertheless deemed to be desirable by the consumer at the time of purchase. Economics frequently avoids this problem by assuming that consumers are rational, in other words, fully informed about the consequences of all their actions. Rationality also ensures that individuals, when faced with an array of affordable commodities, will buy the combination which offers the greatest amount of satisfaction. The term economists use when referring to the enjoyment individuals derive from consuming goods is *utility*.

In later chapters we will consider the economic implications of individuals not being in possession of all the information necessary to make a fully informed choice. Although consumers may be willing to buy a good or service, they may not necessarily have the financial means to convert their desire to enjoy the properties of a commodity into an effective demand for it. For example, while many people would like to own a Rolls Royce motor car, few have the financial means to do so. Thus, for the manufacturer, it is not the people who would *like* to own such a car who are of interest but those who are also able to afford one which will determine how many cars are made ultimately.

This chapter will be organised so as to outline initially the factors which are likely to influence a consumer's willingness and ability to buy a commodity. As well as price, it will be seen that, depending upon the product in question, there are a whole variety of factors which will determine what combination of goods and services a consumer will ultimately demand. Examples include income, the consumer's perception of the product in question (which may be moulded by the effects of advertising or media attention), access to transport, the weather, the relative price of other goods, and so on. We shall then consider how economists formalise the relationship between these variables through what is known as the demand function. Utilising the principle of the demand function, two specific relationships will be highlighted. First, that between the amount of a commodity demanded and its price, and second, that between the quantity demanded and changes in consumers' income. Throughout, reference will be made to some of the leisure items which feature regularly in household spending. The final sections of the chapter will formalise the analysis of the consumption decision through the use of indifference curves. Indifference curve analysis will then be used to look more closely at individual choices between spending time at work and devoting their time to leisure activities.

## WHAT DETERMINES QUANTITY DEMANDED?

### Own price of a commodity

As we have already seen, there are a whole range of factors which can determine how much of a product (if any) a consumer is willing and able to buy. Most obvious is the price of the commodity itself. It is normal to assume that individuals are *price takers*. This means that a given person is not in a position to influence a commodity's price. This is a reasonable assumption to make – when we visit a shop or leisure centre, prices are displayed on a ticket or tariff and the consumer has a 'take it or leave it' decision to make. In some cultures, buyers need not be price takers in the truest sense. Where bartering is an accepted norm, the consumer has the opportunity to buy the good at a range of prices such that the final price will be dependent upon his or her bargaining skill. Nevertheless, we can argue intuitively that the lower the unit price of the good or service in question, the larger the demand we can expect for it. This relationship will form the basis of later discussion.

## Consumer's income

For any given set of prices, our income will determine what combinations of goods and services are affordable. Often our spending is guided by our expectation of income in the future. A windfall gain, for example from a successful bet on a horse race, is unlikely to cause an individual to change his or her spending behaviour on a regular basis. In contrast, an increase in salary may encourage such a change. Income which can be guaranteed over a period in time is usually referred to as *permanent income*. As our real income rises, so does our ability to purchase goods and services. When constrained by income, our consumption decisions have an *opportunity cost*. If we have the financial resources to buy a new set of golf clubs, the opportunity cost is the forgone enjoyment from the next-best alternative, such as a new fishing rod. The assumption of rationality implies that the golf clubs provide greater utility than the fishing rod (assuming similar financial outlays).

## The price of other goods

Changes in the relative prices of goods and services often exerts an important influence upon what we buy. Often we need to categorise goods according to necessity. The need to spend our money on food, clothing and shelter will usually get priority over such luxuries as going to the cinema or going on holiday. Thus, a rise in the relative price of necessities can be expected to detract from our spending upon leisure activities. A similar line of argument can be applied to goods and services which fall within the same general category of spending. This is because some activities necessitate the consumption of two or more products to be consumed at the same time. For example, a camera will need some sort of film before it can be used to take photographs. Thus, if the price of cameras increases rapidly so that they are out of the financial reach of many consumers, then it will reduce ultimately the demand for films and the developing of photographs, even if the prices of film and developing remain constant. Commodities which are used jointly in this way are known as *complementary* goods. Other examples of complementary goods are golf clubs and golf balls, cars and petrol or beer and peanuts.

Sometimes, two or more goods are perceived as alternatives for each other. Again, their relative prices may affect an individual's consumption decision. Assume two people have traditionally set aside Saturday afternoons for playing sport and they are equally fond of playing squash or badminton. If the prices of squash and badminton courts are the same, then they may decide to alternate between the two activities for the sake of variety. However, if the price of the squash court increases rapidly while that of the badminton court remains constant, then the individuals are more likely to concentrate upon the latter activity. In this case, squash and badminton are *substitute* activities for the individuals concerned. Other examples of substitute goods include gas cookers and electric cookers, tea and coffee, and Saturday afternoon shopping and attending a football match.

**Individual preferences**

Our preferences for different products or combinations of products to consume play a very important role in deciding what we ultimately demand. Faced with a whole array of different products, it is reasonable to assume that everyone will have differing opinions about the relative merits of individual goods. For example, some consumers prefer coffee to tea whereas others prefer to drink tea. Similarly, some people prefer watching a game of soccer to being a spectator at a golf championship whereas others may prefer to be present at the golf tournament. Sometimes our preferences may be conditioned by what we see portrayed in the media, such as on the television. For example, Olga Korbutt's performance in the 1972 Olympic Games tempted thousands of children into taking up gymnastics. Likewise, reports of violence at football matches has been identified as a factor contributing to a decline in the number of supporters attending games. In both cases individuals' attitudes to a particular sport has been affected by media attention, either positively or negatively. Of course, the most overt attempts to change our preferences occur through the use of advertising by firms. Commercial television stations rely upon advertising for their revenue. Thus, while watching television, viewers are also encouraged to change their drinking and eating habits, buy a different type of car or visit a particular theme park.

Although for ease of analysis economics prefers to assume that individuals show consistent preferences over time, there are many examples of commodities which become fashionable for a short period of time and are then viewed as undesirable. In the early 1970s, it was necessary for men to own a pair of flared trousers and platform shoes to be noticed. A few years later these items of clothing were gathering dust at the back of the wardrobe yet, at the time of writing, they are becoming fashionable once again. Thus, fashion can play an important role in determining whether or not a product is desirable to own. The sports industry is no different from any other industry. The frequent changes which are made to the style of soccer teams' strips is a constant reminder of how manufacturers try to increase their profits by manipulating consumers' perception of what is and isn't fashionable.

## The availability of leisure time

The availability of time is not often included in textbooks as a factor which will exert an influence on the demand for a product. However, in sport and leisure, activities may not only be associated with the pure financial cost of consumption but also a need to invest significant amounts of time. If this time is not available, it may be irrational to make a financial outlay even if the product can be afforded. For example, it would be inappropriate for an individual to buy a set of golf clubs if he or she did not have enough continuous time to play a round. The time-intensive nature of some activities encourages some individuals to spend their money on labour-saving devices such as washing machines and dishwashers or even to hire somebody to undertake the housework. The need for time to facilitate the consumption of sport and leisure (as a participant or spectator) is an important issue in recreation economics and therefore one we shall consider in more detail later, in particular how the leisure industry should respond to the differences in the leisure time people have at their disposal.

## The availability of transport

The availability of transport is another factor which is extremely important for consumers of sport and leisure activities. For example, many visitors to sites of special interest, such as a national park, need to travel significant distances in order to enjoy the scenery. Even within towns and cities, there may be a need to travel some distance before certain facilities can be consumed. Although squash courts or a swimming pool may be easily accessed, other specialised facilities such as dry ski-slopes or ice-rinks may be more sparsely located. The growth in demand for many recreational facilities has stemmed from the increased availability of private transport, itself facilitated by rises in real income. For example, in 1961, 60 per cent of the total distance travelled in Great Britain was by private vehicle whereas by 1991 this figure had risen to almost 90 per cent (*Social Trends*, 1993). Individuals reliant on public transport may have few problems getting to or from a local leisure centre but may experience significant difficulty in getting to more remote areas offering scenic beauty. The private car has opened up large parts of the countryside and, with it, generated a new industry geared towards satisfying the needs of the visitor. However, it should be remembered that this increase in the mobility of the public has also meant that facilities are more likely to get congested, which may lead to a reduction in the quality of scenery originally made attractive by its remoteness.

### Seasonal factors

Seasonal factors will often play an important role in the demand for sport and leisure activities. For example, the demand for municipal pitch-and-putt courses will be at its greatest during the summer months when the evenings are light and the weather is warm. Similarly, interest in many holiday resorts is also seasonal, but not necessarily for the same reasons. The demand for skiing facilities and accommodation will be at its greatest during the winter months when large falls of snow can be expected, whereas the desire to visit seaside resorts (particularly those in the UK) will increase with the likelihood of sunshine. The fact that the demand for holiday destinations and sporting facilities has a seasonal dimension will encourage individuals involved with the marketing of these products to try and minimise this variation in demand. This may take place through cut-price offers or increased advertising.

### THE DEMAND FUNCTION

All the variables which can influence the quantity demanded of a product are set out in what economists call the *demand function*. The demand function describes the variables which can influence the demand for a particular product, such as own price, income, availability of leisure time and so on. Demand functions may be written down as complex mathematical statements specifying exact inter-relationships between variables. However, more often than not, economists will simply list out the variables they see as being relevant to the determination of demand for a particular product without identifying the exact relationship between them. For example we may write:

$$Q_d = f(P, Y, P_o, Pr, L, T, S)$$

where $Q_d$ denotes quantity demanded, f means 'is a function of', $P$ denotes own price of the commodity in question, $Y$ is income, $P_o$ is the price of other goods, $Pr$ denotes preferences, $L$ is leisure time available, $T$ is access to transport and $S$ denotes seasonal factors. In this case, quantity demanded (on the left-hand side of the equation) is known as the dependent variable whereas variables such as own price, income and leisure time (on the right-hand side of the equation) are known as independent variables. Within this text, no attempt will be made to specify the exact functional relationship between all the independent variables and the resulting demand for a commodity. However, it will be seen that when less complex functional relationships are specified precisely, such as between quantity demanded and price, it is relatively easy to consider numerical changes in each of the variables.

One of the problems economists face is that all the independent variables within the demand function are unlikely to be static over a given period of time. Within a dynamic world, there will be changes in the income of some individuals, there will be changes in the relative price of other goods, and added to this, there will be the fleeting effects of fashion, advertising and the weather. In economics, researchers often want to understand the effect a change in any one of these variables will have on the demand for a particular product. To counter this problem, it is therefore assumed that all the independent variables within the demand function are held constant except one, namely the variable we are interested in. By imposing this constraint, known as the *ceteris paribus* assumption,[1] it is possible to identify the individual influence of one independent variable upon the dependent variable. Once this is done for each variable in turn, it is possible to aggregate these effects and establish what is happening in the real world, when in reality all the independent variables are changing at the same time.

At this stage, we shall use a diagrammatic approach to look more closely at the relationship between quantity demanded and two of the variables identified in our general discussion of the demand function. The first of these variables is price while the second is income. Readers who have studied a little economics before will recognise these relationships in terms of the *demand curve* and the *Engel curve* respectively.

**The relationship between quantity demanded and price**

*The demand curve*

A demand curve measures the number of units of a particular commodity that is demanded over a particular period of time as the price of that product changes, *ceteris paribus*. They can be constructed to depict responses from single individuals or from larger groups of people, for example within a region or country as a whole. Thus, in the former case we would simply be considering the response of one person to a series of price changes, whereas in the latter case the emphasis is on a group response to a particular price change. The formal distinction between what economists call individual demand curves and market demand curves will be explored in detail within the next chapter. For the purposes of this analysis, we shall only consider demand from the perspective of an individual person.

When drawing demand curves, it is conventional to measure changes in price along the vertical axis of the graph and changes in quantity along the horizontal axis. The way in which we calibrate the graph will depend upon the nature of the commodity under consideration. The units we use for quantity may be in terms of weight (for example, flour), boxes (eggs), litres/pints (beer), visitors (squash club) and so on. Similarly, for low-priced goods it may be better to calibrate graphs in units which reflect price movements of a few pence whereas for relatively more expensive goods it may be more appropriate to think in terms of units of £1, £10 or even £100. Intuitively, we would expect the relationship between price and quantity to be a negative one. In other words, as the price of a good rises, quantity demanded will fall. This is demonstrated

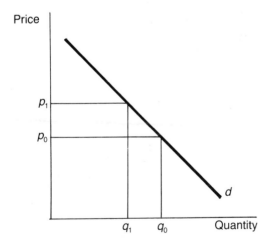

*Figure 2.1* The demand curve

in figure 2.1 where the letter '$d$' is used to denote the demand curve for the individual.

It can be seen in both cases that a fall in price from $p_1$ to $p_0$ leads to an increase in quantity demanded, $q_1$ to $q_0$. However, the degree to which quantity demanded will respond to a given fall in price will depend upon the specific characteristics of the good or service.

### Shifts in the demand curve

As we have already seen, demand curves are drawn under the assumption that all other variables within the demand function do not change, in other words, utilising the *ceteris paribus* assumption. Thus, we are simply mirroring the two-dimensional relationship between quantity demanded and price. However, we can look at the basic demand relationship in terms of movements in other variables within the demand function, such as income, fashion, advertising levels and so on. The effect of a change in any one of these variables, *ceteris paribus*, will be to cause the demand curve to shift, either left or right. This is shown in figure 2.2.

Assuming that $d_0$ is our original demand curve, a rightward shift in the demand curve (to $d_1$) would mean that more of a particular commodity is being demanded at any given price (such as $P_0$), whereas a leftward

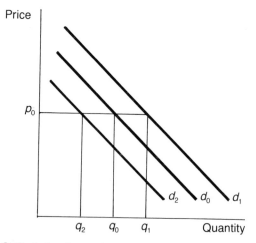

*Figure 2.2* Shifts in the demand curve

shift (to $d_2$) implies the opposite. Such rightward shifts can be prompted from a variety of sources. If the commodity in question is receiving positive media attention, individuals are likely to be encouraged to consume more of it at any given price. Were the media attention to be negative, then the reverse would be true. In either case, media attention is acting as a shift parameter. We have already identified a series of variables which act as shift parameters within the demand function, including income, the price of complementary or substitute goods, the weather and changes in fashion. Variation in any of these variables can have the effect of shifting a demand curve, either to the right or to the left. The exact effect of such movements will again depend upon the nature of the good in question and the magnitude of the change in the variable. Furthermore, because the demand for certain products is inter-related, a change in a variable can shift the demand curve of more than one product. For example, a successful advertising campaign for one brand of a product would have the effect of shifting the demand curve outwards but may at the same time shift the demand curve for competing brands to the left.

From the point of view of understanding the mechanics behind the demand curve, it should be emphasised that a change in the price of a commodity will lead to a movement along the demand curve whereas a change in any other variable within the demand function has the potential of shifting the demand curve, either to the right or to the left. A more detailed analysis of the implications of one or more shifts in the demand curve will be explored in the following chapter.

The next stage of the analysis will be to consider the relationship between quantity demanded and income. In terms of the demand curve, income operates as a shift parameter, though for the purpose of the analysis to follow, we shall employ a different, but broadly similar, methodology to consider how income changes influence the demand for goods and services. This involves the construction of Engel curves.

**The relationship between quantity demanded and income**

*The Engel curve*

The Engel curve derives its name from the nineteenth-century German statistician, Ernst Engel, who derived a now famous law that the proportion of income spent on food diminishes as incomes rise. Less well documented are his assertions that the proportions spent on clothing and housing will remain constant and the proportions of income spent on

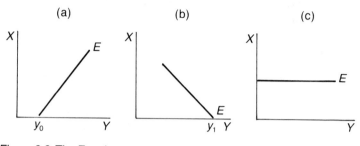

*Figure 2.3* The Engel curve

all other goods will increase. Generally, the Engel curve is used to summarise the relationship identifying the effect of income changes upon the consumption of different goods and services. When drawing Engel curves it is the convention to depict income ($Y$) on the horizontal axis of the graph and the commodity in question on the vertical axis ($X$). Three possible shapes for an Engel curve ($E$) are given in figures 2.3a, 2.3b and 2.3c.

In figure 2.3a, it can be seen that the Engel curve has a positive slope. Thus, as income rises beyond $y_0$, the demand for the commodity in question also rises. For incomes less than $y_0$, no units of the product are consumed. Products whose demand increases as a consumer's income increases are known as *normal goods*. It is very easy to think of products which we buy more of as our income rises. Indeed, examples are often associated with leisure-related activities: the consumption of restaurant meals, the purchase of 'designer' clothing, travelling on foreign holidays, watching video games and so on. In contrast, the Engel curve depicted in figure 2.3b is negatively sloped, such that less of the good is consumed as income rises. When income reaches $y_1$, no units of the product are consumed. Goods and services whose demand is negatively correlated with income are known as *inferior goods*. Examples of inferior goods tend to be associated with low quality. For example, as incomes rise, individuals are likely to buy fewer bottles of inferior wine and fewer items of inexpensive clothing. Thus, the degree to which a specific commodity is inferior will often depend upon the number of higher price/quality substitutes which are available. Some goods may be neither normal nor inferior, resulting in a completely horizontal Engel curve, as in figure 2.3c. Typical examples include such things as salt, pepper and matches. Economists do not make sweeping generalisations about whether a commodity is either normal or inferior. It is more likely that goods and services may be deemed normal at low levels of income but become inferior at higher levels of income as consumers have the ability to switch to higher-quality alternatives. Thus, the Engel curve for many products is likely to exhibit both positive and negative sections, as is depicted in figure 2.4.

The main problem with the Engel curves depicted so far is that they are defined in terms of the unit change(s) in the demand for a specific good as income rises or falls. However, the present format does not lend itself to practical application for two reasons. First, economists tend to be interested in broader categories of goods and services for which there is no common unit of measurement. As we have already seen, the items which can be included in a general category of 'leisure goods and services' are extremely varied. Second, consumers may not change the actual number of units they consume of a particular commodity in response to a change in income but simply switch between high- and low-quality brands within the same product category. For example, a rise in salary may prompt a squash player to have his or her weekly game at a private squash club as opposed to the local public leisure centre. Thus, although the number of games played has not actually changed, the amount of money spent on the activity has. A way of circumventing this problem is to use an Engel expenditure curve.

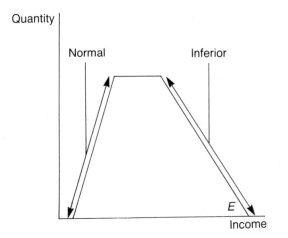

Figure 2.4 An Engel curve for a good with normal and inferior properties

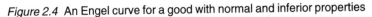

*The Engel expenditure curve*

The Engel expenditure curve focuses upon changes in the level of *expenditure* on a commodity or group of commodities as income changes rather than upon changes in the number of units consumed. Thus, on the horizontal axis we still measure income, but on the vertical axis we now measure consumer expenditure on a commodity or specific group of commodities. Furthermore, unlike the basic Engel curve, it is customary to include an extra line on the graph depicting an Engel expenditure curve. This is known as the 45° line. Assuming that the vertical and horizontal axes are calibrated using the same unit scale (e.g. pound for pound, dollar for dollar), any movement along a 45° line extending from the origin will depict points on the graph where income is exactly equal to expenditure. This can be seen in figure 2.5, where the 45° line is labelled $E = Y$ (expenditure equals income).

If the Engel expenditure curve coincides with this 45° line, then it means that all a consumer's income is being spent on the category of good defined upon the vertical axis. This is extremely unlikely. We would expect consumers to allocate their spending across a variety of commodity groups which would include food, clothing, shelter, travel, leisure and so on. Thus, it would be reasonable to expect the Engel

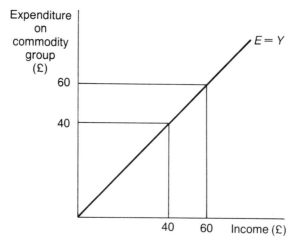

*Figure 2.5* The 45° line

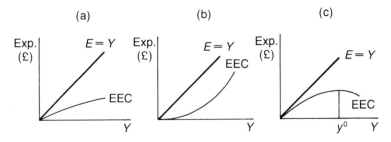

*Figure 2.6* The Engel expenditure curve

expenditure curve to lie below the 45° line. Three possible outcomes are outlined in figure 2.6.

It can be seen that in figures 2.6a and 2.6b the Engel expenditure curve, labelled EEC, is upward-sloping. This means that the commodity group as a whole has normal properties since expenditure on it is rising as income rises. However, it is possible for commodities within the overall category to be inferior, but these commodities are relatively less important to the individual in question than those which have normal properties. The overall effect is that the Engel expenditure curve still slopes upwards. Figures 2.6a and 2.6b differ in terms of the relationship between the Engel expenditure curve and the 45° line. In the first case, it can be seen that although the Engel expenditure curve is upward-sloping, it is deviating away from the 45° line. This means that the commodity group in question is absorbing an increasingly smaller proportion of income. An example of this type of commodity may be food consumed at home. In figure 2.6b, the Engel expenditure curve is bending towards the 45° line. This represents a situation where expenditure on the commodity group in question is an increasing function of income. An example of this would be spending on leisure activities. In figure 2.6c, the Engel expenditure curve begins to assume a negative slope beyond income level $y_0$. This means that the commodity group tends on average to contain what are deemed to be inferior goods. It is not really possible to think of a broad category of goods which would fit this outcome. Examples would therefore be limited to more restricted definitions of commodities, for example expenditure on bus travel, rather than travel in general.

There are two difficulties which arise when trying to establish a link between demand and income in practice. The first is that expenditure on a commodity or group of commodities will depend upon the size and

Table 2.1 Household expenditure, by socio-economic group of head, 1991

| | | | | | | Percentage of expenditure | | | | |
|---|---|---|---|---|---|---|---|---|---|---|
| Socio-economic group | Housing | Fuel light & power | Food | Alcohol & tobacco | Clothing and footwear | H/hold goods & services | Motoring & fares | Leisure goods & services | Other goods & services miscellaneous | Average total expenditure (£ per week) (= 100%) |
| Professional | 17.8 | 3.2 | 15.4 | 4.1 | 5.8 | 13.3 | 18.5 | 17.7 | 4.2 | 399.88 |
| Employers & managers | 17.8 | 3.7 | 16.0 | 5.5 | 6.8 | 12.6 | 15.6 | 17.4 | 4.6 | 406.78 |
| Other non-manual | 18.4 | 3.9 | 16.2 | 5.7 | 6.8 | 13.5 | 17.9 | 13.0 | 4.6 | 306.72 |
| Skilled manual | 17.1 | 4.3 | 19.3 | 8.2 | 6.5 | 11.6 | 17.9 | 10.7 | 4.3 | 282.32 |
| Semi-skilled manual | 18.3 | 4.8 | 19.3 | 8.1 | 6.3 | 12.6 | 15.3 | 10.5 | 4.7 | 234.14 |
| Unskilled manual | 17.9 | 6.1 | 21.0 | 8.5 | 5.4 | 12.5 | 14.7 | 9.5 | 5.2 | 203.27 |
| Retired | 26.1 | 7.1 | 18.8 | 4.3 | 4.6 | 12.9 | 10.6 | 11.3 | 4.5 | 151.80 |
| Unoccupied | 17.7 | 6.0 | 19.6 | 7.2 | 6.2 | 12.8 | 14.0 | 11.9 | 4.6 | 203.81 |
| Self-employed | 20.3 | 4.3 | 17.7 | 6.3 | 5.9 | 13.5 | 14.0 | 13.6 | 4.3 | 339.27 |
| All households* | 19.4 | 4.7 | 17.8 | 6.2 | 6.1 | 12.8 | 13.2 | 4.5 | 259.04 | |

Source: Social Trends, 1993, table 6.3, p. 83

Note: *Includes those where the head was in the armed forces, on a government training scheme, or had never worked, which are not shown separately.

composition of households (as well as such things as age and level of education). In other words, demand is not a simple function of income level. Economists have tried to compensate for this by adopting various weighting procedures. For example, in the case of food consumption, attempts have been made to weight demand according to nutritional requirement, for example by assuming that females have lower food requirements than males. However, this approach assumes a high degree of rationality on the part of consumers. It is unlikely that expenditure will be planned in such a way in reality.

The second problem reflects the day-to-day fact that people are usually reluctant to reveal household income accurately. Thus, it is more usual for studies to compromise and use total expenditure on the horizontal axis since it is a more accessible alternative variable. If the researcher has access to data indicating the relationship between total expenditure and income, for example from a different study, figures may subsequently be modified. However, it should be pointed out that it may be inappropriate to introduce data generated from a different group of consumers without being satisfied that this information is representative in terms of the sample in hand.

As was noted in Chapter 1, an insight into the composition of household expenditure in the UK by household income and general socio-economic group can be obtained from the *Family Expenditure Survey* or *Social Trends*. Table 2.1 is taken from *Social Trends, 1993*, itself derived from the 1991 *Family Expenditure Survey*, and it identifies differences in spending patterns between different socio-economic groups. It can be seen from column eight of the table that expenditure on leisure goods and services does vary between socio-economic groups, so that only 9.5 per cent of expenditure by households headed by unskilled manual workers is directed towards such commodities whereas for professional workers the corresponding figure is 17.7 per cent. In absolute terms this means that professional groups spend almost £68 per week on leisure items, whereas unskilled manual workers are only able to spend less than one-third of this figure. Lower income groups are forced to devote greater percentages of their income to necessities such as fuel, light and power.

## INDIFFERENCE CURVES

So far, the chapter has highlighted some of the independent variables which can influence the demand for a product, such as own price and income. However, we have yet to consider in detail the reasons why some consumers will choose to buy a particular product at a certain price or level of income while others will not. Everyday experience suggests the basic reason for this is that we are all different. We each have different tastes, so one person will enjoy consuming a particular good whereas others may not. One way in which this can be seen is in what we choose to wear. Thus, we will only buy a good or service if its price is less than or equal to the value that we ourselves attach to it. There is no point in purchasing it if the price exceeds our own valuation of it.

All the information which relates to the enjoyment consumers derive from consuming individual commodities or groups of commodities in combination is contained within the utility function. Utility functions are time-specific in that one which characterises our desire for goods and services over a year will differ significantly from one embracing 24 hours. This reflects the greater possibility of experiencing the benefits of a greater diversity of goods and services the longer the time period involved. In the nineteenth century, economists (for example William Stanley Jevons and Leon Walras) believed that individuals were not only able to compare alternative combinations of goods and services but were also able to ascribe a rigid set of values to the amount of utility offered by their consumption. This is referred to in the literature as a *cardinal* system of utility. Thus, if a pint of milk is deemed to offer a person eight units of utility while a pint of orange juice offers only four units of utility, then it can be deduced that a pint of milk is not only preferred to a pint of orange juice but also that the person enjoys the pint of milk twice as much as the same amount of orange juice. In other words, measuring utility becomes no different from making comparisons between objects in terms of differences in their temperature, light intensity or weight. However, this assumption confers a high degree of ability upon individual consumers to be able to measure exactly the utility they derive from different commodities. Twentieth-century economists (most notably, Sir John Hicks and Vilfredo Pareto) have preferred to assume that consumers make choices by *ranking* the utility differences between alternative combinations of goods and services. This is known as the *ordinal* approach. This is like saying that Frank Bruno is heavier than Barry McGuigan but not saying by how much. Although this assumption is less restrictive and appears 'less scientific', it does not prevent consumers from selecting the combination of goods and services which maximises their utility.

When consumers are making comparisons between alternative bundles of commodities, one of the most important constraints upon their behaviour is the amount of money they have available to spend. For some people, such as those on a student grant, this will be small, and therefore what to buy and not buy may be fairly clear-cut, emphasising the basic necessities for survival. For others, perhaps on large salaries, the choice is wider since more goods are affordable, even after their requirements with respect to food, clothing and shelter have been satisfied. Nevertheless, whatever sum of money we have at our disposal, big or small, it is still limited, thereby forcing us to make choices about what we spend it on. The analysis which follows focuses upon the way in which economists depict individuals and households when they make consumption decisions. This involves deriving two fundamental concepts, the *budget constraint* and the *indifference curve*.

### The budget constraint

For simplicity, let us assume that a consumer has to allocate his or her fixed money income between two types of commodity: food and sports goods. Both have a fixed unit price over which the consumer has no control. It should be recalled that in such circumstances we say that the individual is a price taker. The budget constraint or budget line shows all the combinations of goods which an individual can afford with a fixed amount of income. All the money can be spent on one or other of the commodities or, alternatively, some combination of the two. For example, let us assume that the individual has £100 and the unit prices of food and leisure goods are £2 and £5 respectively. If the consumer buys nothing but food, then 50 units can be afforded. Similarly, 20 units of leisure goods can be purchased if no food is bought. It is more likely, however, that the individual would rather purchase a combination of the two commodities; after all, variety is the spice of life!

The options open to the consumer can be set out diagramatically. In figure 2.7, units of food are measured along the horizontal axis of the graph while leisure goods are measured along the vertical axis. Each point on the graph therefore indicates some bundle or combination of the two goods. Points along either of the two axes denote a bundle containing all of one good and none of the other. Other points describe a bundle containing both the goods, with the relative quantities varying as we move within the bounds of the graph. The budget line joins together all the bundles of food and leisure goods which can just be afforded from a fixed level of income. Thus, using the figures in the earlier example, it will be a straight line extending upwards, right to left, from 50 units of food to 20 units of leisure goods. Any combination of food and leisure goods along the budget constraint will completely

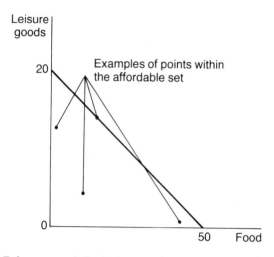

*Figure 2.7* A consumer's budget constraint

exhaust the income available to the consumer. Should the consumer choose not to spend all the income that is available, then it will involve a choice of one of the combinations which lie inside the budget line. These combinations, plus all the points lying along the budget constraint itself, are known as the affordable set. Any bundle of goods which lies outside, to the right of the budget line, cannot be afforded given the fixed prices and the income that is available to the consumer.

The budget constraint which confronts each individual need not be static over time. There are two factors which can lead to its position changing. The first is an increase in income. Assuming that prices remain fixed, an increase in income will cause the budget line to shift outwards, away from the origin. Its final position will be parallel to the original. For example, let us assume that the consumer's income increases from £100 to £120. With the same prices, this means that the consumer can now afford to buy 60 units of food *or* 24 units of leisure goods *or* some combination of the two (such as 30 units of food and 12 units of leisure goods). The increase in the affordable set of the consumer can be seen in figure 2.8. Decreases in the income of the consumer will analogously cause the budget line to move inwards towards the origin (while remaining parallel to the original), leading to a reduction in the affordable set of the consumer.

The other factor which can affect the position of the budget line is a

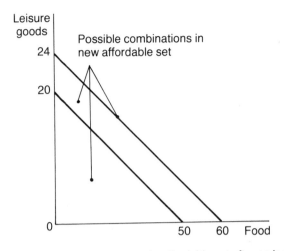

*Figure 2.8* An increase in a consumer's affordable set after an increase in income

change in price levels. For simplicity, let us consider the effects of a decrease in the price of foodstuffs, assuming income and the price of leisure goods remain the same. Rather than initiating a parallel shift in the budget line, a change in one of the prices will cause the budget line to pivot outwards. Let us consider why. If the price of foodstuffs falls, then the maximum number of units of food which can be afforded will rise. However, since this is the only price which has fallen, the maximum number of leisure goods which can be afforded is the same as before. Thus numerically, if it were assumed that the price of foodstuffs fell from £2 to £1, then a maximum of 100 units could be afforded, rather than 50 units before the price change. In contrast, the maximum number of leisure goods which can be bought with the fixed budget remains at 20. As can be seen in figure 2.9, the affordable set has increased by the wedge shape between the two budget lines. As before, it also includes all points along the new budget line. Of course, the reduction in the price of foodstuffs does not necessarily mean that this improvement in circumstances will be completely channelled into the purchase of extra foodstuffs. The consumer might initially have consumed at point *A* in figure 2.9 but responds to the fall in price by moving to point *B*, thereby increasing his or her consumption of both commodities. This reflects the

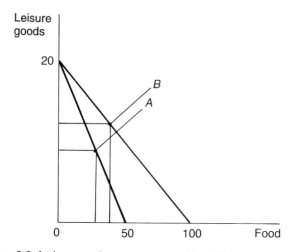

*Figure 2.9* An increase in a consumer's affordable set from a fall in the price of food

consumer's greater consumption opportunities in the face of an expanded attainable set.

For ease of illustration, the discussion has focused upon changes in the consumer's income or a movement in relative prices in isolation. Of course, it is possible for movements in both prices (both real and relative) to be taking place at the same time as fluctuations in the individual's available income. Thus we may witness an outward shift in the line caused by an increase in income together with a reduction in both sets of prices. If the prices change by different amounts, then the new budget line will not only lie completely outside the previous one but will also cease to be parallel to it. Conversely, an increase in the affordable set brought about by a rise in income may be counteracted by a rise in prices, leaving the affordable set the same or even smaller. Although it is possible to incorporate simultaneous changes in all the variables which contribute to the consumer's ability to buy goods or services, it is much easier to focus upon changes in one of the variables in isolation, without detracting from the meaning of the analysis.

So far, we have concentrated upon the factors which contribute to a consumer's ability to consume goods. Let us now turn to a consideration of how we might determine which bundle of goods out of all the bundles that are affordable the consumer will choose. For this purpose, economists use indifference curves. The next stage of the analysis is to define therefore the properties of an indifference curve and how the concept can be used to show that for any given affordable set, there will only be one combination of goods which will maximise a consumer's utility.

## Properties of indifference curves

An indifference curve traces out combinations of two goods which give an individual the same amount of utility. Thus if five units of leisure goods and six units of food provide consumers with exactly the same amount of utility as four units of leisure goods and eight units of food then both bundles will lie on the same indifference curve. Strictly speaking, there is no predefined shape for indifference curves to take. The fact that every individual will have a different utility function which will reflect his or her own particular set of tastes and preferences means that each person will value alternative combinations of commodities in a slightly different way. Nevertheless, we can derive intuitively a general shape which we might expect indifference curves to take.

The axes of the graph in figure 2.10 again measure units of leisure and food. It will be assumed that both commodities are deemed desirable by the consumer, such that additional units consumed will generate greater

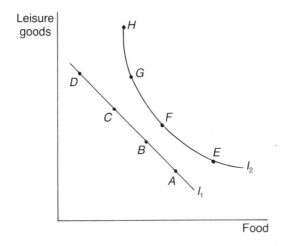

*Figure 2.10* Potential indifference curve shapes

levels of utility (the implication of situations where one or both of the commodities in question are not desirable will be discussed shortly). Two potential shapes for indifference curves have been inserted. Indifference curve $I_1$ is a negatively sloped straight line, whereas indifference curve $I_2$ is curvilinear, convex to the origin.

In the case of $I_1$, it can be seen that, by definition, combinations $A$, $B$, $C$ and $D$ all offer the consumer identical amounts of utility. Thus, for the consumer's level of satisfaction to be constant, an increase in the consumption of one commodity has to be matched by a reduction in the consumption of the other. The rate at which one good must be sacrificed for another in order to maintain a fixed utility will depend upon the consumer's own preferences and is known as the *marginal rate of substitution* (MRS). It can be seen from the graph that as we move from right to left up $I_1$, the MRS of leisure goods for food remains constant regardless of the relative quantities the consumer has, so that, for example, a reduction of one extra unit of sports goods always has to be matched by a two-unit reduction in foodstuffs if the individual is to enjoy the same level of utility. However, this is not the case with indifference curve $I_2$. It can be seen that the rate at which food is given up for leisure goods varies along the indifference curve. Specifically, it can be seen that for the move from $E$ to $F$ the individual is willing to give up a relatively large number of units of food in order to get an extra unit of leisure goods, whereas for subsequent moves from $F$ to $G$ and $G$ to $H$ he or she is willing to give up progressively smaller amounts of food for the unit increment in leisure activity. The rationale behind this is that at point $E$, the individual is relatively abundant in food and scarce in leisure commodities. Thus, he or she is assumed to place a lower valuation on a unit of food than a unit of leisure goods. As we move from $F$ to $G$, the consumer is becoming progressively less abundant in food and therefore his or her unit valuation of that product increases while his or her valuation of units of leisure activity decreases as this commodity becomes less scarce. In this situation we say that the indifference curve is exhibiting a *diminishing marginal rate of substitution*. As before, the rate at which one good must be given up for increments in the other to maintain the same level of utility will depend upon the individual's own utility function. Since this scenario conforms to many real-world situations, it will be assumed that indifference curves are negatively sloped and convex to the origin.

Since, in theory, there are an infinite number of alternative combinations of the two highlighted commodities, there will also be an infinite number of indifference curves for each individual, each associated with

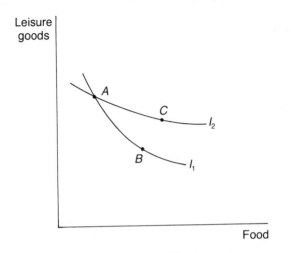

*Figure 2.11* Two (incorrectly) crossing indifference curves

a different level of utility. Since both goods are assumed to be desirable, the further we are away from the origin of the graph in a north-easterly direction, the better off the consumer will be. Thus, the further to the right an indifference curve is, the greater the level of utility it commands. However, indifference curve analysis is an ordinal approach to measuring utility, so we do not know by how much combinations on one indifference curve are preferred to combinations which lie on the indifference curve immediately to the left or the right of it.

Although every conceivable bundle of goods will have an indifference curve passing through it, an important property of indifference curves is that they can never cross. Let us consider why by looking at the implications of allowing (incorrectly) two curves to cross. It can be seen in figure 2.11 that the two indifference curves intersect. Three points are highlighted, $A$, $B$ and $C$. Two implausible situations therefore arise. First, point $A$ falls on both curves yet, by definition, the two indifference curves are associated with different levels of utility. Second, point $C$ is preferable to point $B$ (since it offers more of both commodities) yet the consumer is supposed to be indifferent between either of these points and $A$: clearly a nonsense.

To summarise this section, it should be noted that we have highlighted four main propositions:

1    indifference curves are assumed to be convex to the origin,
     displaying a diminishing marginal rate of substitution;
2    there is an indifference curve passing through every conceivable
     bundle of goods (some texts refer to indifference curves as being
     'everywhere dense');
3    indifference curves can never cross;
4    indifference curves are an ordinal measure of utility.

One further point should be noted. It has been assumed throughout that
the commodities are both desirable. In other words, consumption of each
item generates positive utility. It is possible to modify the shape of
indifference curves so that they can also take account of 'undesirable'
commodities which produce negative utility for the consumer in
question. Our perception of what goods fall into this category may be
shared, such as exposure to pollution and crime, whereas in other cases
it may simply reflect personal taste. Let us consider the implications for
the shape of an indifference curve when one of the commodities is
undesirable in the sense described above. It can be seen from figure 2.12
that the indifference curve which results ceases to be convex to the
origin. In this example, the 'undesirable' commodity is measured along
the horizontal axis. To remain on the same indifference curve and hence
derive the same level of utility, increments in the desirable good must be

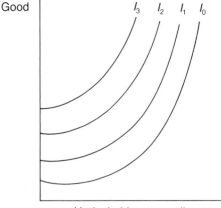

Undesirable commodity

*Figure 2.12* Indifference curves when one commodity is undesirable

met by increments (rather than reductions) in the 'undesirable' commodity. In this case, utility increases as we move in a north-westerly direction. However, such cases are rare and for the purposes of the discussion to follow, we shall concentrate upon situations where both commodities are deemed to be desirable.

We are now in a position to determine which point in a consumer's affordable set will maximise his or her utility. In figure 2.13, we have superimposed a set of indifference curves on to the budget constraint which was derived earlier. It can be seen that two of the indifference curves lie completely outside the budget constraint. This means that no combination of goods along them can be afforded. Utility will be maximised at the point where the most north-easterly indifference curve is just tangential to the budget constraint. In the diagram this is indifference curve I*. Some combinations lying on indifference curves to the left of I* can be afforded, because they coincide with the affordable set, but offer a reduced level of utility. It can be seen that there is only one combination of food and leisure goods which maximises utility, namely $F^*$, $L^*$. Any other combination offers less utility to the consumer or cannot be afforded.

This basic framework can be applied to a variety of different situations where the consumer is constrained with respect to his or her consumption choices. For the purposes of this text, we shall consider a

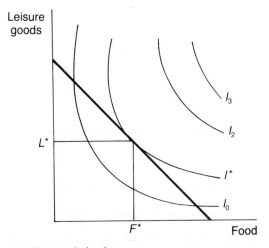

*Figure 2.13* Utility maximisation

situation of direct interest to many researchers concerned with the demand for leisure, specifically the demand for leisure time.

## THE DEMAND FOR LEISURE TIME

For the purposes of this analysis, it will be assumed that individuals can be characterised by a utility function containing just two variables. The first is income, assumed to be derived from paid employment (sometimes referred to as market work). Although working is likely to cause a degree of disutility arising from, for example, the monotony of the tasks involved and the constraints it imposes on lifestyle, the income that it generates can be used to provide positive utility. It can be converted not only into a variety of commodities, ranging from the basic necessities of life such as food and shelter, but also into recreation activities such as tourism, playing sport or videogames and gambling. Obviously, the higher the income that is available to us, the greater the spending options there are. The second variable we shall include in the consumer's utility function is leisure time itself. This can also be

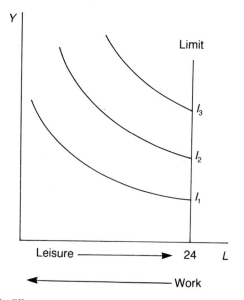

*Figure 2.14* Indifference curves and the choice between income and leisure time

assumed to be desirable since it provides the opportunity to enjoy the commodities which can be afforded. Thus, we may define the utility function as $U = f(Y, L)$, where $U$ denotes utility, $Y$ represents income and $L$ denotes leisure time. This can be shown diagramatically by drawing a family of indifference curves for a representative individual. In figure 2.14, income ($Y$) is represented on the vertical axis while increments of leisure time ($L$) are measured along the horizontal axis. However, because the analysis is concerned with measuring the availability of leisure time within a set period of time, for example a day or a week, the $x$ axis will contain an upper bound. For the purposes of this analysis, it will be assumed that this limit is set at 24 hours. It can therefore be seen that a move from left to right along the horizontal axis simultaneously represents an increase in leisure time and a reduction in working time since both activities are being met from the fixed stock of available time. Conversely, a move towards the origin implies an increase in work time and a fall in available leisure time. This limit on time available also means that the family of indifference curves which have been inserted on figure 2.14 cannot extend beyond the 24-hour limit. Since both income and leisure time are desirable commodities, the indifference

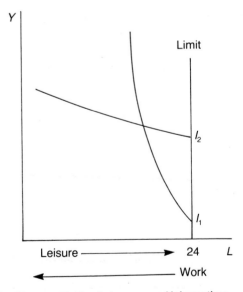

*Figure 2.15* Different attitudes to income and leisure time

curves are negatively sloped (a gain in one of the commodities must be met by a loss in the other if constant utility is to be maintained). Their convexity to the origin indicates a diminishing marginal rate of substitution between the variables. In other words, as the relative abundance of either income or leisure time increases, the lower the value we place on additional units of it.

At this point it should be re-emphasised that individuals have distinctive utility functions. In terms of this analysis, they will differ in their relative valuation of leisure time and income. Some people, for example, will place a high premium on the amount of leisure time they have at their disposal such that at any given level of utility a large reduction in income is compensated for by a comparatively small increment in leisure time. This scenario is reflected in the shape of indifference curve $I_1$ in figure 2.15. Conversely, there are people who place a relatively higher value upon their income who can be compensated for a large reduction in their leisure time by a seemingly small increase in income. This can be seen in the case of indifference curve $I_2$ in figure 2.15.

In our earlier analysis of indifference curves it was acknowledged that consumers will be constrained in their choice of goods and services by the budget available to them over a given time period. Rational individuals were seen to choose the point on this budget constraint which afforded them the greatest possible utility, namely the point at which the budget constraint and indifference curve are tangential. We can construct a similar type of framework for the scenario in hand. To begin, let us construct the budget constraint. At one extreme, the greatest amount of leisure an individual can consume is if no work is done at all, namely the entire 24-hour period. At the other end of the spectrum, there is a limit upon the amount of income which can be earned from any given occupation. In theory, the most which could be earned is the hourly wage rate multiplied by 24. In practice this is obviously impractical since no one could work effectively for 24 hours a day. Nevertheless, the greater the hourly wage rate of a given occupation, the steeper the budget constraint facing the consumer (for any given calibration of the graph) and the larger the number of attainable leisure time/income combinations. This can be seen in figure 2.16 where line $A$ reflects the opportunities afforded by a poorly paid occupation and constraint $B$ represents the budget constraint from highly paid employment. It can be seen that the maximum amount which could be earned from 24 hours work in the lower paid job ($Y'$) could be earned by someone in the higher paid employment within $H$ hours. When the consumer's indifference

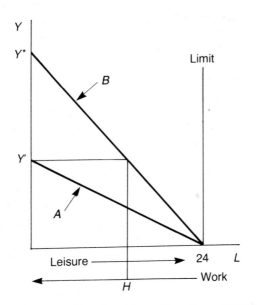

Figure 2.16 Budget constraints from high paid and low paid work

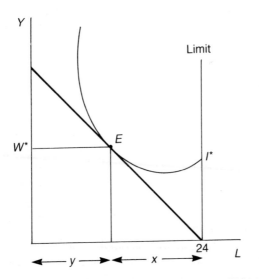

Figure 2.17 Utility-maximising combination of income and leisure time

curves are superimposed upon this budget constraint, we can see that there is a unique utility maximising leisure time/income combination. This is identified in figure 2.17 as point $E$. It can be seen that at the utility-maximising point, $E$, the consumer will work $x$ hours, leaving $y$ hours as leisure time. The income from this paid employment is $W^*$.

The next stage of the analysis will focus upon what will happen if the consumer faces a change in the hourly wage rate. In terms of the framework set out above, such a change will alter the slope of the budget constraint, so that it will be flatter for a reduction in the hourly rate and steeper if there is an increase. Let us look at how a utility-maximising individual will react to an increase in the hourly wage. It is possible to isolate two effects. First, any change in the real wage will have an impact upon the opportunity cost of leisure time. In this case, the opportunity cost will increase since it is now more expensive to take an extra hour of leisure due to the higher forgone earnings. Demand theory would suggest that the individual in question will consume less leisure than before due to its higher price. Economists refer to this as the *substitution effect*.

The second implication of the increase in the wage rate is that it adds to the combinations of leisure time and income which are available. In this case there is no *a priori* hypothesis as to how the individual will respond to these enhanced opportunities. It will depend upon the individual's utility function. However, it would not be unreasonable to expect the consumer to take advantage of the increase in the wage rate not only to add to his or her daily stream of income but also to increase the amount of leisure time available each day. This is referred to as the *income effect*, reflecting the fact that the consumer is now better off. It must be stressed once again, however, that whereas we can predict the direction of the substitution effect, the income effect is dependent upon the preferences of the consumer. The sum of the substitution effect and the income effect is known as the *total effect*.[2] The income and substitution effects are demonstrated diagramatically in figure 2.18 and discussed in more detail shortly.

The increase in the hourly rate of pay is denoted by the upward pivoting of the budget constraint. This provides the opportunity for the individual concerned to experience a higher level of utility, reflected in the new point of tangency, $F$. Thus, the consumer in question has been made better off than before since in this example, he or she has not only been able to expand the amount of available leisure time but also to increase income.[3] For this individual, this point of tangency provides more utility than any other income/leisure time combination on the new

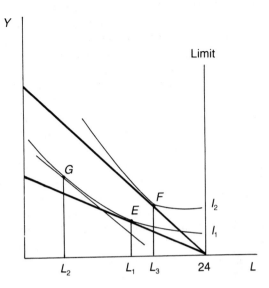

*Figure 2.18* Income and substitution effects

budget constraint. The total effect of this change is therefore the shift from $E$ to $F$ in figure 2.18.

We can highlight the substitution effect brought about by this increase in income by adding an artificial budget constraint to the diagram which reflects the new wage rate (and hence price of leisure time) but is drawn tangential to the old level of utility, characterised by indifference curve $I_1$. This identifies the pure substitution effect since any gains in utility from the extra income and leisure time has been suppressed. By making the consumer neither better nor worse off than before, we are isolating the consumer's response to the pure change in relative prices. Thus, we may define the move from point $E$ to point $G$ in figure 2.18 as the substitution effect and this reflects the fact that the individual will consume less of the more expensive commodity (namely leisure) and undertake more work.

We are now in a position to identify the second of the two changes brought about by the change in the wage rate, namely the income effect. It should be recalled that this focuses upon the fact that the change in the wage rate has widened the consumer's attainable set. We can therefore compare points $G$ and $F$ in terms of the change in the consumption of income and leisure time which has been brought about by a change in the real income of the consumer. The magnitude of increase in real income is mirrored in the distance between the artificial budget constraint and the new budget constraint. The fact that we have now suppressed the change in relative prices is reflected in these two lines being drawn parallel to each other. When the income and substitution effects are combined, we get the total effect and this is the change in equilibrium positions from $E$ to $F$. In terms of the changes along the horizontal axis of figure 2.18, the substitution effect is the move from $L_1$ to $L_2$, while the income effect is the move from $L_2$ to $L_3$. In this example it can be seen that the income effect outweighs the subsitition effect such that the consumer chooses to work fewer hours than before.

Provided it is reasonable to assume that leisure time is a normal good, then we may state without fear of contradiction that the income and substitution effects will work in opposite directions.[4] However there is no theoretical basis to guide us as to which effect will dominate the other in the final outcome, but we may expect that much will depend upon the wage rate. For people on low hourly wages, it is likely that, although leisure is perceived as being normal, the substitution effect will outweigh the income effect. This will result in an increase in the wage rate leading to an increase in the number of hours worked. This

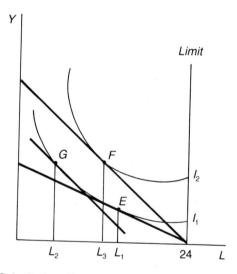

Figure 2.19 Substitution effect greater than income effect

scenario is demonstrated in figure 2.19 where the substitution effect leads to a reduction in leisure time from $L_1$ to $L_2$ and the income effect operates from $L_2$ to $L_3$. At high wage rates, it is more likely that an increase in wage rates will reduce the overall number of hours worked. This is because the individual concerned would already be earning sufficient money to finance both necessary and luxury expenditures and is also seeking to improve the overall quality of life by adding to the available leisure time. In this case, the income effect is not only positive (as expected for a normal good) but is also sufficiently large to outweigh the substitution effect.

Some readers may feel that the framework used in this analysis is somewhat abstract and does not really reflect the choices which confront individuals in real life. For example, time is here simply broken down into leisure time and work time whereas in reality time is also used for eating, sleeping and housework. Furthermore, there is also the possibility of unearned income, arising from accumulated savings or from state benefits. These possibilities should not be seen as a problem. Extremely complex budget constraints *can* be calculated to take account of the even greater interaction between taxes and welfare benefits (such as family income supplement, child benefit and housing benefit) as they apply to households of different individual compositions. These are often used by labour economists to show visually how the benefit system may actually produce disincentives to work amongst the low paid. Estimated constraints contain large plateaux or even dips when paid work leads to the removal of certain benefits. However, the inclusion of such effects would merely serve to complicate the basic analysis.

A point which should be considered, however, is that most individuals do not have an infinitely free choice with respect to the number of hours they work during the basic working week/working day. Usually, the hours that each employee works is determined in advance and offered on a 'take it or leave it' basis. The result is that many individuals do not have the opportunity to maximise their utility. In other words, they are constrained to consume an amount of leisure time which lies on a lower indifference curve than they would prefer to be on. Thus a more realistic outcome is the one depicted in figure 2.20. In this example, it can be seen that the contractual obligations imposed by the employer force the individual to consume $L_1$ units of leisure time. This contrasts with the optimal amount of leisure time for this consumer of $L^*$. In other words, the consumer only receives the utility associated with indifference curve $I_1$, rather than that of $I_2$ which is just tangential to the time budget line.

One group of workers for whom this problem is likely to have a

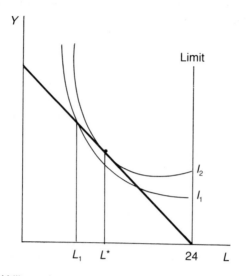

*Figure 2.20* Utility and contractual obligation

significant effect is women, particularly working mothers. This is because the burden of many household tasks falls upon women. For example, domestic requirements, particularly with respect to the needs of children, can place highly complex constraints upon the types of job women can apply for. Thus, although females in full-time employment tend to work fewer hours than males in full-time employment, they undertake significantly more tasks within the home and consequently have less leisure time at their disposal. Figures produced by the Henley Centre for Forecasting (reproduced in *Social Trends, 1993*) show that women undertook an average of 42.3 hours of 'essential activities' (defined as childcare, shopping, cooking, personal hygiene and appearance) per week in 1991–2 whereas the corresponding figure for males was only 26.8 hours per week. Indeed, women working part-time average 57 hours per week of non-market work. The implications of this unequal division of labour within the household can be seen in table 2.2 which not only provides a breakdown of free time for males and females in employment (part-time and full-time) but also for 'housewives' and retired people. The statistical section of the *Employment Gazette* can be used to provide evidence that the leisure sector is an important employer of women, particularly in terms of part-time work. This can be seen in table 2.3. These figures highlight two important characteristics with

*Table 2.2* Leisure time in a typical week, by employment status and sex, 1991–2

| | Full-time Males | Full-time Females | Part-time Females | Housewives | Retired |
|---|---|---|---|---|---|
| Free time per weekday | 4.8 | 3.3 | 4.7 | 7.0 | 11.6 |
| Free time per weekend day | 11.3 | 8.3 | 8.7 | 9.0 | 12.6 |
| Total free time | 46.5 | 33.0 | 41.0 | 53.5 | 83.0 |

*Source: Social Trends, 1993,* table 10.3, p. 140

*Table 2.3* Employment in selected leisure services, December 1992 ('000s)

| | Male Part-time | Male Full-time | Female Part-time | Female Full-time |
|---|---|---|---|---|
| Restaurants, cafés and snack bars | 51.4 | 74.1 | 120.1 | 49.1 |
| Public houses and bars | 74.1 | 34.7 | 186.8 | 33.7 |
| Nightclubs and licensed clubs | 34.1 | 17.8 | 73.9 | 11.5 |
| Hotels and other short-stay accommodation | 36.1 | 76.9 | 87.6 | 70.7 |
| Sport and other recreation activities (incl. libraries, museums and art galleries) | 56.0 | 123.0 | 122.2 | 78.9 |

*Source: Employment Gazette,* April 1993, statistics section, table 1.4

respect to the employment opportunities leisure does offer. First and generally, part-time work is an extremely important contributor to all five of the identified sectors. This should be no surprise. The characterisitics of such services as hotels, public houses and restaurants clearly lend themselves to this mode of employment. Thus taking 'hotels and other short-stay accommodation', there are over 271,000 employees, of which 45 per cent are part-time. Furthermore, for 'sport and other recreation activities' the respective figures are 380,000 and 47 per cent. The second and more specific feature of these figures is the importance of female employment within the overall totals. Again taking 'hotels and other short-stay accommodation' and 'sport and other recreation activities', female employment (part-time and full-time combined) represents

58 per cent and 53 per cent of the total respectively. However, in terms of part-time work, the respective percentages of female employment are 71 per cent and 68 per cent. Conversely, for males full-time jobs are dominant in all five categories. For means of comparison, we may cite the relative contribution of part-time work to manufacturing and overall service employment. In the former case only 27 per cent of the 20,889,600 jobs are part-time whereas in the overall service sector (including leisure), 35 per cent of the 15,159,400 jobs are part-time.

The fact that women not only have a smaller amount of leisure time available but also are more likely to be subject to a more complex set of constraints imposed by non-market work means that it is harder for them to participate in leisure activities outside the home. Thus, as we shall see in later chapters, Sports Council objectives to increase the level of active participation by women in sport and leisure will require leisure providers to be flexible with respect to the opening times of facilities and the provision of childcare facilities.

## QUESTIONS FOR DISCUSSION

1   Draw a hypothetical demand curve for any good or service produced by the leisure industry that you consume on a regular basis. What will be the effect upon it of:

   (a)  an increase in the price of the commodity you have chosen?
   (b)  an increase in your real income?
   (c)  changes in weather conditions, for example between summer and winter?
   (d)  increased media attention given to the need to be fit and healthy?

2   What factors prevent many women from participating in leisure activities outside the home?

# Chapter 3

# Estimating demand and the market for leisure activities

## INTRODUCTION

The analysis conducted in Chapter 2 identified some of the factors that will determine which goods and services an individual will choose to consume. This chapter builds upon this framework and considers the relationship between the demand curve of an individual consumer and that describing the demand from a *group* of consumers. Having established the theoretical relationship between the two, the discussion will turn to consider some of the problems economists face when trying to derive such a demand curve in practice. Specific reference will be made to the problems economists face when trying to estimate the demand for parks and reservoirs, facilities which can be used for a variety of leisure pursuits including angling, sailing, water-skiing, walking or just having a picnic. However, demand is only one side of the equation. A consumer's ability to enjoy the benefits of a given commodity will depend upon the willingness and ability of suppliers to produce it. Thus, the remaining sections of the chapter will consider, first, the factors which prompt suppliers to produce goods and services and, second, the economic properties of the marketplace, where consumers and producers ultimately communicate with each other. As an example, specific reference will be made to the demand for and supply of golf courses.

## THE RELATIONSHIP BETWEEN INDIVIDUAL AND MARKET DEMAND

The overall or market demand for a particular commodity at different prices can be estimated by adding together the individual demands of all the consumers who express a willingness and ability to consume it. To

*Table 3.1* Differences in individual demand in a three-person world

| Price (£) P | Individual A Q | Individual B Q | Individual C Q |
|---|---|---|---|
| 9 | 11 | 0 | 12 |
| 8 | 12 | 0 | 16 |
| 7 | 13 | 0 | 19 |
| 6 | 14 | 0 | 23 |
| 5 | 15 | 1 | 28 |
| 4 | 16 | 2 | 35 |
| 3 | 17 | 3 | 40 |
| 2 | 18 | 4 | 65 |
| 1 | 19 | 5 | 90 |

illustrate, let us consider a simple three-person world. Table 3.1 depicts the amount of a good or service the three individuals demand as the price falls from £9 to £1. It can be seen that each individual wishes to consume a different amount of the product in question at each price. For example, if the price is £8 then the total demand from our three individuals would be 28 units: 12 demanded by A and 16 demanded by C. At that price individual B does not buy any units at all. However, if the price falls to £5, individual B would also be tempted to buy the product, albeit one unit. The overall demand on this occasion would be 44 units, with 15 units bought by consumer A and 28 units by consumer C also. By the same process, a fall in price to £1 per unit would lead to an overall demand of 114 units.

The principle that the market demand for a product can be estimated by adding together all the individual demands for a product can also be demonstrated using a graph. In figure 3.1, a demand curve for a typical individual is labelled *d* while a section of the demand curve appertaining to the whole market is labelled *D*. The discontinuity in the *x* axis is drawn to emphasise the fact that whereas changes in individual demand to a change in price may only be in terms of a few units, changes in market demand to a given price change may reflect thousands, hundreds of thousands or even millions of units. To emphasise the fact that changes in market demand are likely to mirror significantly larger changes in demand, the market demand curve has been given a relatively flatter slope. Consider a fall in the price from $P_0$ to $P_1$. Such a change will elicit a response from each individual, such as the one defined by demand curve *d*. In aggregate, however, the demand curve is identifying the collective response of all individuals who reveal a preference to buy

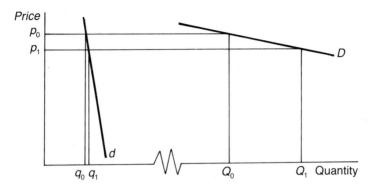

*Figure 3.1* Individual and market demand curve

the commodity. Economists say that the market demand curve is a *horizontal sum* of all the individual demands. In other words, we are summing across quantities rather than prices.

A final point to note with respect to the construction of demand curves, whether they are at an individual or at a more aggregated level, relates to the definition of the commodity on the $x$ axis. If it is too general, the information which the demand curve is providing, with respect to the relationship between price and quantity demanded, may not be as meaningful as it could be. Consider as an example the demand for indoor swimming facilities. Over the last few years there has not only been a significant increase in the number of conventional swimming pools, but also a growth in the number of leisure pools. Although the novelty factor may mean that they are initially substitutes for each other, Johnson (1990) argues that ultimately they become complementary facilities, with standard pools catering for the serious swimmer and leisure pools attracting a younger, more casual user. In other words, it is inappropriate to think in terms of a general demand curve for indoor swimming pools but instead, two demand curves for two different kinds of facility: 'conventional' pools and leisure pools. Despite the fact that leisure pools are more costly to run and that there is survey evidence to suggest that leisure pool users are willing to pay more for a swimming session, there is a tendancy for the prices of conventional and leisure pools to be broadly similar. We may draw upon CIPFA's *Charges for Leisure Services Statistics 1992-93* to back this point up. For a peak-time adult session at a conventional indoor pool, prices in their sample range from £1.05 to £1.75, with charges at 50 per cent of the pools no more than £1.35. Prices for a peak adult session at a leisure pool range from £1.08 to £3, with 50 per cent of prices no higher than £1.63. In other words, despite discernible differences in the basic profile of users at each type of facility (and hence in the relative shape of their demand curves), local authorities still seem to be treating swimmers as an amorphous group of consumers, thereby missing revenue-raising opportunities.

## AREAS UNDER THE DEMAND CURVE

Now that we have outlined specifically what a demand curve is, either as it appertains to one consumer or, in its more aggregated form, depicting the demand of a large number of individuals, it is possible to define two terms which will underpin the analysis in this and subsequent chapters. The first is *total revenue* (or *total consumer expenditure*) and the second is *consumer surplus*. Both can be explained with reference to figure 3.2 which depicts a demand curve for local swimming pool during a given week.

For simplicity, let us assume that there is a single price which is charged to all consumers of the pool, regardless of their age or the time they use the facility. This is *P*. Our demand curve tells us that at that

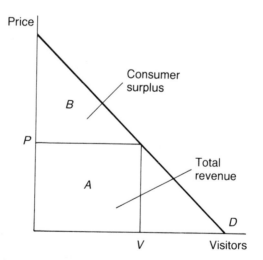

*Figure 3.2* Total revenue and consumer surplus

price, $V$ visitors will go to the pool. The total revenue which the owner of the pool will receive is the entrance fee that is levied multiplied by the number of people using the pool, numerically $P \times V$. Visually, the revenue which the swimming pool owner receives (or the total amount consumers spend on that facility) will be the rectangle labelled $A$. As we have already seen, a change in the price of the pool will bring about a change in the number people who are willing and able to visit it. This will not only lead to a change in the shape of the revenue rectangle when compared with $A$, but is also likely to lead to a change in the revenue which is collected. The way in which total revenue can change as we move up and down a demand curve will be explored in more detail in Chapter 5.

The second term to be identified in this section is consumer surplus. Put simply, consumer surplus is created when individuals are able to pay less for a good or service than the value they actually place upon it. For example, a consumer may be prepared to pay £1.50 to swim, yet the price he or she actually has to pay may only be £1.20. In this case we say that the value of the consumer surplus is 30p. To illustrate this more formally, let us refer again to figure 3.2. It can be seen from the demand curve that there are consumers who are willing and able to pay a price in excess of $P$ to visit the swimming pool. Specifically all visitors to the left of $V$ are actually willing to pay more than $P$ for their swim. Since the demand curve is downward-sloping, it can be seen that the amount of consumer surplus enjoyed by swimmers as we move along the $x$ axis diminishes since each person is willing and able to pay a smaller amount to use the pool (though still greater than $P$). The $V$th swimmer values his or her swim at exactly $P$ and therefore receives no consumer surplus. Consumers to the right of $V$ are not willing and able to pay $P$ for a swim (though they would be encouraged to swim if the price was reduced) and therefore neither consume the product nor enjoy consumer surplus. The total value of the consumer surplus may be calculated from the triangle which lies immediately above the total revenue rectangle and below the demand curve. In figure 3.2 this is labelled $B$. Thus, if the price of using the swimming pool increases, the consumer surplus triangle will have a smaller area.

On many occasions we encounter situations where we do not have to pay directly for the goods and services we use (though we may pay indirectly via local or national taxes). In the case of leisure activities, visits to the countryside or trips to a local playground are free of charge as are many other activities we consume during our free time. If people are willing and able to pay to use a particular facility there will be a demand curve for it even if no entrance fee has to be paid. In this case the consumer surplus will be the entire area under the demand curve since everyone who is willing and able to pay an entrance fee is able to consume the facility at zero cost.

In order to estimate the relationship between price and total revenue and that between price and consumer surplus for a good or service, we need information about the nature of the demand curve. However, deriving a demand curve in practice is significantly more difficult than it is in theory because of the simultaneous changes which are taking place within a given product's demand function every day. Nevertheless, given the almost endless variety of commodities which are bought and sold every day, it is perhaps no surprise that there are hundreds of studies in the economics literature which have attempted to estimate market demand curves. Some researchers have tried to isolate their study from some of the potential biases which may occur by trying to estimate demand curves using individuals' responses to *hypothetical* questions. Others have used genuine data, but in doing so have incorporated all the different biases which can simultaneously affect demand in the real world. Within the next section, four approaches will be highlighted in order to provide a flavour of the types of study which can be found in the general economics literature. This is followed by a more detailed analysis of a study found in the recreation economics literature which incorporates two such techniques, *contingent valuation* and the *travel cost method*.

## THE EMPIRICAL ESTIMATION OF DEMAND

### Surveys

Few people have avoided being confronted with a questionnaire to answer or a survey form at some point in their lives. This reflects the fact that producers are never completely aware of the demand function associated with their product. The need for socio-economic information which may allow them to *target* their product more successfully is paramount, particularly where taste and fashion can play an important role in determining sales. Limited surveys can be used by large and small companies to obtain specific pieces of information about their product, for example general consumer satisfaction or how service delivery could be improved. More complex forms can be constructed to provide more detailed information, such as how much of a given commodity respondents would buy or expect to buy at different prices. In theory, this can provide sufficient information for a demand curve to be estimated. Unfortunately this approach is likely to produce biased results because of the snap judgements consumers are being asked to make. Thus, although individuals may *want* to give the correct information, when placed in a hypothetical situation they may simply be unable to reproduce what their true behaviour would be. In contrast, there may be *interviewee bias* if consumers believe that the questions they are being asked are likely to lead to price rises for the product. In such a situation, respondents may understate their true willingness to pay for various quantities of the product in question.

Surveys are often used in the leisure and recreation industry in order to gain information about the demand characteristics of a particular facility, for example a leisure centre or park. The most elaborate questionnaires tend to have been constructed by economists in order to provide insights into the demand function associated with a particular resource but also its value as defined by the consumer surplus it generates. This may be prompted by a variety of reasons which include pure academic interest, the desire to analyse the possibilities of introducing a new or theoretically more effective charging system or because competing needs are casting doubt over the future of the resource.

An insight into these issues can be obtained by employing an approach known as *contingent valuation*. There are two basic approaches which such a study can take. One is to try and ascertain the maximum amount people are willing to pay for a particular outcome, for example an improvement in scenic quality. An alternative approach is to estimate the minimum that individuals are willing to accept in compensation for a change, such as the closure of a local park. In either case the survey involves an iterative bidding process whereby an imaginary starting price is raised or lowed incrementally until the individual's *willingness to pay* or *willingness to accept* is established. This can raise problems with respect to the starting price since respondents may readily accept bids within the vicinity of the intial price in order to keep the 'game' as short as possible.

Rather than force consumers to make an instant decision, some researchers have adopted laboratory-style exercises where individuals are given a sum of money as an inducement to participate and then asked to undertake a series of imaginary shopping trips (more sophisticated exercises will use real money to enhance the realism of the exercise). For each shopping trip, which may involve several hypothetical vendors, the prices of the commodities under analysis are changed in order to establish various points on the demand curve. Where users may be unfamiliar with the commodity in question, as may be the case with areas of scenic beauty, photographic insights can be used in order to establish respondents' understanding. However this approach does not remove the speculative nature of the exercise nor any problems of interviewee bias. Nevertheless, it may lead to more considered responses than what would be derived from a simple survey.

**Direct market experiments**

Using this approach, the price of the product is varied in shops (or adverts) and the response of consumers monitored. Clearly, this needs to take place over large geographical regions to prevent individuals in one locality finding it advantageous to travel to another area in order to pay the lower price. Assuming that there are a number of representative geographical areas, in that they have similar socio-economic profiles to the overall market, it is possible to extrapolate an overall market demand curve. Although consumers do not feel that they are part of an experiment, this approach is bound to incorporate all the biases arising from the real world, for example the pricing behaviour of firms selling complementary or substitute commodities and any media effects which may influence the purchasing behaviour of households. Furthermore, from the point of view of an entrepreneur, there is the possibility that consumers may be lost after the raising of a price thereby discouraging the use of such experiments for long periods and over a large number of regions. Together, this may result in an insufficient number of observations being gathered.

**Time-series comparison**

The rationale behind this approach is to obtain data relating to the variables within the demand function for a product over a number of years. A comparison can then be undertaken to estimate quantity demanded as appropriate variables change, including price. Taken at face value, however, this approach imposes the dubious assumption that the demand curve is unaltered over a period of time. If this is an incorrect presumption to make, then the resulting study will be subject to the identification problem. This is best understood with reference to figure 3.3.

For simplicity, assume that a study has been undertaken using observations over a five-year period. To the unwary, a demand curve ($D$)

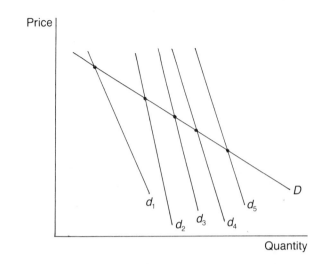

*Figure 3.3* The identification problem

could be estimated by fitting the 'best line' through the five data points. However, as we can see, the five points used to construct this demand curve are points on five unique demand curves $d_1$ to $d_5$. Thus, if a firm uses demand curve $D$ as the basis of its pricing strategy, then the outcome is likely to be highly inappropriate. In practice, econometricians are able to hold the shift parameters constant, thereby allowing the relationship between price and quantity demanded to be estimated. However, the techniques they use are beyond the scope of this book.

**The travel cost method**

Unlike the approaches outlined above, the travel cost method (TCM) has been developed almost entirely from one perspective, namely the desire to estimate demand curves for recreational sites. Given its continued prominence within the recreation economics literature, it would be appropriate to spend some time looking at the basic implications of the technique.

As we have already seen, a problem which many researchers face with respect to estimating a demand curve for many outdoor recreation sites, such as national parks or beauty spots, is that there is no explicit entry fee. This makes it difficult to derive a demand curve for the site in question since there are no price data available. One approach which can be taken is to ask people how much they are willing to pay, referred to earlier as contingent valuation. However, this approach can incorporate a variety of biases (intentional or unintentional) into its final results, primarily because respondents are being asked to suggest prices for something for which they have previously enjoyed at zero cost. The TCM is an approach which partly avoids this particular source of bias since it relies upon the observed behaviour of individuals rather than hypothetical responses. Although it has its own restrictive assumptions, the TCM provides an alternative means of placing a value upon a site by referring to the consumer surplus which can be derived from the estimated demand curve. Care should be taken not to see the contingent valuation and the TCM as alternative approaches. Given the difficulties of estimating the demand characteristics and value of leisure and recreation sites, the two should be seen as complementary techniques which allow the researcher to obtain as much information as possible about the facility or resource in question.

As its name suggests, the main data required for this technique are the travel costs incurred by visitors to the site in question. The basic rationale underlying the approach is as follows. If the cost of gaining admittance to a site is zero, or low relative to the travel costs which are incurred, then the effective price of the site visit is the journey cost. Since the original development of the technique by Clawson (1959) and Clawson and Knetsch (1966),[1] the TCM has been subject to an ever-widening set of circumstances. This has allowed the technique to evolve as refinements have been made in order to overcome specific character-istics of individual recreation sites. However, a review of the literature would suggest that the most successful applications have involved sites whose catchment areas extend several hundreds of miles, since this permits a wider variation in visitors' travel costs. Having outlined briefly the rationale which underpins a very simple travel cost model, we shall undertake a brief survey of some of the main problems researchers have encountered over the last three and a half decades.

*Deriving a travel cost demand curve*

The first stage is to draw a series of concentric circles around the site in question, each subsequent zone being associated with a higher travel cost. This is depicted in figure 3.4. Since each zone will cover increasingly large geographical areas, it would not be unreasonable to expect zones to contain higher populations the greater the distance they are from the site in question. Thus, although the travel cost may actually

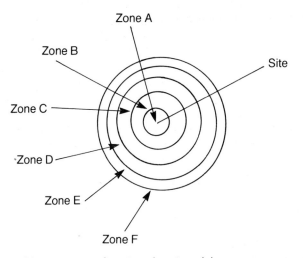

*Figure 3.4* Distance zones for a travel cost model

be increasing, there is the possibility that a move to a zone further away from the site will initiate an absolute increase in the number of people visiting the site. To take account of this, the next step is to estimate the relationship between the *visit rate* of each zone and the associated travel cost. These two variables can be expected to be negatively correlated, provided that the socio-economic characteristics across zonal populations are broadly similar.[2] When depicted on a graph, the relationship between these two variables is known as the initial demand curve.

The final stage of the TCM involves transforming the information given by the initial demand curve into a conventional demand curve, known as the final demand curve, depicting the relationship between the entrance fee of a site and total visits (as opposed to visit rate). This exercise rests upon the assumption that consumers are indifferent between a change in travel costs and an equal (hypothetical) monetary change in the site entrance fee. For example, if site entry is free and the travel cost associated with zones A, B and C is £1, £2 and £3 respectively, it is postulated that if the charge to use the site is £1, then those consumers in zone A, now facing a total cost of £2 (£1 entrance fee and £1 travel cost), will exhibit the same visit rate as those people in zone B had done when site entry was free (£0 entrance fee and £2 travel cost). By the same logic, when a hypothetical fee of £1 is assumed, those people in zone B can be postulated to react in the same manner as individuals in zone C had done at a zero entrance fee and so on. The exercise continues by assuming further hypothetical increases in the entrance fee such that, for example, when a levy of £2 is assumed, zone A people (who now face a total cost of £3, a £2 entrance fee and £1 travel expenses) are hypothesised to react in the same way as individuals in zone C had done when they faced travel costs of £3 and a zero entrance fee. Further points on the final demand curve can be established in a similar manner. An assumption which underpins this process is that consumers do not derive utility or disutility from their journey. If, for example, consumers are actually deriving pleasure from a particular

*Table 3.2* Hypothetical cost and visitation data to construct a travel cost method

| Zone | Distance | Travel cost (£) | Population | Visit rate (per 100,000) |
|------|----------|-----------------|------------|--------------------------|
| A | 10 | 1.00 | 100 | 650 |
| B | 20 | 2.00 | 200 | 475 |
| C | 30 | 3.00 | 300 | 310 |
| D | 40 | 4.00 | 400 | 220 |
| E | 50 | 5.00 | 500 | 105 |
| F | 60 | 6.00 | 600 | 0 |

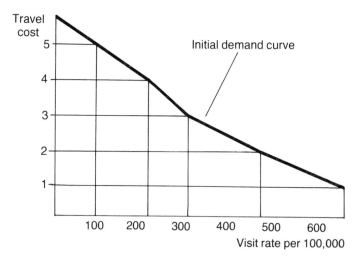

*Figure 3.5* The initial demand curve

journey then the one-to-one trade-off between a £1 spent travelling and a £1 spent on an entrance fee ceases to apply.

To illustrate the basic approach outlined so far, let us consider the figures in table 3.2. It will be assumed that the site in question has no entrance fee. The number of zones are limited to six for ease of computation and all numbers are hypothetical. The initial demand curve is constructed with reference to columns three and five, with travel cost measured along the vertical axis and visit rate on the horizontal axis. This is depicted in figure 3.5.

As noted above, the final demand curve depicts the relationship between admission price (hypothesised) and total visits. Let us begin by calculating total visits when the price of site entry is zero. This is estimated by multiplying the visit rate by the population of each zone and aggregating across zones as follows:

| | | |
|---|---|---|
| Zone A | $1 \times 650$ | 650 visits |
| Zone B | $2 \times 475$ | 950 visits |
| Zone C | $3 \times 310$ | 930 visits |
| Zone D | $4 \times 220$ | 880 visits |
| Zone E | $5 \times 105$ | 525 visits |
| Zone F | $6 \times \quad 0$ | 0 visits |
| | | |
| Total | | 3,935 visits |

Thus, 3,935 visits is the total number of visits which occurs when there is no site entrance fee.

The next stage of the analysis is to calculate how many visits there would be if a £1 fee is levied. As we have already seen, this requires us to assume that individuals visiting the site from zone A will now behave, in terms of their visit rate, as visitors in zone B had done when facing a zero entrance fee. This logic applies to visitors in zones B, C, D and E, such that there are now no visitors from zone E:

| | | |
|---|---|---|
| Zone A | $1 \times 475$ | 475 visits |
| Zone B | $2 \times 310$ | 620 visits |
| Zone C | $3 \times 220$ | 660 visits |
| Zone D | $4 \times 105$ | 420 visits |
| Zone E | $5 \times \quad 0$ | 0 visits |
| | | |
| Total | | 2,175 visits |

It can be seen that 2,175 visits are predicted if an entrance fee of £1 is charged. The next step is to assume a site entrance fee of £2. In this case, individuals in zone A are assumed to behave as visitors in zone C had done when a zero entrance fee was assumed. Following this through, there will now be no hypothesised visits from zone D:

| Zone A | $1 \times 310$ | 310 visits |
|--------|------|------------|
| Zone B | $2 \times 220$ | 440 visits |
| Zone C | $3 \times 105$ | 315 visits |
| Zone D | $4 \times \ \ \ 0$ | 0 visits |
| | | |
| Total | | 1,065 visits |

It can therefore be seen that by doubling the hypothesised price from £1 to £2 reduces total visits by over 50 per cent. This would mean that the rise in price would actually lead to a reduction in revenue rather than an increase (£2,175 would be raised from a £1 levy while only £2,130 would be amassed from a £2 fee). As we shall see in later chapters, price increases do not necessarily mean an increase in revenue for the supplier. It all depends upon the number of consumers who continue to patronise the facility after the price rise.

Let us now move on by calculating the remaining points on the final demand curve. This involves hypothesising three further prices: £3, £4 and £5; the latter will be seen to reduce total visits to zero. Thus for £3 we get:

| Zone A | $1 \times 220$ | 220 visits |
|--------|------|------------|
| Zone B | $2 \times 105$ | 210 visits |
| Zone C | $3 \times \ \ \ 0$ | 0 visits |
| | | |
| Total | | 430 visits |

and for £4 and £5 we get the following respectively:

| Zone A | $1 \times 105$ | 105 visits |
|--------|------|------------|
| Zone B | $2 \times \ \ \ 0$ | 0 visits |
| | | |
| Total | | 105 visits |
| | | |
| Zone A | $1 \times \ \ \ 0$ | 0 visits. |

All the estimated total visits can be used to estimate the final demand curve, depicted in figure 3.6. This demand curve may be used to determine the consumer surplus accruing from the site. Since the site in reality has a zero entrance fee, this may be calculated by estimating the area under the entire demand curve.

As already noted, the TCM has undergone considerable refinement, particularly over the last 20 years or so. These changes have reflected the greater variety of situations to which the TCM has been applied. For

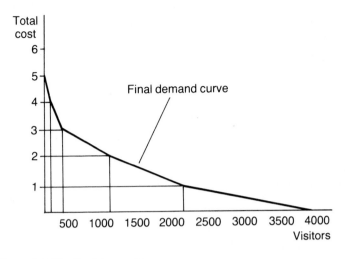

*Figure 3.6* The final demand curve

example models and techniques have been developed to take account of such things as the possibility of not being admitted to a site on arrival due to congestion, the implications of competing sites nearby, and visitors who do not see the site in question as the primary objective for their journey. Others have reflected concern about the competing economic and statistical properties of the model, for example the nature of its functional form.

Perhaps the most fundamental problem for any researcher interested in using the TCM is the question of what actually constitutes a travel cost. This debate takes us down two avenues, the first relating to the costs of running a car, the other involving the valuation of travel time. In the case of valuing a car journey, many studies have utilised estimates provided by the major motoring organisations, such as the Automobile Association (AA) or the Royal Automobile Club (RAC). However, it is unlikely that drivers are fully aware of all the costs they actually incur when making a journey. Although it is likely that they know the cost of the fuel that is used, based upon the knowledge accumulated through repeated purchases, we can expect motorists to be less conversant with the general running costs they are incurring, such as wear and tear. Thus, there may be a difference between the final demand curve derived from official estimates of journey costs and that based upon what individuals perceive to be their journey cost.

Second, some readers may also have noticed that the only journey cost used in the previous example was the monetary cost of travel. However, all journeys, whatever their duration, will be also associated with a time cost. If this is omitted from calculations, the true cost of the journey is understated, as will be any consumer surplus calculated from the resulting demand curve. However, one of the major problems the economist faces is that leisure time does not have a conventional market value. In situations where commodities do not have an explicit market value, some way must be found of estimating a surrogate value, usually referred to in the literature as a *shadow price*. In theory, we already have an insight as to how we might overcome this problem, using the analysis undertaken at the end of Chapter 2 with respect to the consumer's trade-off between leisure time and income. Assuming that a consumer is free to choose his or her hours of work, then at the margin the value of one hour's leisure time is equal to the benefits (financial) from one hour's work. Thus, economic theory suggests that the value of leisure time is less than the pre-tax wage rate, specifically it is equal to the post-tax wage rate minus the marginal disutility of undertaking that one hour's work. Unfortunately, we do not have a consistent shadow value for leisure time since different researchers have used different methods and samples of the population to derive their estimate. Generally, the economics literature has tended to suggest a figure which falls somewhere between 25 per cent and 50 per cent of the wage rate. The Department of Transport (1987) has recommended an average value of 43 per cent of earnings as an appropriate figure. However, in a recent paper, Cooke (1993) estimated the value of leisure time to be less than 10 per cent of the wage rate in the case of urban recreationalists. In a classic study, Cesario and Knetsch (1976) compared consumer surpluses estimated from travel cost models which included and excluded the costs of travel time for 11 national parks in Pennsylvania. Assuming the value of leisure time to equal one-third of the average wage rate, it was found that the inclusion of leisure time led to an increase in consumer surplus of between 15 and 35 per cent.

To conclude this section, we shall consider briefly a classic study taken from the recreation economics literature by Bishop and Heberlein (1979). Their work provides a particularly useful insight because it combines both a travel cost and a contingent valuation exercise. The study focuses specifically upon estimating the value to hunters of goosehunting permits. Although permits are free of charge, their availability is restricted for ecological reasons. For one period in the hunting year, a sample of 900 hunters was identified and subdivided

*Table 3.3* Average consumer surplus derived from goosehunting
permits, using contingent valuation and travel cost models

|  | *Consumer surplus/permit ($)* |
| --- | --- |
| Cash offers | 63 |
| Hypothetical offers from CV | |
|   (a)  willingness to sell | 101 |
|   (b)  willingness to pay | 21 |
| Travel cost estimates | |
|   (a)  zero time value | 11 |
|   (b)  time = 25% wage rate | 28 |
|   (c)  time = 50% wage rate | 45 |

*Source*: Bishop and Heberlein (1979, p. 929)

into three groups. One group received actual cash offers for their
permits. These were conveyed by mail as cheques ranging in value from
$1 to $200, with an instruction to return the cheque or the permit (one
must presume that it was not possible to retain both!). A second group
of hunters received mail questionnaires designed to estimate their
willingness to pay for and willingness to sell their permit. The final
sample received questionnaires designed to extract sufficient information to estimate travel costs. The average consumer surplus derived from
goosehunting permits estimated from each of the three samples is given
in table 3.3.

It can be seen that the responses to the cash offers suggested an
average consumer surplus per permit of $63. This contrasts with the
estimates derived from the contingent valuation sample where the
suggested willingness to sell averaged $101 while the average will-
ingness to buy was $21. Assuming that the figure from the cash offers
is the 'best' estimate, then the former estimate is significantly biased
upwards while the willingness to pay is biased downwards. This
suggests the existence of the biases which can be introduced into
contingent valuation studies. In part it may be a problem of respondents
being unable to place a value upon something which they have normally
received free of charge, as well as an almost inevitable example of
strategic behaviour. The travel cost equations also provided a variety of
estimates, highly dependent upon the degree to which the cost of travel
time is assumed to play a role in the equation, such that at the limits, the
average consumer surplus per permit can be magnified fourfold. We
should not be surprised that such a diversity of figures was estimated,

given the different assumptions which have been applied to derive each one. The authors were trying to place a value on something with no explicit market value. By using travel cost and contingent valuation estimates as complementary approaches, a range of estimates were derived which provided an insight into how much hunters valued their goosehunting permits.

## DEMAND, SUPPLY AND THE MARKET

Concern about how an individual or a group of individuals will respond to changes in the variables influencing their demand for a commodity is only one part of the equation. These demands will not be realised if there are no producers who are willing and able to supply the commodities which consumers desire. If buyers and sellers are able to make contact with each other, a market is formed.

Often it is assumed that the term 'market' refers to an observable geographical location. In the case of a shop, the market is observable since buyer and seller meet in a tangible geographical location. In contrast, many people respond to adverts in a newspaper or offers in mail-order catalogues. Although the buyer and seller need not now meet face to face, a market has still been created. If there is a choice between buying a commodity in a shop and buying it more conveniently via some sort of advert, many people still prefer the former since the characteristics of the commodity in question can be observed more easily. This is despite the additional journey costs which may be involved.[3] Many leisure commodities cannot be stored and have to be consumed at the marketplace itself. For example, whereas a video can be enjoyed anywhere which has the appropriate equipment, a swimming session will be both paid for and enjoyed at the same time. Other commodities also fall into this category of goods, for example a restaurant meal, spectating at a sports event and a visit to the cinema. In such cases, the market may need a booking system to operate effectively. If there is a high degree of uncertainty as to whether admittance will be gained to a particular facility, people are less likely to use it, particularly if large distances have to be travelled.

Having looked more closely at some of the characteristics of a market, we shall now consider some of the factors which will induce a firm to supply a product to the market. The analysis will be similar to that used when identifying the factors which influence demand, though of course it will be undertaken from the point of view of the producer rather than the consumer. Thus, as with demand, the starting point will be to look at some of the variables which can play a role in determining the quantity supplied.

## SUPPLY

Just as demand refers to the willingness and ability of an individual or group of individuals to consume a product, supply reflects the amounts that a producer or group of producers plan to sell in a particular time period. It does not refer to the quantity of a good or service that is actually sold. Thus, entrepreneurs' plans may not be realised if there is insufficient demand for the product in question. The variables which influence a producer's decision to supply a good or service to the market are contained within the *supply function*.

### Which variables determine supply?

*Own price of the product*

The basic law of supply states that the higher the price of a commodity, the greater will be the quantity supplied, everything else held constant (*ceteris paribus*). The intuition behind this statement is that, providing the unit costs of producing a good or service remain the same, an increase in price will generate a larger profit per unit for its supplier. Thus, as prices rise there is a greater incentive to increase supply. This relationship is characterised by the upward-sloping supply curve (denoted $S$) depicted in figure 3.7. The position of the supply curve on the diagram should be noted carefully. In this case, it is suggested that the firm will not wish to supply the good or service below a price of $p_0$. A supply curve which cuts the $x$ axis suggests that the firm is willing and able to supply a certain quantity of products to the market at zero price.

Sometimes we may wish to distinguish between supply in the short term, for example over a few weeks or months, and supply in the long term, perhaps extending over a number of years. For some goods and services, production cannot be increased at short notice, even if the price of the product rises rapidly. The result is that the supply curve will appear as a very steep slope in the short term when viewed alongside its long-run counterpart. For example, if the price of a particular type of house increases rapidly, builders will not be able to respond instantaneously to the change. For example, finance needs to be raised (from banks or recycled profits), planning permission has to be obtained, land

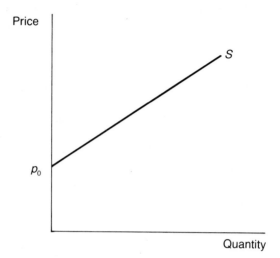

*Figure 3.7* The supply curve

has to be bought, cleared and levelled, workers and equipment need to be hired and only then can the property be built. The production of some goods and services may be relatively more responsive to price changes in the short term. Thus, provided that raw materials can be obtained quickly, either from the stocks in the warehouse or from a supplier, a manufacturer may simply be able to increase the speed of the production line. Neverthless, when viewed alongside its long-run counterpart, the short-run supply curve will appear to have a steeper slope.

At this stage it is appropriate to emphasise one important point about the 'steepness' of supply curves (or demand curves). When this type of comparison is made, it assumes that the supply (or demand) curves are being compared within the same set of axes. Otherwise it is possible for short-run and long-run supply curves to have identical gradients, distinguished only by the calibration of the quantity on the $x$ axis. This point will become clearer when we consider the market for golf facilities at the end of this chapter.

Summing up, a change in the price of a product will bring about changes in the amount a producer is willing and able to supply to the market. The degree of responsiveness to price change may vary according to whether the analysis is reflecting producers' responses over a short or long time period. Whatever the characteristic of the good or service involved, this can be representated by a movement *along* the supply curve. However, there are a number of variables which will affect the position of the supply curve. As with our analysis of demand, these variables are known as shift parameters. It is these variables to which the analysis now turns.

## Prices of other goods

The supply of one product will be influenced by price changes affecting other commodities which can be produced by a firm. Two scenarios may be highlighted. The first is where two or more products are *substitutes in production*, while the second refers to situations where products are *complements in production*. To begin, consider a situation where products are substitutes in production. An example of this may arise in the case of a clothing manufacturer which produces tennis, squash and badmintion shirts alongside its range of more traditional short-sleeved shirts. It will be assumed that the machinery and labour skills used to produce each design of shirt is the same. The output mix of the firm will vary according to the relative prices and demand for each type of garment. Thus, for example, if sports shirts command a relatively low price in the shops, then their manufacture may be curtailed in order to increase output of more profitable lines such as tennis or badminton shirts.

The price of other goods is also important when the production of one commodity provides the opportunity to produce another commodity. This relates to the second of our two scenarios, when products are complements in production. For example, if an increase in the price of badminton courts leads to more sports halls being built, then the growth of such facilities may also allow an increase in the number of aerobics classes during times when the badminton courts are not in use.

## Prices of factors of production

In order to create goods and services, firms require what economists refer to as *factors of production*. These are usually subdivided under three basic headings: land, labour and capital. Land refers to any natural resources used in the production process. Most obvious is the land which entrepreneurs use to locate their factories and warehouses. Inputs of labour are required to undertake certain tasks within the production process. These tasks may require an intellectual input, for example designing a marketing strategy to promote a good or service to potential consumers, while other jobs may be more physical in character, for example stacking shelves in a supermarket. In economics, capital refers to the buildings, machines and vehicles which are used during the production of a good or service.

Activities which use a large input of labour relative to capital, for example tea-picking, are said to be *labour intensive*. Conversely, processes which use large amounts of capital relative to labour are said to be *capital intensive*. An example would be the production of nuclear energy. The degree to which production of goods and services is capital or labour intensive will reflect both the state of technology (see below) and the relative prices of capital and labour. For example, if wage rates are relatively high then it is more likely that producers will view capital intensive processes more favourably than if wages are relatively low (providing that capital and labour can be easily substituted for each other). Overall, if the prices of factors of production are high, producers may be deterred from supplying goods and services. Conversely, we would expect that a reduction in the price of factors of production will make it more likely for suppliers to supply goods and services to the market.

*Technology*

Whether it is the result of a lone inventor working in the attic at home or the multi-million pound activities of research and development departments of major companies, the development of new technologies or the refinement of exisiting technologies often enables firms to produce units of a good or service at a lower cost. Improvements in technology can also make it possible to produce output at a lower environmental cost, perhaps in response to new legislation on chemical emissions into the atmosphere or into the rivers. Changes in technology are likely to lead to changes in the relative capital/labour intensity of production.

*The number of producers in an industry*

The amount of a good or service supplied at a given price will also reflect the number of individual suppliers operating in the market. If selling a particular product proves to be profitable for existing firms then it is likely that more suppliers will be tempted into the market. Conversely, if firms experience losses, then we would expect some producers to cease production in that industry (but they may continue production in other industries) or to close down entirely. The degree to which the number of suppliers will increase or decrease in response to changes in economic conditions will depend upon the *structure* of the market.

If an industry is characterised by a few large firms with established brand names then it may be expensive for new firms to penetrate the industry, even in times of prosperity. Thus any increases in supply may only originate from increased production from existing firms. If, on the other hand, the potential costs of entering an industry are relatively low, as has been the case with health and fitness clubs, then aggregate increases in supply may also reflect a growth in the number of producers within the market.

### The objectives of the producer

As we shall see in later chapters, the traditional assumption economists make is that firms aim to *maximise profit*. This is a natural extension of an assumption that we have already employed with respect to the objectives of individual consumers, namely that they wish to maximise utility. In reality, the ability of an entrepreneur to maximise profits necessitates the possession of a high level of knowledge about the environment in which he or she operates, or a high degree of luck. Thus, it is very unlikely that he or she will be aware of the relative importance of all the factors which will ultimately determine the success of a firm. Thus if achieving high profits is to be the goal, it is more realistic for firms to set themselves a target rate of profit and to set output to reflect this objective. Part of this decision involves choices being made concerning whether or not to trade off short-term profits for gains in the longer term. For example, a long-term strategy may require a firm to incur short-run losses through saturating the market with its product. Thus, supply may be higher than that which would be expected if success is to be measured over a shorter time period. Thus, this decision may not only reflect the economic character of the firm, but also its relationship with firms against which it is competing. These and other possible output strategies that a firm can adopt will be discussed in much greater detail in Chapter 7.

### The weather

The weather can play an important role in determining the supply of certain products. The most obvious example is the supply of agricultural produce. Thus, a warm but moist growing season will mean that yields of many crops will be high. Too much sun or too much rain will have the opposite effect. Plants may dry up due to the intense heat or not mature due to a curtailed growing season. Weather plays an important role in determining the supply of certain sporting activities. An individual's ability to go skiing at a particular resort will be dependent upon the amount of snow which has fallen on the slopes. If snow has only fallen on the most elevated ground then the supply of skiing areas will be smaller than if snowfall has been abundant at lower levels of altitude. Furthermore, if the spring is mild, then the rate at which snow thaws will be much greater, gradually reducing the supply of areas suitable for skiing. Similarly, persistent wet weather may reduce the supply of golf courses at certain times of the year. Although the facilities exist in pure physical terms, the need to prevent greens from being damaged may lead owners to prohibit play during the wettest times of the year.

### The supply function

We have highlighted a number of variables which can play a role in determining the amount of a good or service producers are willing and able to supply to a market. These variables (and others, depending upon the nature of the product in question) may be identified as being part of a supply function. Analogous to the demand function, this expression states that the output a firm will supply to a market ($Q_s$) will be a function of the following variables (as before, we shall not identify the precise mathematical relationship between the variables):

$$Q_s = f(P, Po, F, T, N, O, W)$$

where f means 'is a function of', $P$ denotes the price of the product in question, $Po$ denotes the price of other goods produced by the firm (whether complementary or substitutes in production), $F$ depicts the price of the factors of production used, $T$ denotes the state of technology, $N$ measures the number of producers in the industry, $O$ reflects the (potentially different) objectives of each firm within the industry and $W$ depicts the effects of the weather. The supply curve, which we have already identified as depicting the relationship between the own price of the product in question and the quantity supplied, is drawn under the assumption that all the remaining variables which can influence the level of production are held constant (*ceteris paribus*). If any of these other variables does change in value, such as a change in the wage rates (thereby affecting the price of labour) or the introduction of a new production process, the supply curve will move. For this reason, these

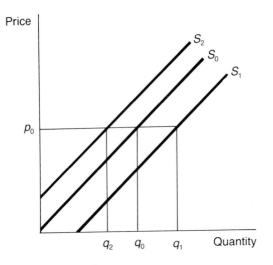

*Figure 3.8* Shifts in the supply curve

variables are also known as shift parameters. Thus, the supply curve of tennis rackets will shift to the right if new manufacturers enter the market ($S$ to $S_1$) whereas it will shift to the left ($S$ to $S_2$) if one or more firms switch to the production of squash rackets (*ceteris paribus*). Both these effects are demonstrated in figure 3.8. It can be seen that after a shift in the supply curve more or less will be supplied for any given price, such as $p_0$.

We have now considered the variables which can influence the level of demand and the level of supply in mutual isolation. The next stage of the analysis will involve bringing the two together so as to create a hypothetical market. We have already seen that the market does not need to have a fixed geographical location. Provided that demanders and suppliers are in contact with each other, whether it is over the telephone or whether it is through adverts within a local newspaper, a market will exist.

## PRICE DETERMINATION IN THE MARKET

The framework constructed so far provides the opportunity to provide a diagrammatic insight into the workings of the market. With the relationship between quantity and price being the central focus of both the demand and supply curve, there is no problem with depicting them

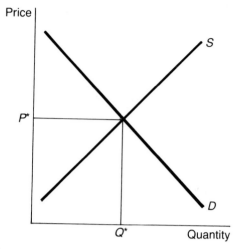

*Figure 3.9* Demand and supply

on the same graph, thereby showing the interaction between them. Price can be retained on the vertical axis with quantity (demanded and supplied) measured along the horizontal axis. The result can be seen in figure 3.9. It can be seen that there is only one price at which demand and supply are exactly equal, namely $P^*$. At all other prices, the quantity demanded either exceeds the quantity supplied or is less than the quantity supplied. The quantity associated with this price can be seen to be $Q^*$. The aim of the discussion that follows is to show that there is a natural tendency for the market to be in *equilibrium* at the price at which demand and supply are equated.

To illustrate this point, figure 3.10 will be assumed to represent the market for training shoes during one month of the year. For ease of analysis we will suppose that all training shoes are of the same quality and offer purchasers the same attributes. To begin, let us assume that the price of training shoes is set at $p_1$ a pair. It can be seen that at that price producers are willing and able to supply $q_1$ pairs per month. However, at that price, the demand curve tells us that consumers are only willing and able to buy $q_0$ pairs of traning shoes.

The problem for producers is that they cannot exert any control over the quantity that consumers buy. Thus if the price remains at $p_1$, $q_0$ pairs of trainers will be sold. Indeed, should producers want to sell all $q_1$ pairs, the price would have to be lowered to $p_0$. Although suppliers would be

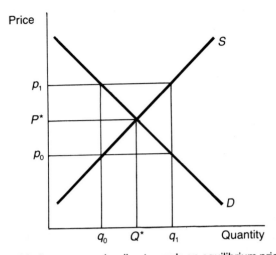

*Figure 3.10* Market pressure leading towards an equilibrium price and quantity

able to sell $q_1$ pairs of trainers if the price is $p_1$, the supply curve shows us that they would actually be willing to sell the $q_0$th pair at a price of $p_0$. Thus, it can be seen that competing firms would be prepared to keep undercutting each other until a price of $p_0$ is reached. Previous analysis has also told us that as price falls, the quantity demanded will rise. Thus, as manufacturers keep cutting their price, more individuals are willing and able to buy the product. However, as suppliers begin to lower the price from $p_1$, their incentive to supply training shoes diminishes, as depicted by the supply curve. Nevertheless, as the price falls, the demand for the product is simultaneously increasing. Thus, in terms of figure 3.10, supply and demand will be equated at a price of $P^*$ and an output of $Q^*$. At that price, the desire of producers to supply and consumers' wishes to buy are exactly the same. Indeed, providing that there are no changes in the variables which characterise the demand and supply functions of consumers and producers respectively, there will be no reason why this situation should not persist over time. For this reason, $P^*$ is said to be the *equilibrium price* and $Q^*$ is known as the *equilibrium quantity*.

The starting point for the above analysis was that the market was originally in a position of excess supply. Of course, the situation could have been reversed. If the price of training shoes had originally been $p_0$

there would have been excess demand equal to the distance $q_0 q_1$. Of course, consumers cannot force producers into supplying the additional training shoes they require at the price of $p_0$. Thus, there will be pressure for the price of trainers to rise. Since the demand curve shows that there are individuals who are willing and able to pay more than $p_0$, the price will be bid up. Faced with the opportunity to receive a higher price for training shoes, producers will be encouraged to increase their supply of the product to the market. However, as the price rises, fewer consumers will be willing and able to pay the increasing price for trainers (as depicted by the demand curve). The result is that the excess demand will continue to fall until the equilibrium price and quantity of $P*$ and $Q*$ respectively are achieved. Again, at this price the desires of buyers and sellers are exactly equated. As long as there is no variation in the parameters characterising the demand and supply functions of consumers and producers, there will be no tendency for this equilibrium price and equilibrium quantity to change. Thus, regardless of whether the market originates in a state of excess supply or excess demand, forces will determine an equilibrium price and quantity at which the market can be said to clear. In other words, the quantity demanded by consumers at that price exactly equals the quantity supplied by producers at that price.

## Consumer surplus (revisited) and producer surplus

Having established the principle of an equilibrium price and quantity within a market, the aim now is to look more closely at the implications of this outcome for the consumers and producers. Let us consider initially the case of consumers. At the equilibrium price of $P*$, it can be seen that there are a number of consumers who are actually willing to pay more than the equilibrium price (that is, a price in excess of $P*$). Each of these consumers will therefore be enjoying a gain equal to the difference between the equilibrium price and the price they are willing to pay, for example the difference between $x$ and $y$ in figure 3.11. This difference between the price a consumer pays and what he or she is willing to pay has already been identified in Chapter 2 and was referred to as consumer surplus. The value of this consumer surplus to all individuals can be estimated by calculating the area of the triangle $AP*B$. This is the sum of all the consumer surpluses enjoyed by people who are willing and able to pay more than $P*$.

A similar exercise can be undertaken from the point of view of the producer. It can be seen from the supply curve in figure 3.11 that for

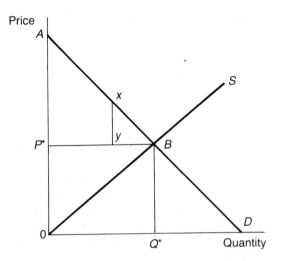

*Figure 3.11* Consumer surplus and producer surplus

quantities below the equilibrium quantity, the producer is actually willing and able to supply at a price lower than $P^*$, the equilibrium market price. The difference between the price at which producers are willing and able to supply goods to the market and the market price is known as *producer surplus*. The overall value of this producer surplus can be calculated by estimating the area of the triangle $P^*B0$.

The total revenue (or total consumer expenditure) which will be received by producers for selling the equilibrium quantity of the commodity in question can be estimated by multiplying $Q^*$ by the equilibrium price $P^*$. In the above diagram, this is the rectangle $P^*BQ^*0$. Two things should be noted at this point. Firstly, by definition, the value of the producers surplus is included in the producer's total revenue. Second, the analysis to date has made no mention of whether producers are actually making a profit in the market in question. No information has been offered with respect to the costs of production and therefore no comment can be made. Such considerations will be addressed in Chapter 6. A further issue which features in many microeconomics texts is the possibility of producers making consumers pay prices which reflect their willingness to pay, partly reducing or even eliminating consumer surplus and thereby increasing their own revenue. This option, known as *price discrimination*, will be addressed in Chapter 5. This is also a great area of interest for people involved with the provision of leisure activities though, as we shall see, price discrimination is also a means by which throughput at leisure outlets can be increased.

## Changes in the equilibrium price and quantity

If a variation in one of the shift parameters within the demand or supply function leads to a change in the position of the demand curve or supply curve then it can be shown that we should expect a change in the equilibrium price and quantity. To illustrate, let us suppose that the market for training shoes is currently in equilibrium at a price of $P*$ and a quantity of $Q*$. We shall first consider the implications of a shift in either the demand curve or the supply curve (the other schedule remaining constant) and then we shall analyse what can happen when both the demand and supply curves move simultaneously. The outcome of all three potential scenarios are depicted in figures 3.12, 3.13 and 3.14.

To begin, assume that there is a rightward shift in the demand curve for training shoes. This may have arisen because of the increased desirability of trainers as a fashion item which encourages more individuals to demand the product at any given price. The effect of the

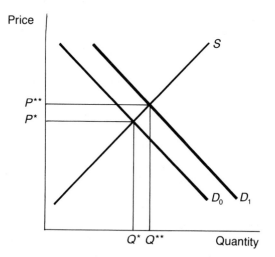

Figure 3.12 A change in the equilibrium price and quantity from a shift in the demand curve

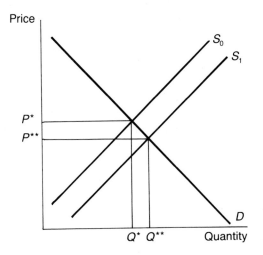

*Figure 3.13* A change in the equilibrium price and quantity from a shift in the supply curve

outward shift in demand is to simultaneously increase the equilibrium quantity and the equilibrium price. What happens is that with the position of the supply curve remaining unaltered, the market has moved from its original equilibrium to a new point of intersection between the demand and supply curves. At the price of $P^*$, there now exists a situation of excess demand, brought about by the shift in the demand curve. Competition between buyers ultimately will drive the price up, thereby encouraging suppliers to expand their output. The result is the higher equilibrium price and quantity, namely $P^{**}$ and $Q^{**}$. This process is demonstrated in figure 3.12. Conversely, had the demand curve for training shoes moved inwards (again assuming a static supply curve), both the equilibrium price and quantity would have fallen. This is because at the old equilibrium price, supply would now exceed demand. As we have already seen, suppliers would be encouraged to reduce their prices in response to reduced public desire to buy their product, ultimately leading to a reduced equilibrium price and quantity.

Let us now consider the changes which are brought about by a shift in the supply curve. A rightward shift in the supply curve may arise because of an improvement in the technology used to make shoes (enabling factories to produce more units at any given price) while an inward shift in the supply curve for training shoes may be caused by a decision by manufacturers to diversify their output to include other types of footwear. In the former situation, the outward shift in the supply curve will lead to an increase in the equilibrium quantity but a reduction in the equilibrium price. This is because the old equilibrium price leads to excess supply after the new technology has been installed. The downward pressure placed on prices leads to increased demand for the product (movement down the original demand curve) and the new equilibrium position described in figure 3.13. Had the supply curve shifted to the left then the equilibrium price would increase and the equilibrium quantity would decrease. This is because the old equilibrium price leads to excess demand. In the face of this shortage, consumers will bid up the price, thereby encouraging producers to increase their output. Ultimately, the market will clear at a higher equilibrium price but at a smaller equilibrium quantity than before.

So far the analysis has assumed that any change in the equilibrium price and quantity within a market is a result of a change affecting one of the two groups of players within the market: either to one or more of the producers, leading to a shift in the supply curve, or to one or more of the consumers, producing a shift in the demand curve. In reality there is no reason why changes should not be taking place for both parties at the same time. After all, the world is a dynamic environment and inevitably there will always be fluctuations in most of the parameters which influence the shape and position of market demand and supply curves. However, when this is taking place it is less easy to predict what the ultimate outcome will be with respect to either the equilibrium price or the equilibrium quantity. For example, imagine a situation where a large group of workers have been able to negotiate higher real wage rates, thereby increasing their employers' labour costs. Thus, assuming that the products they consume are normal (that is, more is consumed as incomes rise), there will be an outward shift in the demand curve while the supply curve will shift to the left (since production costs have risen). From the analysis that has gone before, we can be certain that the equilibrium price will rise. However, the effect of the changes upon the equilibrium quantity cannot be predicted without knowing the relative positions of the two curves and the magnitude of the positional changes. For example, the shift in demand may be so great as to increase the equilibrium price. Alternatively, the leftward shift in the supply curve may completely override the positive effects of increased incomes, leading to a reduction in the equilibrium quantity. Finally, the two curves may shift in such a way that the equilibrium quantity remains unchanged. All three possibilities can be seen in figure 3.14.

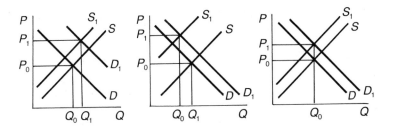

*Figure 3.14* Changes in the equilibrium price and quantity shift in both the demand and supply curves

One factor which will play an important role in determining the degree to which equilibrium values will change is the time horizon assumed within the analysis. To illustrate this point, let us consider an example drawn from the leisure industry, namely the market for golf courses.

## The supply of golf courses

Over the last two decades, there has been a dramatic increase in the desire to play golf, on privately owned facilities as well as on courses run by local authorities. This can be attributed to a number of factors: increasing real incomes, increased transport opportunities, increases in available leisure time and increased media attention, particularly following Europe's good performances in the Ryder Cup during the 1980s. However, despite this surge of interest, the number of golf courses available for people to play on has not been able to respond instantaneously to this increased interest. The reason for this stems from the complex logistics associated with golf course construction. Golf courses are 'lumpy' items which need to be purchased, landscaped, planted and allowed to settle. Only then can people be allowed to play on them. We can draw diagrams to show what is happening from two perspectives, the short term and the long term. The distinction between what is short term and long term is somewhat nebulous and will depend in part upon one's own perspective. For the purposes of this analysis we shall assume the former to refer to changes over one or two years while the latter will refer to changes over half a decade or more. The analysis that follows will be from the perspective of the market for privately owned golf courses. To begin, let us consider the market in the short run, based upon the information given in figure 3.15.

It can be seen in the figure that the supply curve, denoted $S$, is drawn almost vertical to reflect the short-term inflexibility of golf course provision. This reflects the long gestation period which characterises the construction of this type of facility. Assume that the demand for golf is initially described by the demand curve $D_0$. Following on from previous analysis, we can state that the equilibrium price and quantity will be $P^*$ and $Q^*$ respectively. Now, let us assume that there is a rise in interest in golf, brought about by the performances of British and European golfers in major competitions. This may lead to increased demand from existing players, who are encouraged to play more, as well as new demand from individuals who did not previously play golf. Our understanding of demand theory tells us that this will result in a rightward shift in the demand curve, from $D_0$ to $D_1$. This will therefore lead to a new equilibrium price and quantity, denoted $P^{**}$ and $Q^{**}$ respectively. It can be seen that in relative terms, there has been very little change in the equilibrium quantity. Indeed the increase in golf courses which does occur may only have been possible through the foresight of planners who anticipated the need for more courses.

The main change has taken place with respect to price. It can be seen

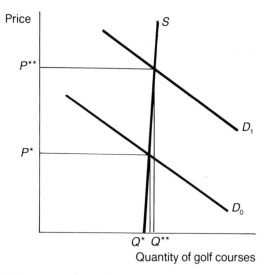

Figure 3.15 The market for golf facilities in the short run

that the rapid increase in demand has led to a significantly greater equilibrium value. If the price of golf were left at the old equilibrium price of $P*$ then it can be seen that there will be a situation of excess demand. Two changes may therefore take place. First, if the size of the membership of each club was fixed then waiting lists would emerge. This may not only reflect demand from entirely new golfers but also from individuals who currently play on public-sector courses but desire a greater commitment to the sport via membership of a club. Second, there is likely to be an increase in the number of games played on each course. This will lead to greater congestion and slow down the progress of play. In the case of public-sector courses, it is this latter effect which will be noticed by users. Obviously, it will be during peak periods (such as weekends) when this will be most noticed, with an increasing number of people being forced into playing during off-peak periods or not at all. The fact that courses are more congested may mean that the demand curve shifts inwards again because of the reduced quality of each game played. In other words, individuals' perception of congestion will act as a shift parameter within the general demand function for golf. To preserve the clarity of the diagram, this additional change has not been shown, though the reader may wish to draw a diagram to incorporate this effect.

If, on the other hand, prices were allowed to rise towards the new equilibrium value then waiting lists would be smaller (or non-existent if the price of $P**$ was levied) and there would be less pressure on golf courses on a day-to-day basis. If the price of playing at private clubs did rise while the levy charged at public-sector courses remained unaltered (or grew less quickly) then this may lead ultimately to increased demand for the (cheaper) substitute facility. As before, this change may lead to a deterioration of the quality of the game available at public-sector courses, again causing the demand curve to shift inwards.

In the longer term, the situation will be somewhat different. In figure 3.16, a long-run supply curve has also been inserted (denoted $S_{LR}$). It can be seen that this is relatively flatter than the short-run curve (now denoted $S_{SR}$) reflecting the fact that if the timescale is sufficiently large, then the supply of golf courses can be seen to increase.

As before, we shall assume that the market is originally in equilibrium at $P*$ and $Q*$. After the demand curve has shifted outwards, it can be seen that the equilibrium quantity has increased (from $Q*$ to $Q'$). Furthermore, the equilibrium price in the long run is much less than it is in the short term since the supply of facilities is now able to expand, specifically $P'$ rather than $P**$. Similarly, some of the problems

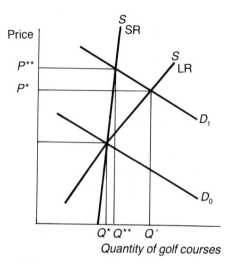

Figure 3.16 The market for golf facilities in the long run

associated with congestion on courses are likely to diminish in the longer term.

## QUESTIONS FOR DISCUSSION

1   'According to the law of demand, the higher the price of a commodity, the less I should buy. However, I always take one holiday per year.' To what extent is the law of demand invalidated by this person's behaviour?

2   How would you estimate a demand curve for a local swimming pool?

# Chapter 4

# Market failure in leisure

## INTRODUCTION

The analysis conducted in Chapters 2 and 3 provided the necessary background from which it was possible to analyse the workings of simple market situations. It was seen that the interaction of rational buyers and sellers will lead ultimately to an equilibrium price and quantity, a position which can only change if there is movement in one of the shift parameters within the demand or supply functions. The assumption which underpinned this analysis was that the behaviour of economic agents, the markets which emerge and the equilibrum price and quantity are all desirable from a societal point of view. If not, markets are said to *fail*. The aim of this chapter is to look at some of the circumstances when markets might seem to fail and, if outcomes are not desirable, whether governments should intervene in markets in order to prompt what is deemed to be a 'more' satisfactory outcome. The degree to which goverments should or should not intervene in our everyday life in this way is a subject which is constantly debated by politicians. The broad aim of this chapter is to identify in more detail the economic implications of market failure situations and to highlight them with special reference to markets for leisure and sport.

This focus for our analysis reflects the importance of leisure activities within our everyday life, exemplified in the 'Sport for All' concept, a policy which has been promoted actively by the Council of Europe since 1968,[1] ultimately leading to the signing of the European Sport for All Charter by 16 European governments in March 1975. Specifically, the development of Sport for All grew from three main concerns. First, that a lack of physical exercise is a major source of ill-health and therefore a fitter society will reduce the pressure on already stretched health and social security budgets. Second, that sport provides individuals with the opportunity to express themselves, thereby avoiding frustration, even at low levels of attainment, and third that sport has tended to be consumed by the 'well-off' and therefore needs to be made more available to less-privileged groups in society. It is through the activities of such organisations as the Sports Council, together with central and local government, that most people come face to face with Sport for All.

Government intervention in sport and leisure in the UK is now the responsibility of the Department of National Heritage. It was formed in April 1992 and is responsible for co-ordinating central government support of sport and leisure-related activities. With its remit, the functions of six government departments now fall under the auspices of one. In its first annual report, produced in 1993, the stated aims of the Department are to create conditions which:

1    will preserve ancient sites, monuments and historic buildings and increase their access for study and enjoyment now and in the future;
2    maintain, increase and make available the national collection of books, works of art, scientific objects and other records and artefacts of the past and of the present;
3    encourage the living arts to flourish – including the performing arts; the visual and plastic arts; broadcasting; film and literature;
4    increase the opportunities for sport and recreation both for champions and for the general public;
5    attract a wide range of people from this country and abroad to enjoy and enrich our national culture.

It is the economic rationale which underpins the fourth of these aims which will occupy the majority of this chapter and, indeed, is the focus of attention for much of this text.

## EXTERNALITIES

The assumption of rationality employed in previous chapters implies that a consumer will only consider buying a good or service if the utility it generates is greater than or equal to the price he or she has to pay for it. Put into stricter economics terminology, an individual is assumed to compare the marginal benefit a commodity will generate with the marginal cost of its consumption. It can be shown that it is rational for people to consume a given product up to the point where marginal costs exactly equal marginal benefits. The implications of this statement can be illustrated in using two approaches, one numerical, the other using a simple diagram.

Table 4.1 Marginal costs and marginal benefits from fitness training

| Time in gym (hrs) | Marginal benefit (£) | Marginal cost (£) |
|---|---|---|
| 0.5 | 2.5 | 1.5 |
| 1.0 | 2.0 | 1.5 |
| 1.5 | 1.5 | 1.5 |
| 2.0 | 1.0 | 1.5 |

Let us assume that a consumer is deciding whether or not to go to a fitness gym for the afternoon. For every half hour the facilities are used, the price charged is £1.50. Thus, a full hour's exercise would cost £3 in total (for the purposes of this illustration, we shall assume away any other costs the consumer may incur, for example out-of-pocket journey expenses). The decision he or she then faces is how long to work out. The individual will compare the half-hourly cost with the level of benefit which he or she expects to receive from each additional half hour spent at the gym. It will be assumed that the benefit the consumer derives from working out, such as the sense of achievement, the general feeling of well-being, the opportunity to meet like-minded people, can be quantified in monetary terms. Details of the marginal benefit (in money terms) which this individual derives from each half hour spent at the gym is set out in table 4.1.

It can be seen that the first half hour of exercise confers benefits of greater value than the £1.50 user fee. Thus, it would be rational to consume this unit. However, as the table shows, the added stress and strain of continuous exercise reduces the enjoyment the consumer gets from working out. The result is that the benefits derived from further activity diminish, such that the next half hour is only valued at £2. Nevertheless, because the cost of using the equipment for a further half-hour is only £1.50, the individual is still deriving a benefit in excess of cost and therefore it would still be rational to undertake the extra half hour's exercise. One and a half hour's exercise is, for this person, the rational stopping point. A further half-hour period in the gym generates less enjoyment (in money terms) than the price which would have to be paid. Thus, we would expect the consumer to spend a total of £4.50 for one and a half hours in the gym. The value of the total benefits derived from the exercise equals £6 (£2.50 + £2 + £1.50). Thus, the value of the net benefit accrued by the consumer from visiting the gym is £1.50.

We can present the same information in diagrammatic form in figure 4.1. Along the x axis we measure time at the gym whereas on the y axis

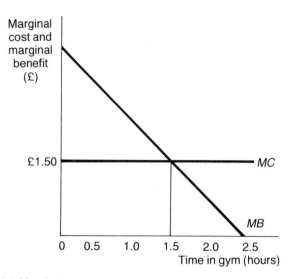

*Figure 4.1* Marginal costs and marginal benefits from fitness training

we measure the money value of the marginal costs and benefits associated with the visit to the gym. It can be seen that the line characterising the marginal benefits (*MB*) is assumed to have a negative slope, whereas the marginal cost curve (*MC*) is horizontal. Based upon the rationale set out above, it can be seen that the optimal stopping point for the individual concerned is where these two lines cross, namely at one and a half hours. For each unit of time spent at the gym, the vertical distance between the marginal cost curve and the marginal benefit curve represents the net benefit received by the consumer. Beyond this point, the individual begins to incur a negative net benefit.

So far, the analysis has focused upon the consumption decision from the point of view of an individual. Thus, the analysis has rested upon a comparison of the private costs and private benefits incurred by the person in question. However, in many situations this approach can be somewhat myopic since many everyday decisions we make also affect other people. They may be restricted to family members or to immediate friends but in some circumstances may extend also to wider groups of individuals with whom we may not be acquainted. When an individual's actions has an effect on the welfare of other people who have had no part in the original decision, we face what is known as an *externality* situation. The theory which underpins the externality literature requires us to analyse consumption decisions from two perspectives rather than one. In particular it highlights the fact that, in many situations, activities by individuals, households or firms can also generate social costs and/or social benefits.

To begin, let us consider the basic framework which economists use to analyse externalities. In the case of individuals or households, they are referred to as external economies of consumption and external diseconomies of consumption, depending upon whether the outcomes are desirable or undesirable for any third party who is affected. To illustrate the former case, we could cite the example of a person deciding whether or not to have an inoculation against 'flu. Ultimately, the decision will involve the individual comparing the private benefits of inoculation (as he or she perceives them) alongside any costs which are incurred, which may take into account the person's tolerance to needles! However, by choosing to have the treatment, the person concerned has not only reduced his or her own chance of contracting 'flu but also the probability of other people getting 'flu. Although others may be gaining a benefit from the inoculation, only the person receiving it bears the cost of treatment, which will include travelling costs and the opportunity cost of waiting time. Thus, if these private costs are perceived to outweigh the private benefits, others will be denied the (social) benefits which could have been generated.

A similar but opposite argument can be made in the case of external diseconomies of consumption. In this case an individual's actions are seen to generate an undesirable outcome for others who played no part in the original decision. An example might be a person choosing to light a bonfire to dispose of some garden rubbish rather than transport it to a local tip. For that person, the costs will seem relatively low and the benefits high, particularly if the local tip is some distance away and he or she has no private transport. However, for neighbours, particularly those downwind of the fire, there is the problem of smell and soot particles in the air. As we all know, the probability of someone lighting a bonfire is directly related to the amount of washing we have on the line and whether we have just painted our outside window frames! In this case, a large number of people may bear the cost of someone else's decision to light the fire without receiving any compensation in return.

Desirable externality situations which arise from the activities of firms are referred to as external economies of production. These may arise if, for example, a firm provides basic training for its employees. Although it is the firm which bears the cost it may find that it is unable to reap all the benefits of its investment if its employees move on to jobs elsewhere.

In this case, the recipients are the workers themselves (who have gained additional skills and therefore are more occupationally mobile) and the firms which ultimately take on these workers, especially if they do not offer training programmes themselves. At the other end of the spectrum, we have external diseconomies of production. These arise when a firm's activities impose costs upon others. The most obvious example is pollution. For example, a number of rivers are subjected to toxic discharges each year and these frequently decimate all but the most hardy forms of aquatic life. This compromises the recreational value of affected rivers and therefore detracts from the enjoyment of thousands of people who use them.

If there is no mechanism by which payments can be made, either to the provider of a desirable externality or to the victim in the case of undesirable externalities, social costs and social benefits will not be recognised in market transactions. Intuitively, we should therefore expect socially undesirable outcomes to be oversupplied by the market since the perpetrators will not be incurring the full cost of their activities. By an analogous argument we would also anticipate socially desirable activities to be underrepresented in the market. This point can be made clearer by referring to figures 4.2a and 4.2b. The graph in figure 4.2a depicts a situation where a person's consumption behaviour has desirable social consequences, while conversely, in figure 4.2b, private consumption behaviour imposes a social cost upon others (a similar analysis can be undertaken from the point of view of a firm's activities).

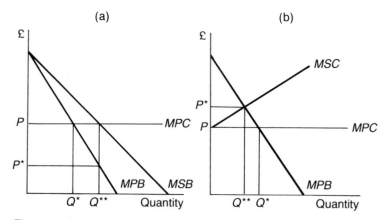

*Figure 4.2* Desirable and undesirable externality situations

In both graphs, the schedules denoting marginal private benefits and marginal private costs are denoted *MPB* and *MPC* respectively. As in the previous graph, it will be assumed that marginal private costs are constant. From the individual's point of view, the optimal level of consumption occurs where the *MPB* and *MPC* curves intersect, namely at $Q^*$. However, in both diagrams the actions of the consumer are assumed to have social implications. The situation depicted in figure 4.2a assumes that the activity under consideration generates social as well as private benefits. This is reflected by the position of the marginal social benefit curve (*MSB*), which lies to the right of the *MPB* curve reflecting the possibility that as the individual's consumption increases, so does the benefit enjoyed by other members of society. Assuming that there are no social costs associated with consuming this desirable commodity, it can be seen that marginal social benefits exceed marginal private costs at $Q^*$, the individual's optimal point of consumption. Indeed, taking society's point of view, it would be desirable for the person to consume at $Q^{**}$ rather than $Q^*$, the point at which marginal social benefits are equated with the marginal cost of consumption. However, this outcome would not be acceptable to the individual since at $Q^{**}$ his or her marginal private benefits are less than the marginal cost of consumption.

Thus, if it is socially desirable for the individual to consume $Q^{**}$ rather than $Q^*$ and the authorities deem it necessary for him or her to do so, three basic options exist. First, the authorities could coerce the individual into consuming the additional amounts of the product. This can be seen in the case of education where there is a legal requirement for parents to send their children to school up to the age of 16. Second, the individual could be provided with a subsidy for each unit consumed equal to $P$ minus $P^*$ such that the marginal private cost becomes $P^*$. Reducing the marginal cost of consumption encourages the additional consumption to take place. The main problem with this solution is that the authorities need to have some idea about the shape of the individual's marginal benefit curve or else an inappropriate amount of the product will still be consumed. The third and final option is for the relevant authorities to initiate an awareness campaign in order to promote the desirable qualities of the commodity in question. An example of this would be the campaigns by the Health Education Authority to encourage people to eat healthier food and to exercise regularly. The rationale behind this approach is to shift the individual's marginal benefit curve to the right so that the marginal private benefit curve and the marginal private cost curve are equated at $Q^{**}$ rather than $Q^*$.

The theory underpinning figure 4.2b is broadly similar to that employed in figure 4.2a, except that in this case the situation involves consumption activity which imposes additional costs upon others. For simplicity it is assumed that the good or service in question does not also generate benefits to society in addition to those enjoyed by the individual in question. Thus, although the marginal private cost is assumed constant, additional units are assumed to impose an increasing level of social cost, thereby causing the marginal social cost curve to lie above and deviate away from the marginal private cost curve. From the individual's point of view, it is rational to consume the product in question up to the point where his or her marginal private costs equate with marginal private benefits, namely at $Q^*$. However, at this point, the costs to society exceed private costs. Taking society's point of view, it is desirable for consumption to take place at the point where the marginal private benefit curve equates with the marginal social cost curve, specifically at $Q^{**}$. Again, without some form of intervention by the authorities, there is no reason why the individual's consumption of the commodity in question should depart from $Q^*$.

The options which are thus available are similar to those considered in the case of a desirable externality. First, there is the possibility of coercion. Traditionally, this has been the approach taken with respect to environmental issues, such that for example, motorists are not allowed to sound their horn between 11 p.m. and 7 a.m. A second approach is to levy some form of tax. The aim of this option is to raise the private costs of consumption so that they reflect the social costs of consumption. This can be seen in the case of the taxes levied on cigarettes. Although the Chancellor of the Exchequer has long recognised that the consumption of any product which is habit-forming will be a good source of revenue, he has frequently made reference in budget statements to the undesirable social costs of smoking. In the case of figure 4.2b, the tax per unit would equal $P^*$ minus $P$. The third way in which the authorities can try and reduce the consumption of goods and services which have undesirable social consequences is again through some form of public-awareness campaign. If successful, such a programme will make consumers recognise that their private cost curve should also reflect social as well as private costs.

## Externalities and sport

Sport and leisure activities are recognised by many commentators as classic examples of commodities which not only produce private benefits but also a variety of social benefits. Few days go by without a newspaper report or television programme informing us of the physical and mental benefits which many leisure activities can confer upon us. These benefits not only apply to carefully managed active sports[2] but also activities which require relatively small amounts of physical exertion, such as angling. Obviously, many of these benefits are private. By engaging in some sort of sporting activity we are likely to feel mentally fitter and physically healthier than we would if we spent all our leisure time in front of the television. In 1978 Fentem and Bassey prepared a statement for the Sports Council providing an authoritive summary of all the scientific evidence on the benefits of exercise.

These benefits are not exclusive to each individual consumer of exercise. They are frequently passed on indirectly to others, thereby generating externality situations of the type identified in the previous section. First, if exercise is positively correlated with good health, then active people are going to make fewer demands upon the health care services. This will therefore free resources for other types of medical problem. Second, families are likely to be placed under less financial and psychological stress if individual members are healthy and not debilitated for long periods of time. Third, a healthy and fit population can also enhance the productive capacity of the economy by increasing worker effectiveness and reducing the number of days taken off sick. Fourth, the consumption of sport and leisure is also seen to generate benefits with respect to general social cohesion.

Over the last 35 years in particular, the provision of sport and leisure facilities has been seen as a means of diverting the attention of teenagers who would otherwise engage in vandalism and other 'undesirable' activities. The rationale for such intervention has emerged for two different reasons over the years. During the 1950s many older people saw a breakdown of societal norms emerging from the growing affluence of teenagers and the new 'rock-and-roll' culture. Nowadays, a similar argument is put forward, but in terms of the diminished employment opportunities which confront school leavers, the availability of violent videos and a decline in parental responsibility. The overall benefits which sport and leisure can provide is best reflected in the statement:

> For many people ... physical activity makes an important contribution to physical and mental well-being. ... By reducing boredom and urban frustration, participation in active recreation contributes to the reduction of hooliganism and delinquency among young people.
>
> (Department of the Environment, 1975, p. 3)

The role of leisure opportunity as a potential 'safety valve' is also a theme of Lord Scarman's 1981 report into the disturbances in Brixton.

In the previous section, it was argued that there are three basic ways of encouraging individuals to consume socially desirable activities. The use of coercion is of limited application in the case of sport and leisure, though the continued inclusion of physical education in the national curriculum does fit into this category. However, once children have left school, the authorities have to rely on alternative means of encouraging them to engage in some form physical activity. The most frequently used approach is price subsidies. The idea behind it is that by reducing the marginal cost of consumption, sporting activities will be attractive to a wider spectrum of people. However, because the consumption of leisure activities is likely to be subservient to the purchase of essential goods, such as food, clothing and shelter, it is assumed that price subsidies may need to be substantial (or even total) if activities are to be consumed on a regular basis by people on low levels of income. Furthermore, as we have already seen, the entrance fee to a particular sports facility is not the only cost that a potential consumer faces. First, we must recognise the travel component associated with getting to and from the facility in question. This embraces both a money cost and a time cost and suggests that there must be a comprehensive network of facilities available if the need to travel is not a deterrent to prospective recreationalists. There may also be a whole series of time constraints which are imposed on individuals by the workplace and family life in general. Thus, facilities need to be open when people can use them, not simply from nine till five.

These and other issues relating to the problems of encouraging people to undertake active leisure pursuits will be addressed in this and later chapters. Nevertheless, it should already be recognised that simply providing a price subsidy may not be enough to promote consumption. The use of price subsidies is frequently complemented by advertising and awareness campaigns. For example, the 1977 White Paper *Prevention and Health* recommends that:

> the relevant Government Departments should actively promote the practice of physical exercise, in a suitable form, for all age groups as a positive contribution to preventive medicine; and that every opportunity should be taken to use the media to educate the public on the value of exercise.
>
> (Department of Health and Social Security, 1977, p. 43)

However, one of the problems with the approach is that it cannot be guaranteed that everyone will be aware of the campaign. For example, leaflets which are made available at local libraries are not going to be read by people who do not visit libraries. Thus a multi-media approach, which embraces libraries, newspapers, radio and television, must be adopted if a particular campaign is to have an impact either locally or nationally. Nevertheless, promoting the benefits of sporting activity within schools may be successful if it leads to good habits later on in life and, moreover, if children pass on information to their parents.

However, the external effects of an individual's decision to participate in some form of sport or leisure activity are not exclusively desirable. As McLatchie (1986) noted, the growth in sports participation has also brought about an increase in sports injuries to the extent that over 2,000,000 people are affected by some sort of sports injury. Serious medical problems arise because people suddenly decide to undertake some form of rigorous exercise without taking expert advice beforehand, thereby risking cardiac and respiratory complications. Others arise gradually from musculoskeletal overload (repetitive micro-trauma) or more abruptly from a direct blow. The likelihood of the more chronic problems will depend upon the interaction between a number of variables which include the nature of the activity together with age, general health, strength of skeleton and the hereditary background of the participant.

The decision to play sport is a classic area of asymmetrical information. Most people will have a limited appreciation of their own well being and their personal capacity to absorb rigorous exercise. Adverse signs, such as the symptoms of an impending heart attack, may be misinterpreted and medical advice is not sought. However, the costs of major medical problems, such as heart attacks, are not borne exclusively by the individual concerned (for example, in terms of lost earnings, pain and suffering). Costs are also incurred by the health service (or insurance company) over a prolonged period of time. Added to this are the financial and psychological costs to that person's family, friends and relatives. In the short term, economic costs may involve out-of-pocket expenses and the general stress of visiting someone in hospital. Over a longer period there may be the additional costs associated with the main income provider within the household being forced to take a lower-paid job or being unable to work again.

Injuries arising from active sport and leisure participation are not usually life threatening and are initially treated at accident and emergency departments in hospitals throughout the country. An unpublished study by Tatem (1988) found that of the 87,339 people who attended the Accident and Emergency Department at the Queen's Medical Centre, Nottingham, in 1987, 7,400 were sport-related injuries.

The majority arose from playing contact sports, particularly soccer, and tended to involve the knee, lower leg, ankle and foot (40 per cent). Injuries to the hands and arms contributed a further 26 per cent to the total while the figures for facial and shoulder injuries were 14 per cent and 12.3 per cent respectively. It was found that most people were able to return to work and play sport again within four weeks (depending upon the severity of the injury). Although over half of the people involved required no further treatment, 26 per cent required three further clinic appointments during the four weeks. Thus, external costs of sports participation are imposed upon the health services (immediate treatment of the injury and any supplementary treatment and physiotherapy),[3] the injured person's employer who bears the costs of the injured person's absences from work, and that person's family and friends.

To date the discussion of externalities has treated the possibility of desirable and undesirable outcomes from an individual's (or firm's) actions as separate issues. Clearly, this is not the case, as illustrated by the example of playing sport. Not only can such activities generate a social benefit but they can simultaneously lead to social costs, particularly if the consumer is ill-informed about the health and safety aspects of participation.

If we wish to combine these effects into a single diagram, for example to illustrate the positive and negative external effects of playing sport, we

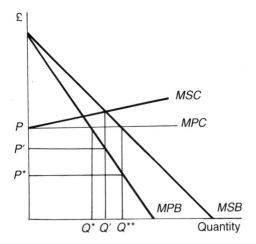

*Figure 4.3* Socially optimal level of exercise

may define a theoretical optimum which reflects the interaction between both the social benefit and social cost curves. This is demonstrated in figure 4.3. The notation adopted in previous diagrams is used here. If the individual only takes his or her own private costs and benefits into account when making the initial consumption decision, the optimal amount of activity is $Q^*$, where the marginal private benefit and marginal private cost curves intersect. If the social cost of sports participation is zero, then it would be desirable for the individual to be encouraged to consume sport at the point $Q^{**}$, where the marginal social benefit curve intersects with the marginal private cost curve. However, as we have seen, the nature of the exercise incurred by the individual's chosen sport or leisure activity may also carry a social cost, reflected in the marginal social cost curve. Thus, the optimal consumption point is where the marginal social benefit and marginal social cost curves intersect, specifically at $Q'$. Given that the social benefits from a carefully managed programme of exercise are likely to exceed the social costs, we would expect $Q'$ to lie to the right of $Q^*$, as depicted in figure 4.3. The subsidy which is required to encourage consumption of $Q'$ is $P$ minus $P'$. Had there been no social costs generated, the subsidy would have to be much larger, equal to $P$ minus $P^*$.

## PRIVATE GOODS AND PUBLIC GOODS

In considering externalities, we have emphasised the need for outside agencies to play a role in determining what quantities of particular goods individuals should consume. Where the external effects are predominantly beneficial, their role is to encourage consumption by coercion, price subsidy and the provision of information so that more informed choices are made. Conversely, when the external effects are predominantly negative, the authorities have the opposite task: to discourage consumption or even to prohibit it. However, there are circumstances where the market is even more unsuited to the production and consumption of certain products due to the characteristics of the goods or services involved. In particular, economists make a distinction between those goods and services for which the majority of benefits are enjoyed by the purchaser to the exclusion of others (even though they may involve external effects) and those goods and services whose benefits can embrace large numbers of people (even extending to the entire population of a country) to a point where one person's consumption does not detract from the consumption of others. An example of the former would be the eating of a bar of chocolate while an example of the latter would be national defence.[4]

Generally speaking, economists use the term *private goods* to describe products for which the purchaser can choose to exclude others and the term *public goods* to define commodities whose characteristics make them difficult to exclude from others. The aim here is to look more closely at the distinction between private goods and public goods and its broader economic implications, particularly with respect to sport and leisure.

Students frequently misunderstand the economist's distinction between private goods and public goods, often assuming that it simply refers to differences in their mode of provision. Thus, many misinformed essays and examination answers refer to the primary characteristic of public goods: that they are supplied by government or local authorities out of the public purse whereas private goods are commodities which are purchased by individuals in a traditional market situation. Although there is a strong element of truth in such a distinction, this explanation does not tell the whole story.

## Private goods

To an economist, private goods are commodities which are consumed solely by the purchaser unless he or she later chooses to donate them to others. Thus, they possess two main characteristics. The first is *rivalry* and the second is *excludability*. Rivalry simply means that for any given unit of a commodity, one person's consumption is at the expense of another person. For example two people cannot consume the same piece of chocolate. Similarly, if an individual is using a set of golf clubs then someone else cannot use them at exactly the same time. The other person may of course use another set, but by definition, this use then becomes rival to everyone else's. Excludability on the other hand refers to the fact that if someone owns a particular commodity then he or she has the option of denying other people the opportunity to use it. Thus, taking the example of the chocolate bar again, it is clear that the purchaser does have the option of sharing it with his or her friends. However, if the consumer wants to, he or she can prevent others from eating it, in other words, exercise the right of exclusion. However, if the bar is shared out, rivalry will still exist with respect to the individual pieces of chocolate which are eaten.

On many occasions, rivalry is not a significant problem since there is usually enough in the shops to go round. However, when a chocolate bar is the only one in a sports centre's vending machine, then the rival demands of individuals become explicit. More seriously, the images we see regularly on television of people starving to death due to shortages of food or medical supplies illustrates the degree to which rivalry and excludability can even result in life or death situations. One person's ability to obtain food or clean water denies someone else the opportunity of nourishment. Similarly, giving one person the opportunity to take scarce medication means that someone else will continue to suffer.

## Public goods

In contrast, public goods are commodities to which the assumptions of rivalry or excludability do not apply. Thus analogously, the first characteristic is that of *non-rivalry*. This means that one person's consumption of the product does not stop someone else from consuming the same unit. The second property of public goods is *non-excludability*, which means that no individual can realistically prevent another from consuming the product in question. Put another way, it would be uneconomical to actually enforce a system of prevention.

An example of a public good is the feeling of pleasure and national unity which is derived by the population from the success of its country's sportsmen and sportswomen. For example, victories by Linford Christie and Sally Gunnell in high-profile athletics events at the 1992 Olympic Games and the 1993 World Athletics Championships led to a general feeling of national pride. This is perhaps indicated by the fact that although relatively few people attend athletics meetings on a regular basis, 11.49 million television viewers saw Linford Christie's near record-breaking 100 metre run at the 1993 World Championships (Broadcasters Audience Research Board). These figures exceeded the audiences of long-standing programmes such as *Home and Away* (Thursday, 11.46 million) and both the Tuesday and Thursday episodes of *The Bill* (11.15 million and 11.40 million viewers respectively). Even people who did not actually see the race live, but instead saw it indirectly as part of television news coverage, are likely to have gained some feeling of pleasure from a British athlete succeeding at the highest level of competition. Generally, this example has classic public good properties since the author's own pleasure derived from the success of British athletes in international competition does not detract from the 'stock of pleasure' which can be consumed by everyone else.

Commodities which fulfil the specific criteria outlined in the previous paragraphs are known as *pure public goods* or *pure private goods*. Although it is fairly easy to cite examples of pure private goods, goods and services which adhere strictly to the requirements of a pure public good are more difficult to find. More often than not, there exists an array of goods and services which are referred to as *quasi public goods*. Consider the case of a National Park such as the Peak District. When there are few visitors to the area, the problem of rivalry is unlikely to be significant, providing that everyone shows a degree of respect for others and the countryside around them. However, as more and more visitors come to the site, designated car parks fill up and since there is no exclusion policy, scenic areas become congested by tourists, particularly during the summer months. In effect, the congestion which arises is a manifestation of the rivalry between competing individuals for a particular beauty spot. Although the same basic experience can be enjoyed by all the visitors, the quality of the visit ultimately deteriorates, such that the Park cannot be defined as a pure public good.

An element of rivalry also exists for the emergency services. Although they can be seen as offering a public good in terms of the peace of mind they provide and the fact that no one is actually excluded from consuming the services they offer, variations in the distance we live from the police, fire or ambulance station will mean that we are bound to receive a slightly different service. Furthermore, during periods of high demand, there is the strong possibility of rivalry. Consider the situation of an outbreak of fire at home. The speed at which the fire station can actually respond to your call will depend upon the distance the fire engine actually has to travel and second whether there are other outbreaks of fire at the same time. If there is a limited number of fire engines then we may find that our request for assistance cannot be acknowledged as quickly as when the outbreak of fire occurs in isolation. Similarly, the ability of the police to respond to an emergency call will depend upon the level of crime within the same vicinity. In high crime areas, rival demand for the police's resources will be particularly evident. Thus, although no formal attempt is made to exclude the potential users from using the emergency services, our rival demands can mean that none of the services falls strictly into the category of a pure public good.

*The demand for public goods*

One of the problems frequently addressed by economists is how public goods and quasi-public goods should be financed, given that they can simultaneously provide benefits to large groups of consumers rather than to single individuals. If people who pay for the good or service are unable to exclude others from consuming it, there is an incentive to *free-ride*. Unless there exists some mechanism by which all consumers of a public good are made to make some payment towards its upkeep, there exists the possibility that the good or service in question will be under-supplied when seen in terms of what is socially desirable.

To illustrate these points, let us consider the example of street lighting. The people most likely to benefit from its existence are those living nearby who not only benefit from the added visibility along the road but also the added security which well-lit areas provide. People who travel on that road infrequently will place a lower value on the lights when compared with local residents. This will be reflected in the demand curve of each individual or household. In figure 4.4, demand curves $d_2$ and $d_3$ characterise the demand for the lighting from two groups of local residents whereas demand curve $d_1$ reflects the demand for the streetlighting from individuals who use the road infrequently. It can be seen that for a given supply of streetlighting, $S$, both groups of local residents are willing to pay more for the facility than non-residents. In the case of a private good we would sum horizontally demand curves 1, 2 and 3 to derive a market demand curve for the lighting such that the quantity demanded at any given price would expand as more people revealed a preference to consume the product. However, in this example, we are considering a public good for which consumption can be shared without detracting from the overall benefits of the commodity. Thus, we are interested in the total amount people are willing to pay for the product. This can be determined by summing the demand curves vertically rather than horizontally. Thus in the case of figure 4.4, the total willingness to pay for the street lighting is $P^*$ ($p_1 + p_2 + p_3$). Having established the total amount people are willing to pay for the service, some mechanism needs to be devised so as to raise the necessary finance.

To begin, let us assume that there is no national or local government. Thus, the system of street lighting would have to be financed by private individuals. However, as we have already seen, local residents will place a higher value upon the benefits of the street lighting than non-residents. If the total amount residents are willing and able to pay is sufficient to finance the cost of erecting and maintaining the street lights then it would go ahead. It would prove administratively impractical to force non-residents to pay a fee to use the lights (by switching off the lights, residents would be denied the benefits; the use of checkpoints at the beginning of each road would cause major disruption). Thus, there is no need for them to reveal their preference for the service, thereby allowing

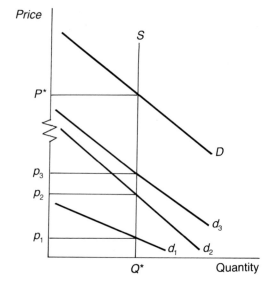

*Figure 4.4* Demand for a public good

them to receive the service free of charge, in other words, to free-ride. However, problems arise if there are an insufficient number of public-spirited individuals to bear the full costs of the lighting system. In this scenario the public good is under-supplied (less than $Q^*$) or not provided at all because the market is unable to extract payment from all those people who would ultimately benefit from it. Since there is an incentive for some consumers to free-ride, it becomes desirable for consumers to assume some sort of collective responsibility for the commodity in question such that everyone who benefits from it can be made to contribute towards its provision. Since people would have every incentive to understate their willingness to pay for the facility in question, the cost of many (quasi-)public goods is met out of local or national taxes. Of course, since people vary in terms of how they value the good or service, some will gain consumer surplus if they end up paying less than they would be willing to pay whereas others may pay more than they would be willing to pay.

## MERIT GOODS AND MERIT BADS

As we have already seen, economics makes the assumption that individuals are rational and able to make fully informed decisions. It is all too apparent that this is inappropriate in real life. Not only are we confronted with insufficient knowledge about the consequences of actions but also we are likely to place inappropriate level of emphasis on the relative importance of the information we do have at our disposal. Repetitive consumption may allow us to modify our purchasing behaviour over time but in many cases individuals continue to make 'inappropriate' consumption decisions perhaps because they are habit-forming, for example drinking or smoking too much. For many goods and services, this outcome will be of no concern to others. The market system will not be perceived as failing even if we make 'mistaken' purchases.

However, there are some products for which other people do take an active interest in our consumption behaviour and argue that on occasions it needs to be modified, if necessary by force. This need can arise for two reasons. First, because we may not take heed of warnings given to us. For example, many children would not engage in active exercise unless they were forced to at school. Second, individuals may under-consume certain commodities because they have insufficient income to demand the 'right' amount. Examples of this type of commodity abound in the social policy literature and include such goods as health care, education and pension provision. Collectively, these items are known as merit goods in the case of desirable commodities and merit bads in the case of undesirable products. Which goods and services should fall into either of these categories is a matter of opinion. What is deemed to be desirable or undesirable rests ultimately upon the paternalistic opinion of others. Nevertheless there seems to be general agreement about the types of goods and services which should be considered to be merit goods or merit bads, even if the exact details about how consumption should be encouraged or discouraged is the subject of political debate, as in the cases of exercise and smoking respectively.

It should already be clear that examples of merit goods and merit bads cross over into the types of commodities usually addressed in the externality literature. Thus in many respects, defining exactly what distinguishes a merit good (bad) from a commodity whose consumption simply generates positive (negative) external benefits is not altogether clear, given that both necessitate some form of government intervention. However, in the case of merit goods and merit bads we can emphasise the role of paternalism by others with regard to the way we live our lives. Put another way, individuals are not necessarily the best judges of what factors contribute to their own (and indeed, society's) well being. The most obvious source of this paternalism is from government, both national and local, though it may also stem from employers.

Examples of commodities which generate positive externalities and are acknowledged by many economists as being merit goods are many active leisure pursuits. Consequently, their consumption is actively encouraged by government, as well as many employers, reflecting their recognition that they can produce desirable externalities. This has already been acknowledged within our previous discussion examining the private and social benefits certain activities can provide with respect to our health and in terms of various government statements which recognise sport and leisure as a means of alleviating vandalism and delinquency. However, we may take this a stage further and argue that many sport and leisure activities have been perceived as merit goods for the last century and a half. Thus, as an early example we may cite Victorian legislation encompassing public libraries and museums (introduced during the late 1840s and early 1850s) which was intended to facilitate greater cultural appreciation by the masses. We can cite the role of the Countryside Commission set up by the Countryside Act of 1968,[5] in promoting general access to 'open air recreation' particularly by publicising country areas outside the National Parks and the development of subsidised leisure provision by local authorities, recently backed up by one of the requirements for the National Curriculum that by the end of 1994 all children should be able to swim 25 metres before they leave primary school.

Current objectives outlined by the Department of National Heritage (1993), with respect to its support of sport within the UK, reflects the ongoing belief that sport can not only have the properties of a public good and a merit good but also be a disseminator of desirable externalities. For example, in its 1993 annual report objectives include: the desire to promote participation at all ages; to encourage participants to better their own performances and provide the environment within which champions can develop; and to enhance the international sporting reputation of the UK. This reiterates the aims of the Sports Council, established almost 30 years ago.

The implementation of these objectives not only involves the work of the Sports Council and local authorities, but also the Department of Health and the Health Education Authority. Furthermore, as we shall discuss in this and later chapters, the government has been placing an increased emphasis on the importance of the private sector working alongside the public and voluntary sectors. The rationale behind this move is set out in the major government policy statement *Sport and Active Recreation* (Department of the Environment, 1991) which emphasises previous goals with respect to encouraging mass active leisure participation and sporting excellence.

Also in 1991, the (football) Pools Promoters Association began funding the Arts and Sports Foundation. Around two-thirds of its £60 million income is directed towards sport, in particular, the building of sports centres. Furthermore, a sports sponsorship scheme, known as 'Sportsmatch' aims to promote grassroots sponsorship of sport, particularly to help young people from ethnic minorities and disabled people, as well as to help develop sport within areas of urban and rural disadvantage. Since December 1992, contributions of £1,000 or more (up to a maximum of £75,000) from first-time sponsors (or in addition to existing sponsorship agreements) of an event enable its organisers to apply for a government grant on a pound-for-pound basis.

At this point of the analysis it is appropriate to look more closely at the role of some of the providers of sport and leisure which have grown alongside the market system. The fact that they have developed alongside the market is a signal that market failure has taken place, reflecting the emergence of incomplete markets and the role of imperfect information on the part of both demanders and suppliers. Specifically, we shall consider the growth and development of indoor public-sector leisure facilities, the existence of what Torkildsen (1992, p. 214) refers to as the 'backbone of leisure and recreation organisation and participation', namely the voluntary sector and public subsidy of the 'arts'. To conclude we shall highlight the role of a different type of market intervention, namely private sector sponsorship of sport and leisure.

## THE GROWTH IN THE NETWORK OF MUNICIPAL LEISURE CENTRES

According to the Audit Commission (1990), local authorities in England and Wales are responsible for running of over 1,700 indoor sports facilities. Although the first sports centre was built as early as 1964, the actual impetus for the growth in public sports centres came from the newly established Sports Council which, in 1968, set out a case for spending £370 million on new provision between 1971 and 1981. Against a backdrop of relative economic prosperity (see Chapter 8), the basic criterion employed was that one centre should be built for every

50,000 population within each local authority, plus a further centre for every additional 40,000 population. The rationale behind this strategy was that the main deterrent for individuals with respect to the consumption of sport and leisure was accessibility and price. Thus, if a wider and more concentrated network of subsidised facilities could be provided, emphasising the merit good status of sporting activity, existing participants would be encouraged to consume sport on a more regular basis and new groups of consumers would be attracted to the new facilities, thereby generating even more private and social benefits. Thus, this was a 'supply-led' initiative. Facility planning took place at local level, with reference to emerging inventories of facilities which were being compiled by nine newly established Regional Sports Councils. Despite the involvement of the main interested parties within the planning process (for example local councils, sports clubs and education authorities), this period of growth was also characterised by a maldistribution of resources such that the Department of the Environment Audit Inspectorate (1983, p. 19) were forced to report

> cases in our small sample where two leisure centres are sited only three miles apart on opposite sides of district/county boundaries.... There are examples of ... regional facilities which could not be justified for the population resident in the authority, drawing upon the population from a number of different authorities, which are being subsidised by ratepayers in one authority without requesting financial assistance from other sources.

During the 1970s, the rate at which facilities were built tended to reflect fluctuations in the general health of the economy. The period 1974–5 was particularly notable with the opening of 137 new sports centres and 190 swimming pools (Sports Council, 1982). Nevertheless, from a base of only 12 sports centres and 440 swimming pools in 1970–1 (ibid.), 61 per cent of the target number of sports centres had been constructed, representing a total of 461 major complexes, whereas for swimming pools the target was exceeded: 964 pools were built as opposed to the target of 857.[6] The general success of this supply-led strategy was seen retrospectively in figures produced in the *General Household Survey.* However, the 1980s saw a change in emphasis, set out in the two Sports Council documents *Sport in the Community: The Next Ten Years* (1982) and *Sport in the Community: Into the 1990s* (1988). Although both papers set out the case for a further programme of expansion for sports facilities in general, more attention was paid to the actual targeting of groups within the population which had failed to respond to the increased leisure opportunities available to them. Particular attention was paid to the general under-representation of women relative to men and the low demand exhibited by people from ethnic minorities, elderly and unemployed persons and individuals who have just left school or who are nearing retirement age. Thus, the emphasis of policy changed from being almost exclusively supply-led, to one which also emphasised the demand characteristics of individual consumer groups. For example, in the 1988 *Sport in the Community* document, the Sports Council not only showed concern that there would be insufficient resources to meet all their facility requirements but also that any which were provided should appeal to target groups and be priced reasonably. Furthermore, in their 1982 report, a target of 800 indoor sports halls was set for the period up to 1988 (in reality less than half this figure came to fruition), of which 150 were to be developed in areas of special social and sporting need. This reflects the continued role of sport as a merit good. The more complex issue of how pricing and marketing strategies may be varied to attract different types of consumer into leisure centres will be addressed specifically in Chapter 5.

## THE VOLUNTARY SECTOR

The definition of the voluntary sector with which the literature seems to be in accord is that by Butson (1983, p. 28): 'The voluntary sector is defined as including non-profit-making sports organisations which are essentially run by, and provided for, amateur sportsmen.' Thus, according to this definition, voluntary organisations fall into an intermediate area between the commercial organisation, for which profit will play some role in determining what facilities are supplied, and the attempts by central and local government to correct for any deficiencies which have subsequently resulted. This implies that they not only have a role in correcting for the market failure which arises from commercial activity but also that governments (at local and national level) are not necessarily providing the precise mix of facilities which society wants, what we might term 'government failure'. Unlike public-sector provision, however, for which low prices are frequently charged to promote use, some voluntary organisations have acquired the traits of commercial facilities by restricting their membership through high prices and/or limits on the number of places.

Voluntary organisations provide the opportunity to participate in religious and youth groups, the arts and sport as well as a whole range of leisure activities. Some groups are highly localised, whereas others are organised regionally or nationally, for example the National Trust. A comprehensive list of the different types of voluntary leisure organisations which exist is provided by Torkildsen (1992, pp. 210–11). One omission from that list is the role of employers in providing subsidised leisure activities for their employees, including sports teams, social clubs and even organised tourism. General increases in income, leisure time and mobility has fuelled a rapid increase in the number and membership of many voluntary organisations embracing 'traditional' and 'non-traditional' activities. For example, the British Orienteering Federation had 114 affiliated clubs and 2,368 members in 1975. By 1989, these figures had risen to 153 and 7,307 respectively (Sports Council, 1991). However, not all organised groups have experienced such increases. In 1950, membership of the British Cycling Federation amounted to 66,528. By 1989, this figure had fallen to less than a quarter of this total. Although *Social Trends* does not provide information with respect to the membership of sport-related voluntary organisations, it does highlight trends in the membership of more general leisure-related groups. Again evidence suggests that while many organisations are experiencing an increase in numbers, others are declining in popularity. For example, membership of the Cub Scouts grew from 265,000 in 1971 to 349,000 in 1991 while that of the Scouts fell from 215,000 to 192,000 over the same period. Similar trends are reflected in the membership of the Brownie Guides and Girl Guides. One area of young persons' voluntary leisure activity which has experienced a strong increase in interest has been the Duke of Edinburgh's Award scheme. In the 20 years between 1971 and 1991, the number of participants increased from 122,000 to 200,000, with the number of bronze, silver and gold awards increasing in a similar proportion (to 35,000, 13,000 and 6,000 respectively).

The importance of voluntary groups as providers of organised leisure within different localities was highlighted in a study by Hoggett and Bishop (1986). In the Kingswood area of Bristol, with its suburban population of around 85,000 people, it was found that there were 300 different groups. Taking a sample of one-quarter of this number, it was found that the largest proportion of voluntary groups, around 37 per cent, were sport-related. Of the rest, 28 per cent were multifunctional (for example, youth groups and senior citizens' clubs), 23 per cent were hobby-related (for example pigeon fancying) and 13 per cent were arts-related (for example drama groups).

One of the problems analysts face when investigating the voluntary sector is the limited amount of empirical data which is available:

By the very nature of voluntary sector activity, assessment of its economic importance is virtually impossible. Many of the inputs into the organisations' activities go unrecorded. This is particularly the case with the labour input since much labour is normally provided free. Equally, the output of such organisations is rarely measured because many voluntary organisations are small and records of their activities are not available except to the organisations' members.

(Gratton and Taylor, 1985, p. 129)

This problem is also acknowledged by the Henley Centre in their investigation into the contribution of sport to the national economy, referred to in Chapter 1. Nevertheless, questionnaire evidence was gathered from clubs operating in six major sport areas: athletics, cricket, football, golf, rugby and sailing, producing 232 replies from an original sample of 600. Responses suggest that the major sources of monetary income for voluntary sport-related clubs are gross bar receipts (48 per cent), subscriptions and fees (32 per cent) and raffles/gaming (9 per cent).

## PUBLIC SUBSIDY OF THE ARTS

Public subsidy of leisure is not simply limited to the leisure activities we find at sports centres and parks. The continued existence of museums, libraries and the arts reflects government intervention at both central and local levels. The rationale for such intervention is similar to that expounded earlier for 'active' sport. At various times in history, the promotion of the arts has been seen as a public good which can help instil a feeling of national identity and pride. In other words, a vibrant network of performing arts, museums, libraries and galleries provides a set of non-excludable benefits similar to those derived from sporting success. This phenomenon can best be seen in Scandinavian countries where a rich literary tradition continues to provide a major source of social cohesion. The arts are also seen by many as an example of a merit good, a product deemed desirable by 'society', yet due to incomplete information is under-consumed by many individuals. The external benefits of the arts may also be seen in terms of improving the education of the population in general. For example, the Department of National Heritage finances 11 national museums and galleries, with a set of objectives which include the promotion of public access and the need to enhance educational facilities (with special reference to the content of the National Curriculum). The benefits therefore extend beyond the private individual to employers and society as a whole. If left to the free market, it is likely that the diversity of the arts would diminish, limited to the work of popular composers or writers, and probably only accessible to the better-off members of society. This would provide inappropriate signals to contemporary practitioners, thereby slowing down the development of the arts. In effect, it could be argued that these costs are not being imposed only upon present but also upon future generations. However, there is an alternative argument to put forward. Only a very small proportion of the population actually goes to the theatre or visits museums and art galleries. For example less than 10 per cent of adults attended a museum or art gallery four weeks prior to interview (*General Household Survey*, 1990). Thus, as we shall see below, hundreds of millions of pounds of public money is being spent subsidising what is effectively a minority activity.

Information about the level of central government expenditure directed towards the arts can be obtained from the *Annual Report* of the Department of National Heritage. For example, it can be seen from table 4.2 that for the year 1993–4, it is committed to spending well over £500 million on this area of activity.

Government support for the arts is largely channelled through the Arts Council of Great Britain whose objectives are: to increase the number and range of people experiencing the arts; to improve the creative standards of the arts and; to promote artistic activity in general. In 1991–2, total expenditure by the Arts Council of Great Britain and the Arts Council of Northern Ireland amounted to almost £215 million, of which a quarter went to the national theatre, ballet and opera companies. Of the remainder, a further 46 per cent of spending is directed towards the Regional Arts Associations, drama and music. Over the last decade, there has been a change in the government's attitude towards the arts, in that there has been an expectation that they should show much greater awareness with respect to the funds they absorb and to the general marketing of their products. This is reflected in the 1993 *Annual Report* of the Department of National Heritage which refers to the development of a series of indicators to measure the 'performance' of the arts. In 1984, the Business Sponsorship Incentive Scheme (BSIS) was launched to promote growth in commercial sponsorship. Monies from first-time sponsors are matched pound-for-pound from a government grant (up to a set limit); second-time-round sponsors attract £1 from goverment for every £2 invested, while for third-time sponsors the ratio is £1 for every £4 invested. According to figures supplied in the 1993 *Annual Report* of the Department of National Heritage, the scheme has succeeded in

Table 4.2 Central government expenditure on the arts (£million)

| | 1985–6 | 1986–7 | 1987–8 | 1988–9 | 1989–90 | 1990–1 | 1991–2 | 1992–3[a] | 1993–4[a] | 1994–5[a] |
|---|---|---|---|---|---|---|---|---|---|---|
| Museums and galleries | 103 | 120 | 122 | 154 | 158 | 182 | 201 | 213 | 213 | 218 |
| Arts[b] | 118 | 150 | 144 | 158 | 162 | 183 | 212 | 237 | 235 | 231 |
| Libraries | 58 | 64 | 76 | 80 | 99 | 114 | 129 | 133 | 114 | 133 |

Source: Department of National Heritage, Annual Report, 1993, p. 1
Notes:
[a]Figures for 1992–3 are estimates while subsequent figures are planned.
[b]Most funds to the arts are distributed by the Arts Council.

bringing £59 million of new money into the arts (including government contributions of £19.3 million) and attracted over 2,700 first-time arts sponsors since its inception. Funding for the scheme was increased from £3.5 million to £4.5 million in 1992–3 and this figure will be maintained until 1995–6. However, this has fuelled concern that business sponsorship will ultimately lead to a reduction in innovative work. As we shall see below, companies are unlikely to sponsor an event if there is no obvious return for them. Thus, assuming that they would not want to be associated with an unsuccessful experimental play or concert, there is the likelihood that firms will exert an increasing influence upon what performances actually take place.

## COMMERCIAL SPONSORSHIP OF LEISURE AND SPORT

As most readers will be aware, commercial sponsorship is not limited to the arts but extends to all forms of sport and leisure. Although commercial sponsorship provides monies which can help to correct market failure which exists in many aspects of sport and leisure provision, it should not be interpreted as philanthropy or in the same terms as a government subsidy since it is intended to lead indirectly to increased profits, market shares and publicity, rather than to correct a potential market failure *per se*. Nevertheless, the effect of commercial sponsorship of events can be similar if it helps correct deficiencies in the market. Furthermore, as we have already seen in the case of the arts, governments themselves intervene in the sponsorship process by providing incentives to encourage the emergence of commercial sponsors. Sponsorship takes place at all levels of leisure activity, ranging from a local hardware store sponsoring a village fête to the financing of national and international cricket. Torkildsen (1992) suggests that major sponsorship deals are often attempts to 'buy' respectability by firms operating in sectors with a poor public image, for example in the tobacco and alcohol industries. Some sports have benefited heavily from sponsorship. For example, during the 1970s and 1980s, commercial sponsorship turned snooker from a minor spectator event to one which is held in prestigious halls and attracts major television coverage.

Gratton and Taylor (1985) view the decision to sponsor an event over a number of years as an investment decision whose returns will be enjoyed over a number of years rather than as a windfall gain. However, gains in terms of increased market share or greater public awareness of corporate image are not certain. One way of measuring the success of sponsorship deals is to identify the number which are renewed. For example, Gillette withdrew its sponsorship from a major one-day cricket competition because it felt that public awareness of the company name was not cumulative. In contrast, Cornhill Insurance have retained their interest in test cricket since 1977, benefiting from increased public awareness of their product and increased premium income.

The fact that sports sponsorship is not philanthropy suggests that sports governing bodies should not become over-dependent upon the involvement of any one company. Furthermore, there is a question as to whether the rules or conventions of a game should be changed in order to satisfy a commercial sponsor. For example, 1993 saw the introduction of coloured clothing for one-day cricket played on Sundays. Test match pitches are now adorned with the Cornhill logo. Although traditionalists may see these and other changes as undesirable, it is unlikely that without sponsorship cricket would have survived as long as it has. Thus, for people who feel that cricket is part of Britain's national heritage, sponsorship, whatever its motives, has served to correct a potential market failure.

## QUESTIONS FOR DISCUSSION

1   Using demand and supply analysis, explain what you understand by the term 'market failure'.

2   Put forward the case for 'Sport for All' from an economist's perspective.

# Chapter 5

# Elasticity and the pricing of leisure facilities

## INTRODUCTION

The analysis in Chapters 2 and 3 identified what economists mean by the terms demand function and supply function. It was seen that these functions specify the relationship between the quantity demanded or quantity supplied and the variables which can exert an influence over them. Thus, in the case of quantity demanded, we considered the influence of such parameters as own price, income, the price of other goods and fashion whereas for quantity supplied such variables as own price, the price of factors of production and the objectives of the producer were acknowledged. The aim of this chapter is to consider the methodology economists use to measure the responsiveness of quantity demanded and quantity supplied to a change in any independent variable. The general term economists use when referring to this sensitivity measure is *elasticity* (of demand or of supply). The general formula for an elasticity calculation is:

$$\frac{\text{percentage or proportionate}}{\text{change in quantity demanded or supplied}} \qquad [5.1]$$
$$\overline{\text{percentage or proportionate change in variable (e.g. price)}}$$

As the focus of the equation is the percentage change in both the denominator and numerator, results from elasticity calculations are not specified in units – the percentage signs simply cancel out.[1]

The most common focus for such calculations is the own price variable, namely price elasticity of demand and price elasticity of supply, and therefore relates to responsiveness as we move up and down the demand curve or supply curve. In particular, it will be seen that price elasticity of demand estimates can provide important insights into the most appropriate way of pricing leisure facilities. We shall also consider elasticity of demand in terms of the income variable (income elasticity of demand) and the price of other goods (cross elasticity of demand).

## PRICE ELASTICITY OF DEMAND

Price elasticity of demand calculations refer to changes as we move along a demand curve. In other words, the key variables are quantity demanded and price. We have already seen that the relationship between them can be expected to be negative in the vast majority of cases (in other words, a higher price will lead to a reduction in quantity demanded and vice versa). It therefore follows that we should expect a negative answer from carrying out most price elasticity of demand calculations. The equation which is used is simply a more definite version of the one outlined in equation [5.1], specifically,

$$\frac{\text{percentage or proportionate change in quantity demanded}}{\text{percentage or proportionate change in price}} \qquad [5.2]$$

Thus, with respect to the negative outcome we would expect from applying [5.2] to real or hypothetical price and quantity demanded data, either the numerator will be negative and the denominator positive (quantity demanded falls as the price rises) or the numerator will be positive and the denominator negative (a reduction in price leads to an increase in demand). It should be noted at this point that not all commentators include the negative sign when reporting the results of price elasticity calculations. However, for the purposes of this text the negative sign will be acknowledged throughout.

At the outset, we may define three basic outcomes from such a price elasticity of demand calculation:

1    When the percentage or proportionate change in quantity demanded exceeds the proportionate (but opposite) change in price. This will produce a figure in excess of $-1$. In these circumstances we say that demand is *price elastic*. At the most extreme, we may highlight the (trivial) situation where a change in price results in an infinite change in quantity demanded. Here, demand is deemed to be *infinitely price elastic* and would, for example, result from a calculation based upon a completely horizontal demand curve.

2    When the percentage change in quantity demanded exactly equals

the proportionate (but opposite) change in price. On these occasions, we refer to the situation as one of *unitary price elasticity* (of demand) since an answer of −1 will result.

3    Finally, there is the situation of *price inelastic demand*. This arises when the percentage change in quantity demanded is less than the proportionate change in price. Consequently, a price elasticity of demand calculation will have produced a figure of less than −1. Again, there is an extreme outcome, this time when a change in price has no effect on the quantity that is demanded. In this case a figure of zero would result in a situation referred to as *infinite price inelasticity*. For example, such an outcome may be expected if the demand curve is completely vertical.

To illustrate how each of these outcomes may arise, let us consider three worked examples. In each case, we require information about the percentage or proportionate change in quanitity demanded (for the numerator in equation [5.2]) and the percentage change in price (for the denominator in equation [5.2]). Thus, we need to know the quantity demanded at the original price and the quantity demanded after the change in price. It is important that the change in both price and quantity demanded are expressed in percentage terms. To illustrate why, let us assume that a given price rise leads to a 50 unit fall in quantity demanded. Had quantity demanded originally been 60 units, then a 50 unit fall is extremely significant, since it represents a high percentage of the original total. If, on the other hand, a 50 unit fall arises when the initial quantity demanded is 28,000 units, the change is much less significant.

We may define the proportionate change in any variable by dividing the absolute change by the original value. Thus, in the first case, the proportionate change would be 50/60 which equals 0.83 or 83 per cent. In contrast, in the second case the proportionate change is 50/28,000 which equals 0.0018 or 0.18 per cent. Following on therefore, we may redefine equation [5.2] algebraically as:

$$\frac{\Delta Q/Q \ (\times \ 100\%)}{\Delta P/P \ (\times \ 100\%)} \tag{5.3}$$

where $\Delta Q$ and $\Delta P$ denotes change in quantity and price respectively, while $Q$ and $P$ signify the original quantity and price. The percentage signs simply cancel out.

We are now in a position to carry out a price elasticity calculation. Consider the case of a hypothetical product for which 150 units are demanded at a price of £15. Now assume that the price increases by £5 to £20. We would expect, given the law of demand, that the quantity demanded will fall, let us say to 120 units. The absolute reduction in quantity demanded is 30 units (150 units minus 120 units). Substituting these figures into our price of elasticity of demand equation [5.3] we get the following:

$$\frac{30/150}{5/15} = \frac{0.2}{0.33} = (-)0.6.$$

By the definitions set out above, we may say that demand in this case is price inelastic because the answer is less than unity. In other words, the proportionate change in quantity demanded is less than the proportionate change in price.

Let us attempt another calculation. Let us assume that at a price of 30p, 100 units of a commodity are demanded. When the price rises to 36p (an absolute price change of 6p), quantity demanded falls to 80 units (an absolute reduction in demand of 20 units). Again, substituting into the price elasticity equation we get:

$$\frac{20/100}{6/30} = \frac{0.2}{0.2} = (-)1.$$

In this case we are witnessing a situation of unitary price elasticity, that is, the proportionate change in quantity demanded exactly equals the proportionate change in price.

Rather than go through the detailed mechanics of a third worked example to demonstrate price elastic demand, we shall simply supply the figures so that the reader may carry out his or her own calculation. In this case, assume that a price fall from £24 to £20 and that the quantity demanded rises from 50 to 80 units. If the calculation is completed correctly, a figure of 3.75 should result. Put another way, the proportionate change in quantity demanded is in excess of the proportionate change in price.

There are no hard and fast rules to guide us as to whether particular goods or services are more likely to be associated with price elastic or price inelastic demand. Nevertheless, four factors are frequently highlighted in textbooks as likely to exert an influence upon a product's price elasticity. However, it should be recognised at the outset that each point is extremely generalised and consequently represents 'rules of thumb' rather than scientifically proven facts.

First, there is the availability of substitutes for the commodity in question. In particular, we would expect that as the number of substitutes for a product increases, the greater will be its price elasticity of demand. For example, an increase in the price of carrots (for which there are numerous alternatives) will generate a more significant reduction in demand than a similar increase in the price of salt, for which there is no close substitute. However, much depends upon how closely the product is defined. General definitions such as 'food' and 'leisure' are more likely to be associated with price inelastic demand than specific commodities within those categories such as 'coffee' or 'watching football matches'.

The second variable assumed to influence the price elasticity of demand for a product is whether a commodity is deemed to be a necessity or a luxury. Generally, necessities are products which we need for basic survival whereas luxuries are products which improve our general quality of life. Of course the definition of which products fall into which category is a matter of opinion. Forty years ago, a television set was viewed as a luxury whereas nowadays it is perceived by most people as a necessity. Similarly, much of the food we eat is not necessary. The prevalence of convenience foods and unhealthy snacks in most people's shopping baskets bears witness to this. Nevertheless, rule of thumb would suggest that necessities are more likely to be associated with price inelastic demand than luxuries.

Third, it is often argued that goods which make small incursions into our everyday budget will have a lower price elasticity of demand than products which require greater outlays of money. The relatively low-priced products which permeate the literature are also characterised by having relatively few close substitutes, for example salt or matches.

Finally, commentators often refer to the period of time under consideration. Demand over relatively short periods of time is likely to be more price inelastic than demand over the longer term. The classic example to cite is that of the oil price increases which emerged during late 1973 and 1974. These price rises were engineered by the oil producers' cartel OPEC (Organisation of Petroleum-Exporting Countries) after the Arab–Israeli War. Although the price of oil quadrupled to $12 per barrel, the demand for oil changed little since both consumers and industry were locked into using oil-intensive technologies. In the case of consumers, rising real incomes together with the low fuel prices offered by relatively cheap oil in the past had encouraged the purchase of fuel-inefficient cars. Thus, rather than leading to a large reduction in oil demanded, the quadrupling of prices only led to a 5 per cent reduction in world demand. From previous definitions, this should suggest highly price inelastic demand. Over the long term however, the uncertainty brought about by the first major oil 'crisis' led both consumers and industry to move away from oil-intensive technologies, thereby increasing the price elasticity of demand for oil.

So far we have established how to carry out a simple price elasticity of demand calculation and considered how we might interpret the figures which result. Since price elasticities are not expressed in units, they allow economists to compare the relative responsiveness of demand to given price changes for any number of commodities, regardless of whether they are consumed in kilograms, litres, boxes or by time. However, the usefulness of the price elasticity of demand concept does not stop there. It can be shown that price elasticity of demand calculations can also provide extremely important information for a supplier as to whether it is desirable to increase or decrease the price of his or her product. To show why, we need to redefine the basic price elasticity equation. Recall the basic equation [5.3]:

$$\frac{\Delta Q/Q}{\Delta P/P} \qquad\qquad [5.3]$$

This may be restated as:

$$\frac{\Delta Q}{Q} \div \frac{\Delta P}{P} \qquad\qquad [5.4]$$

which is also equivalent to:

$$\frac{\Delta Q}{Q} \times \frac{P}{\Delta P} \qquad\qquad [5.5]$$

and may be rearranged to get:

$$\frac{\Delta Q}{\Delta P} \times \frac{P}{Q} \qquad\qquad [5.6]$$

Equation [5.6] is a useful restatement of the price elasticity equation. It is made up of two basic components. The first, $\Delta Q/\Delta P$, refers to the ratio of the change in quantity to the change in price. This is simply the gradient (slope) of the demand curve. The second component, $P/Q$, describes the actual point on the demand curve at which the price elasticity calculation is being measured. This suggests that the only piece of information required by a decision-maker is the equation of the demand curve associated with the product in question, which tells us what the gradient is. In the case of an equation specifying a linear demand curve, the slope is constant. This means that to estimate price elasticity for any point lying on a demand curve, we simply need to divide the appropriate price by the quantity and multiply by the coefficient of the equation. To illustrate, let us consider the equation of a very simple demand curve:

$$Qd = 10 - P \qquad\qquad\qquad [5.7]$$

In this case, the gradient of the demand curve is −1. Using the equation, we can determine quantity demanded from any given price. For example, if we want to calculate the price elasticity of demand when the price equals 4, it can be seen that quantity demanded is 6 units. Substituting these figures into equation [5.6] we get:

$$-1 \times \frac{4}{6} = \frac{-4}{6} = -0.66$$

This tells us that at that point on the demand curve, demand is price inelastic. If this calculation were replicated for every price/quantity combination on the demand curve then an extremely important result emerges: price elasticity varies along the entire length of the demand curve. Indeed this result unambiguously applies to *any straight-line demand curve.*[2] This is illustrated in table 5.1 which uses equation [5.7] as a basis for its estimates. It can be seen that there are four columns of information. In the first two columns the degree to which quantity demanded changes as the price changes is measured as we move from left to right down the demand curve. In column three, the level of consumer expenditure or total revenue (as defined in Chapter 3) has been estimated by multiplying each price–quantity combination together. Finally in column four, figures denoting the price elasticity of demand at each point along the demand curve are presented. The reader should attempt to replicate each figure using the price elasticity of demand equation before proceeding to the next section of the chapter.

It can be seen that the demand curve is associated with a complete range of price elasticities, ranging from zero (completely inelastic) to infinity (totally elastic). Some readers may be puzzled by derivation of the two extreme points: when price elasticity equals infinity and zero. In the first case the ratio $P/Q$ in equation [5.7] will have a zero as its denominator. Since zero divides into 10 an infinite number of times, it

*Table 5.1* Changes in price elasticity and consumer expenditure along a
straight-line demand curve

| Price | Quantity | Consumer exp. | Price elasticity |
|-------|----------|---------------|------------------|
| 10 | 0 | 0 | infinity |
| 9 | 1 | 9 | −9.00 |
| 8 | 2 | 16 | −4.00 |
| 7 | 3 | 21 | −2.33 |
| 6 | 4 | 24 | −1.50 |
| 5 | 5 | 25 | −1.00 |
| 4 | 6 | 24 | −0.66 |
| 3 | 7 | 21 | −0.42 |
| 2 | 8 | 16 | −0.25 |
| 1 | 9 | 9 | −0.11 |
| 0 | 10 | 0 | 0.00 |

will naturally produce a figure of infinity when multiplied by −1 (the
demand curve coefficient). Similarly, when the price is zero, 10 units
will be demanded. Thus, the ratio *P/Q* is 0/10. Since zero divides by 10
zero times, this figure, even when multiplied by −1 (to complete the
price elasticity calculation), will still produce a figure of zero. The
information given in columns one, two and four is replicated in figure

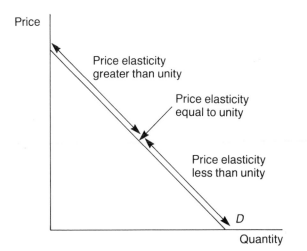

*Figure 5.1* Changes in price elasticity along a straight-line demand curve

5.1 which shows that price elasticity of demand declines as we move down the demand curve from left to right.

Closer inspection of columns three and four of table 5.1 reveals a very important relationship. When the price elasticity is less than one, an increase in price will produce an increase in consumer expenditure (or revenue to the producer). For example, a price rise from 3 to 4 leads to an increase in consumer expenditure from £21 to £24. Similarly a reduction in price within the inelastic section of the demand curve leads to a fall in consumer expenditure. However, within the price elastic section of the demand curve, the reverse is true. In other words, an increase in price leads to a fall in consumer expenditure whereas a drop in price would increase consumer expenditure. It can also be seen that consumer expenditure is maximised at the point where price elasticity of demand equals unity.

The fact that the direction of change in consumer expenditure after a price change can be predicted with reference to the price elasticity of demand can also be demonstrated graphically. The two diagrams depicted in figure 5.2 show the response of consumer expenditure to a rise in price on the price elastic and price inelastic sections of the demand curve respectively. In figure 5.2a, the extra expenditure by people who continue to use the product in question is less than the fall in consumer expenditure brought about by the reduction in demand. In figure 5.2b, the extra money paid by existing users outweighs the expenditure of people who have been deterred from consuming the

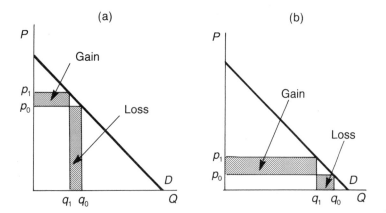

Figure 5.2 The relationship between price elasticity and total revenue

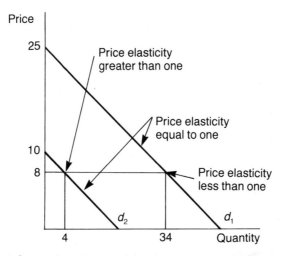

*Figure 5.3* Comparing price elasticity along two parallel demand curves

product by the higher price. Although, in this case, the price increase brings about the same absolute reduction in quantity demanded, its importance relative to the initial demand is greater in figure 5.2a than it is in figure 5.2b, hence the distinction resulting between the price elastic and price inelastic sections of the demand curve.[3]

So far, the discussion has focused upon price elasticity in terms of one demand curve. It is also important to consider how best to interpret price elasticities when the analysis incorporates a comparison of two or more different demand curves. To begin, take for example the two demand curves drawn in figure 5.3, $d_1$ and $d_2$. It can be seen although they start and end at different points on the graph, they have exactly the same slope. In terms of their respective equations, this means that they will have exactly the same coefficient. In this case, $d_1$ could be characterised by the expression $Q = 50 - 2P$, while $d_2$ could be defined by the equation $Q = 20 - 2P$. Although they both have the same slope, the price elasticity of demand will be different at any given price (since we are comparing demand curves it is assumed that we are making comparisons over prices which are common to both demand curves). For example, we might ask what the price elasticity of demand is when $P$ equals 8. By substituting 8 into both equations we can estimate the quantity demanded in each case. It can be seen that the respective quantities are 34 and 4 resulting in price elasticities of −0.47 and −4.0.[4] Thus, when $P$ equals 8 we are on the price inelastic section of the outermost demand curve yet on the price elastic section of the demand curve closest to the origin, despite the fact that their slopes are identical. This illustration highlights a very important rule. If we are confronted by two parallel demand curves, the one which is furthest away from the origin will always be more price inelastic at any given price. Indeed, this is part of a more general rule: that if we are comparing any two straight-line demand curves, regardless of their relative slope, it is the one which cuts the $y$ axis at the highest point which will be most price inelastic at any given point. The reader may wish to test this statement mathematically by calculating the price elasticity of demand for two non-parallel demand curves described by the equations $Q = 50 - 2P$ and $Q = 40 - 3P$ when $P$ equals 10 or any other price he or she chooses.

At this point, it is appropriate to dispel an area of ambiguity which often creeps into student essays when demand responsiveness is being discussed. To illustrate, consider the demand curves drawn in figure 5.4. It can be seen that, relative to $d_2$, $d_1$ is extremely steep (though not completely vertical) while $d_2$ is extremely flat relative to $d_1$. Often students will label the former demand curve as 'price inelastic' and the other as 'price elastic'. The reason for this is the visual information which the demand curve seems to be suggesting: demand seems very

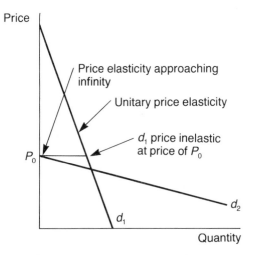

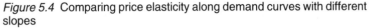

*Figure 5.4* Comparing price elasticity along demand curves with different slopes

unresponsive to price changes along $d_1$, hence its steepness, while conversely demand is very responsive to price change along $d_2$. However, as we have already seen, not all the demand along the curve $d_1$ is price inelastic, just as not all demand along $d_2$ is price elastic. Both curves will exhibit a range of price elasticities which will approach infinity and zero at the extremes. In figure 5.4, it can be seen that as the price increases towards $P_0$, price elasticity along demand curve $d_2$ is approaching infinity yet in the case of $d_1$, demand is still price inelastic. In such cases it should simply be commented that at any given price (such as $P_0$), demand is *more* price inelastic along $d_1$ than it is along $d_2$. To say that demand curve $d_1$ is price inelastic and demand curve $d_2$ is price elastic is simply misleading.

## INCOME ELASTICITY OF DEMAND AND CROSS ELASTICITY OF DEMAND

There are two other variables within the demand function which are often used as a focus for elasticity calculations: income and the price of other goods. In both cases, the mechanical exercise of calculating these elasticities is identical to that set out in the previous section when price elasticity of demand was being considered. Thus, the following discussion will tend towards providing an insight into the economic meaning of these calculations. To begin, let us consider income elasticity of demand.

### Income elasticity of demand

The basic income elasticity of demand equation is:

$$\frac{\text{percentage or proportionate change in quantity demanded}}{\text{percentage or proportionate change in income}} \qquad [5.8]$$

Calculations based upon this expression will again produce three general outcomes:

1   When the percentage change in quantity demanded exceeds the percentage change in income. This will produce a figure in excess of unity and is known as *income elastic demand*. At the extreme we may highlight a situation of infinite (or complete) income elastic demand though, as in the case of price elasticity of demand, this case is trivial.

2    When the percentage change in quantity demanded is less than the percentage change in income. This is known as *income inelastic demand* and will be associated with a figure of less than unity. At the extreme, there is the mathematical possibility of obtaining a figure of zero. This suggests that demand is completely unresponsive to income change. Again, this is trivial since such a situation is extremely unlikely.

3    Finally, there is *unit income elasticity*. This arises when the percentage change in quantity demanded exactly equals the percentage change in income. By definition, such a situation will produce an income elasticity figure equal to 1.

The feature which distinguishes the outcome of price elasticity calculations from the outcome of income elasticity calculations is that estimates ranging from plus infinity to minus infinity can be derived. It may be recalled from Chapter 2 that commodities fall into two basic categories: normal goods and inferior goods. In the case of normal goods, there will be an increase in demand as income rises, whereas for inferior goods the reverse is true; specifically, demand falls as income rises. Thus, in terms of our income elasticity equation, the percentage change in quantity demanded may increase or decrease after an income change depending upon whether the commodity in question is viewed as being normal or inferior. This means that it is possible to derive a positive or negative figure from an income elasticity of demand calculation. Mathematically, this range extends from plus infinity (completely income elastic and normal) to minus infinity (completely income elastic and inferior). The importance of indicating whether an income elasticity calculation has resulted in a positive or negative figure is therefore paramount.

To illustrate these general points, let us consider two examples. Initially, let us assume that for a given commodity a change in income from £47.50 per week to £50 per week leads to a fall in quantity demanded from 60 to 53. Substituting these figures into our income elasticity equation [5.8], we get −11.6 per cent/5 per cent, which produces a figure of −2.3. The negative figure not only shows what we already know, that the product in question is inferior, but also that it is income elastic (since the result exceeds unity). However, had the same rise in income brought about a change in quantity demanded from 60 to 70, this would have resulted in a figure of (+)17 per cent/5 per cent or (+)3.4. Again, our calculation has produced an income elastic figure (exceeding unity) but instead the product fulfils the conditions of a normal good.

As with the price elasticity of demand equation, we may redefine the expression for income elasticity, this time so that it relates directly points along the Engel curve (or Engel expenditure curve). By manipulating equation [5.8] in the same way we rearranged equation [5.3] we get the following expression:

$$\frac{\Delta Q}{\Delta Y} \times \frac{Y}{Q} \qquad\qquad [5.9]$$

where $\Delta Q/\Delta Y$ reflects the slope coefficient of the Engel curve and $Y/Q$ is the point of calculation. Since the principle which underlies the use of this equation is exactly the same as that expounded during the analysis of price elasticity of demand, no further worked examples will be considered here. However, it should be reiterated that demand may not only be income elastic or income inelastic but also that Engel curves can be positively sloped or negatively sloped according to whether the good is normal or inferior.

As was noted in Chapter 2, researchers encounter informational difficulties when trying to derive Engel curves in practice since survey respondents tend to give unreliable responses to questions which involve income. Thus elasticities derived in the literature are what we should really term total expenditure elasticities rather than the income elasticities discussed in most textbooks. A classic study which attempted to estimate a series of Engel curves and subsequently estimate the associated income (total expenditure) elasticities was undertaken by Prais and Houthakker (1955). Their study partly involved the selection of an appropriate functional form for their Engel curves. Although this had no bearing on whether figures were income elastic or income inelastic *per se*, functional form did, to a limited extent, have an effect upon the resulting elasticity figures. Nevertheless foods such as vegetables were income inelastic, producing estimates around +0.6. Meat and fish were similarly found to be income inelastic with figures around +0.65 and +0.8 respectively while fruit was found to be marginally income elastic (+1.08). A more recent study by Deaton (1975) discovered food items to be more income inelastic with meat, vegetables and fruit generating figures of +0.79, +0.26 and +0.52 respectively. Leisure items such as books and magazines produced a figure of +0.95 while car travel and foreign travel (predictably) produced more income elastic figures of +1.23 and +3.32 respectively. Intuitively one would expect the luxury status of certain goods to be an explanation for their income elastic demand, as in the case of foreign travel, and commodities such as food to exhibit income inelastic demand. In the latter case, there is a limit to the amount we can eat and drink and hence it will absorb a diminishing proportion of household expenditure. The main problem is that there have been very few across-the-board studies which have calculated income elasticities for the entire range of goods and services bought by individuals.

One example from sport to which economists have applied the concept of income elasticity of demand is soccer attendances. A feature of the game since the Second World War has been the long-term decline in attendances. For example during the season 1948–9 total attendances at English league matches totalled 41.3 million (Football Trust, 1992). Over the next 20 years attendances fell, so that by 1968–9 the figure had dropped to 29.4 million and by 1988–9 it had fallen even further to 18.5 million. Although recent trends suggest that spectators are showing increased interest in the game, such that 20.5 million spectators attended league games in 1991–2, this overall decline has occurred during a period during which there has been a growth in real incomes, thereby suggesting that during the post-war period, spectating at soccer matches has assumed the characteristics of an inferior good. Indeed Bird (1982) estimated income elasticity to be −0.6. In some respects, this should not be a surprise. The post-war period has been one of increasing leisure opportunity, so that the leisure budget, albeit an increasing one, can be spread around more commodities. However, one must be careful when employing this argument since some leisure activities may not be perceived by consumers as a direct substitute for watching soccer, for example spending money on a foreign holiday as opposed to one in the UK. In effect, we are looking for a reason why some consumers have stopped spending their Saturday afternoon at a football match.

One possibility may be that of image. Until recently, the quality of most football grounds in the UK has been poor. Improvements have been prompted by necessity, namely the need to fulfil the recommendations of the Taylor Report after the Hillsborough disaster. Furthermore, the game does have an image problem because the basic product has not evolved in line with the changes in tastes of its target audience, in particular their desire for a more sophisticated product. Although soccer matches have always provided an outlet for a violent minority, the increased media attention given to problems in the 1980s has served as a deterrent for some spectators. A further point to note is that although attendances at soccer matches have fallen, the desire to participate in soccer matches has not diminished and indeed has continued to grow. For example, in 1975 there were 37,461 clubs affiliated to the English

Football Association whereas by 1990 this figure had risen to 42,000 (Sports Council, 1991). Adopting the assumption that each club operates an average of 1.4 teams and that there are 18 players within each team, this suggests that there are over one million adult males playing organised soccer on a regular basis in England, an increase of over 100,000 since 1975. Over the five-year period between 1985 and 1990, the number of clubs affiliated to the Women's Football Association has risen from 200 to 250, with the number of players registered rising from 6,000 to 7,000, 7 per cent of the total adult players.

### Cross elasticity of demand

The final elasticity measure to be discussed in this section is cross elasticity of demand. This measure can be used to show the degree to which the demand for two products is related; in other words, the degree to which they are complements or substitutes for each other. The basic equation follows the same principles as before:

$$\frac{\text{percentage or proportionate change in the quantity demanded of product 1}}{\text{percentage or proportionate change in the quantity demanded of product 2}} \qquad [5.10]$$

If the resulting figure has a positive sign, then the two goods may be viewed as being substitutes for each other. Put another way, an increase in the price of one good is encouraging people to demand more of the other. In contrast, the sign for complementary goods will be negative. Thus, an increase in one product's price will not only bring about a reduction in its own demand but also in the demand for any good which is consumed at the same time. The logic which underlies these statements is no different from that employed in Chapter 2 during the discussion of the basic demand function. The size of figure which is produced from a cross elasticity calculation (whether positive or negative) will reflect the degree to which any two goods are substitutes or complements for each other. We would therefore expect a cross elasticity calculation to produce a figure approaching zero if the products were not strongly related to each other (either as complements or substitutes) and figures of increasing magnitude the greater the degree to which the products are related. Thus, for example, we might expect the cross elasticity of demand to be greater for two brands of training

*Table 5.2* Elasticity of demand for electricity

|  | Price elasticity | Income elasticity | Cross elasticity |
|---|---|---|---|
| Residential | −1.3 | +0.3 | +0.15 |
| Commercial | −1.5 | +0.9 | +0.15 |
| Industrial | −1.7 | +1.1 | +0.15 |

*Source*: Chapman *et al.* (1972, p. 705)

shoe than for a pair of training shoes and a more formal pair of lace-up shoes.

Unfortunately there have been few attempts to calculate a consistent set of cross elasticity estimates for any type of product, let alone those associated with products produced as part of the leisure industry. Nevertheless, one study, undertaken by Chapman, Tyrell and Mount (1972), provided estimates for all three types of elasticity calculation as they applied to the demand for electricity. Their study classified electricity demand into residential, commercial and industrial uses. The cross elasticity figures relate to the demand for the competing fuel, gas. Consider the figures in table 5.2. In all three situations, residential, commercial and industrial, electricity can be seen to be a normal good (positive income elasticities) and that it is a substitute for gas (positive cross elasticities). Perhaps most surprising are the price elasticity figures which suggest, contrary to standard opinion, that the demand for electricity is price elastic rather than price inelastic.

So far, the analysis has focused specifically upon the responsiveness of demand to changes in one of the variables within the demand function. We shall now consider one other elasticity measure, this time relating to supply. Although we could technically consider the responsiveness of supply to a number of variables within the supply function, it is customary to focus upon the specific example of own price.

## PRICE ELASTICITY OF SUPPLY

The basic mechanics of carrying out a price elasticity of supply calculation is broadly similar to that used for the three demand elasticity measures (own price, income and cross price). Thus, the term price elasticity of supply refers to the responsiveness of quantity supplied to changes in the price of a good or service. The equation therefore takes the following form:

$$\frac{\text{percentage (or proportionate) change in quantity supplied}}{\text{percentage (or proportionate) change in price}} \quad [5.11]$$

Just as price elasticity of demand calculations can be expected to produce negative estimates (though some authors choose to suppress the negative sign), price elasticity of supply can be expected to generate positive outcomes. This is because the supply curve invariably slopes upwards from left to right, such that an increase in price is expected to bring about an increase in the quantity economic agents are willing and able to supply. Thus, we may expect three main outcomes:

1   When the percentage change in quantity supplied exceeds the percentage change in price, supply is said to be *price elastic*. In these circumstances the outcome exceeds unity. Thus, if the quantity supplied increases by 20 per cent in response to a 5 per cent increase in price, we get a figure of 4.0. Thus, in this case, supply is said to be price elastic. At the most extreme, there is the possibility that supply is *completely* price elastic. This means that producers are willing to supply any amount of a good or service at a given price and suggests that the supply curve is horizontal. In these unlikely (trivial) circumstances a figure of infinity would emerge.

2   Conversely, when the proportionate change in price exceeds the proportionate change in quantity supplied, supply is said to be *price inelastic* and a figure less than unity is derived. Thus, if quantity supplied increases by 2 per cent after a 10 per cent increase in price, a price elasticity of supply estimate of 0.2 would result. There is the possibility that no matter how much a product's price increases, the producer does not increase supply. Supply is then said to be completely price inelastic and would be characterised by a completely vertical curve.

3   If the percentage response of supply is identical to the percentage change in price then the price elasticity of supply is said to be *unitary*. It can be shown that any straight-line supply curve which passes through the origin has a price elasticity of supply equal to one throughout its entire length.

To illustrate this third point, let us use the following example. In table 5.3, a number of price and quantity combinations have been given for two straight line supply curves, I and II, both of which pass through the origin. Let us take the price increase from 3 to 4 on the first of the two

*Table 5.3* Price and quantity combinations for two supply curves passing through the origin

| Curve I | | Curve II | |
|---------|---------|---------|---------|
| Price | Quantity | Price | Quantity |
| 0 | 0 | 0 | 0 |
| 1 | 3 | 1 | 2 |
| 2 | 6 | 2 | 4 |
| 3 | 9 | 3 | 6 |
| 4 | 12 | 4 | 8 |

supply curves. We can see that this leads to an increase in supply from 9 units to 12 units. Substituting these figures into our elasticity of supply equation [5.11] we get (3/9)/(1/3) which equals one. Alternatively, we could calculate the price elasticity of supply over a larger increase in price, let us say from 1 to 4. Again, substituting the appropriate figures into our basic equation we get (12/3)/(4/1) which again equals one. Let us now attempt a calculation based upon the second supply curve, for a price change from 2 to 4. Substituting the appropriate figures into equation [5.11] we get (4/4)/(2/2) which again equals unity. Indeed, if we were to undertake identical calculations for the price quantity combi-

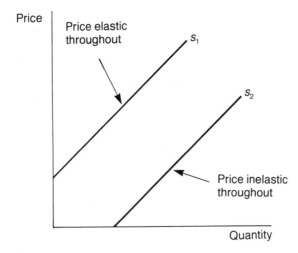

*Figure 5.5* Price elasticity and straight-line supply curves

nations along supply curve II, the same result would emerge. Readers should attempt further calculations if they remain unconvinced about this property.

This is not the only rule which applies to straight-line supply curves. We can also predict whether a supply curve which does not pass through the origin is price elastic or price inelastic. Specifically the rule which can always be applied is that if a straight-line supply curve passes through the vertical (price) axis, as does curve $s_1$ in figure 5.5, it will display a price elasticity of supply in excess of unity throughout. Conversely, if a straight-line supply curve passes through the horizontal (quantity) axis, as in the case of $s_2$, it will have a price elasticity of supply below unity throughout its entire length.

We may test this hypothesis by considering some of the price and quantity combinations associated with the two supply curves in table 5.4. The price elasticity of supply along curve I exceeds unity throughout its length whereas supply is price inelastic all the way along curve II. Taking an arbitrary price change along supply curve I, say from 6 to 7, we can substitute the appropriate figures into equation [11]. We get (2/4)/(1/6) which equals 3. Alternatively, if we take the price change from 3 to 4 along curve II, we get (1/9)/(1/3) which equals 0.33. The reader should replicate this analysis for other price/quantity changes along curves I and II. Within the constraints outlined above it should also be noted that the slope of the supply curve will have a bearing upon the price elasticity of supply. In either case, the flatter the supply curve, the more price elastic is supply for any given change in prices (price elasticities along curve II remain price inelastic but are closer to unity for any given price change). If a supply curve is not a straight line but

*Table 5.4* Price and quantity combinations for price-elastic and price-inelastic straight-line supply curves

| Curve I | | Curve II | |
|---|---|---|---|
| *Price* | *Quantity* | *Price* | *Quantity* |
| 4 | 0 | 0 | 6 |
| 5 | 2 | 1 | 7 |
| 6 | 4 | 2 | 8 |
| 7 | 6 | 3 | 9 |
| 8 | 8 | 4 | 10 |
| 9 | 10 | 5 | 12 |

instead is curved, such that it bends towards either the $x$ axis or $y$ axis, then it can contain both price elastic and price inelastic sections.

To date, the analysis has utilised expression [5.11] to draw out the key points which relate to price elasticity of supply. However, as with price elasticity of demand, we can rearrange the basic elasticity equation to create a formula which allows us to calculate the price elasticity at any point on the supply curve, provided that we have the equation of the supply curve. Specifically, price elasticity of supply equals:

$$\frac{\Delta Qs}{\Delta P} \times \frac{P}{Q} \qquad\qquad [5.12]$$

where $Qs$ denotes quantity supplied. To illustrate, assume that the equation of a supply curve equals:

$$Qs = 72 + 2P \qquad\qquad [5.13]$$

and we are asked to calculate the price elasticity of supply when $P$ equals 20. From the equation we know that the gradient of the supply curve is $+2$ and that when $P = 20$, $Q = 112$. Substituting these numbers into [5.12] we get $2 \times 20/112 = 0.35$. We should not be surprised that supply is price inelastic in this example since the equation tells us that the quantity supplied equals 72 when the price is zero and hence the supply curve cuts the horizontal (quantity) axis.

There are two main variables which will exert an influence upon whether the supply of a product is price elastic or price inelastic. The first is the ease with which each producer can substitute the supply of one good for the supply of another. For example, assume that a supplier owns a number of large multipurpose outdoor playing areas which are capable of providing the space for a number of sport and leisure activities, including five-a-side football, netball, hockey, cricket and tennis. At some times of the year, there may be sufficient numbers of teams and individuals to support the supply of playing areas for all these activities on a commercial basis. However, if there is a rapid increase in what consumers are willing to pay for a particular activity (due to media coverage), then it would be relatively easy to convert, for example, a football pitch into several tennis courts or vice versa. Thus, in this case, it would be reasonable to assume that the supply of all these facilities is relatively price elastic. In contrast, the owner of a swimming pool does not have the same flexibility. If there are rapid increases/decreases in demand for swimming, suppliers cannot respond in the same way and increase/decrease the area available for swimming in response to price changes. The choice simply becomes a decision as to whether or not to remain open. Price elasticity of supply would therefore be extremely low.

The second factor which will have a significant influence upon the price elasticity of supply is time. This variable played a significant role in the supply of skateboards during the 1970s. In the short term, exisiting producers were somewhat unprepared and therefore unable to cope with the growth in demand as the craze took off. Supply elasticity was therefore low. In the longer term, the supply of skateboards increased as existing firms increased their rate of production and new entrants entered the market thereby increasing the elasticity of supply. The distinction between supply in the short term and supply in the long term has already been made with respect to the supply of golf courses. In Chapter 3 it was noted that Europe's success in the Ryder Cup, together with increases in disposable income, led to a rapid increase in demand for both private and municipal golf courses. In the short term, suppliers have not been able to respond since golf courses require large tracts of (scarce) land, together with significant periods for planning, construction and land-scaping. Price inelasticity of supply in the short term has led to waiting lists to join private clubs and off-course and on-course queues to play on public courses.

Having considered elasticity as an economic principle, the next stage of the analysis will be to look in more detail at its implications for the provision of sport and leisure facilities. Much of the discussion that follows will focus upon the fact that users of leisure facilities exhibit different price elasticities of demand for facilities and that if a supplier is to be successful in promoting a facility, it is information about this variable which may well determine how successful a facility is likely to be in terms of raising revenue and/or increasing throughput. Suppliers may choose to exploit these differences in demand elasticity by adopting policies which economists refer to generally as price discrimination. The aim of the final stage of this chapter is to highlight the theory and application of this approach with specific reference to the provision of publicly run leisure facilities.

## PRICE DISCRIMINATION

If there are numerous small suppliers of a highly standardised product, then we can expect individual producers to be price-takers. In other words, the price of the product in question will be determined by market forces, which, in an unregulated market, will be the equilibrium price.

The producer has then to decide how much to produce at this given price (if any) and this will be based upon his or her costs. An example of such a situation might be an open-air fruit and vegetable market, where usually there are few differences between the prices being charged on different stalls since the product in question will display little variation in quality. In markets where there is a smaller number of suppliers, firms competing for market share usually attempt to make their product different from that of their competitors. Thus, although the general characteristics of the products of rival firms may be intrinsically the same, brand advertising and gimmicks play an important role in determining what consumers buy. Thus, we may see rival product brands sitting alongside each other on the supermarket shelf with widely differing prices. When firms are able to exert a degree of power over the market in this way, they have the opportunity (within reason) to play an active role in determining the price of the product they sell, rather than rely upon the market. Thus, prices can be set according to perceptions about a variety of factors which will include the expected behaviour of rivals, as well as the perceived demand curve for their product.[5] However, firms are not obliged to choose a single price for the product they sell. In everyday life, we frequently encounter situations in which different prices are charged for the same product. For example, prices may vary according to the time of day the product is bought or according to the type of consumer making the purchase. When firms choose to sell their output to consumers at different prices for reasons unrelated to the cost of producing the product, economists use the term price discrimination. One of the aims of this section will be to show that such a policy can be used to increase a firm's revenue above that which would be achieved if a single price were charged.

Firms can apply price discrimination to individual consumers or to specific sections of the population. Examples of the former approach are frequently seen in supermarkets as 'multi-buy' or 'multi-saver' schemes where selected product lines can be purchased in single units or at a cheaper unit price if a set number of units are bought at the same time. Another example is the season ticket system operated by football clubs which provides individuals with the opportunity to pay less to see matches if they are prepared to commit themselves to a larger number of games over the season. Good commercial examples of the second approach, where different groups of buyers are charged different prices for the same product, can be seen with respect to British Rail which, amongst other schemes, may charge different prices to pensioners and non-pensioners for the same journey. Other examples can be seen with respect to the distinction made between commercial and domestic users of electricity and telephone services and the different admission prices paid by adults and children to gain entry to the cinema. Examples of both these types of price discrimination can usually be witnessed at our local sports centres. In this case, individual consumers may be charged different prices according to whether they use the facilities at peak or off-peak times, while at the same time certain sections of the population (such as the unemployed) are given the opportunity to engage in activities at lower prices than the standard (peak or off-peak) admission charge.

Some readers may already have recognised a potential problem for using discriminatory pricing policies. Specifically, producers will need to ensure that consumers who are supposed to pay a relatively high price for the product in question are not able to obtain it at one of the preferential prices. There are two basic possibilities: one in which the 'wrong' person finds some way of buying the good or service at the lower price directly from the seller, or alternatively where people who qualify for a lower price are able to resell the product to people who would normally pay the higher price. The ability of the supplier to prevent one or both of these problems from occurring will depend upon the nature of the product being sold. In situations when the price differential reflects the time of consumption, discrimination between users is relatively easy, as in the case when different peak and off-peak prices are charged at a swimming pool. In supermarkets, it is often possible to buy a product at a lower price providing that a certain number of units have already been purchased at a higher price. In these situations, consumers are usually expected to supply some proof of purchase (within a given period of time) before they are allowed to buy (additional) units of a commodity at the preferential price. Differential pricing which distinguishes between different groups of the population can be more difficult to monitor and therefore will usually require the consumer to supply some form of identification. For example, a pensioner would be expected to show his or her pension book before getting a preferential bus pass or concessionary ticket to a concert. Of course, no system is completely foolproof – ingenious readers will already have thought up countless ways of getting round the safeguards listed above!

Formal economic analysis of price discrimination tends to focus upon the advantages of adopting such a policy from the point of view of the producer, specifically in terms of the opportunity it provides to increase revenue by making incursions into consumers' surplus. In contrast, for many providers of sport and leisure outside the commercial sector, the use of price discrimination reflects the merit good status of many activities, with the emphasis given to encouraging consumption by sections of society who have traditionally had a low propensity to consume sport and leisure. The aim of the remainder of this section will be to identify the three main types of price discrimination which exist, to assess the economic advantages and limitations of each approach and finally, to consider the degree to which price discrimination has been successful with respect to the provision of leisure within the public sector.

There are three main types of price discrimination known (somewhat unimaginatively) as first-degree, second-degree and third-degree price discrimination. Realistically, first-degree price discrimination is only viable as a theoretical option since it requires the producer to charge individuals the exact price they are willing (and able) to pay for the commodity in question, as defined by the market demand curve. The economic implications of this approach can be seen in figure 5.6. If the producer decided to charge consumers a single price, let's say $P^*$, then $Q^*$ would be demanded. As we have already seen, the revenue accruing

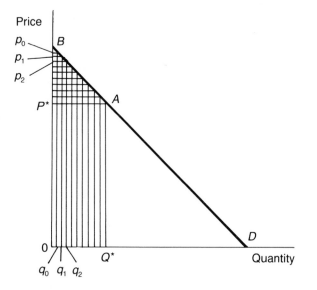

Figure 5.6 First-degree price discrimination

to the producer can be measured in terms of rectangle $0Q^*AP^*$, while the consumers' surplus is depicted by triangle $P^*AB$ which lies above it. First-degree price discrimination involves the producer being able to identify individuals on the demand curve so that he or she is able to charge $p_1$ for the first unit, $p_2$ for the second unit, $p_3$ for the third unit and so on all the way down to $P^*$. If applied successfully, this policy would lead to all area $B$ being transferred from the consumers to the producer such that total revenue now equals $0Q^*AB$.

Second-degree price discrimination is a less precise approach than that outlined above and involves the supplier selling a product at different prices according to the number of units the consumers actually buy. Consider figure 5.7. Were the producer to charge $P^*$ for the commodity in question, $Q^*$ units are purchased, the revenue equals the rectangle $0Q^*AP^*$ and the value of the consumer surplus would be triangle $P^*AB$. However, the producer could choose to sell the first $Q'$ units at the price of $P'$ and the subsequent $Q'$ to $Q^*$ units at $P^*$. In doing this, it can be seen that the producer has increased its revenue by the amount $P^*ECP'$. It can be seen that this rectangle is surrendered directly from consumer surplus. Of course, the producer must ensure that the first $Q'$ units are purchased before subsequent units are sold at the lower price. Examples of second-degree price discrimination can often be seen in local supermarkets, particularly for food items. Essentially, on the

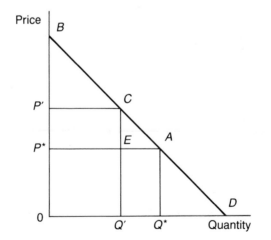

*Figure 5.7* Second-degree price discrimination

purchase of the first unit of a good the consumer sends off a label and receives a token which allows the purchase of a further unit of the commodity at a reduced price. A variation on this principle is the multi-buy purchases which have been adopted in supermarkets since the introduction of automatic scanners at cashouts.

The final type to consider is known as third-degree price discrimination and involves charging different groups of consumer a different price for the same product. As with first- and second-degree price discrimination, standard economics textbooks stress this approach as a means by which producers can increase their revenue. However, in the case of marketing a variety of products, including public and private sector leisure facilities, third-degree price discrimination has been a particularly important method of encouraging the use of facilities during off-peak periods. Before turning specifically to the case of leisure, let us consider the advantages of employing third-degree price discrimination, using a simple example. For simplicity it will be assumed that production is a costless activity. The inclusion of such costs does not alter the basic rationale underlying the principle.

For the purposes of this example it will be assumed that the demand for a firm's output comes from two discernible groups of consumers, A and B, who differ with respect to their relative price elasticity of demand for the product in question. Specifically, the demand from group A is more price inelastic than that of group B. As we have already seen in Chapter 3, the market demand curve can be calculated by summing horizontally the demand curves of the two groups of consumer. The aim of the example will be to show that more revenue will be raised if the firm sees its market in terms of two distinct groups of consumer instead of a single market demand curve. The overall market demand for prices from £12 to £0 are set out in column two of table 5.5 while the respective demands from consumer groups A and B are outlined in columns three and four respectively. Thus, by adding the quantity demanded in columns three and four we get the aggregate demand depicted in column two. The revenue that the firm receives at each price/output is set out in columns five (aggregate demand), six (consumer group A) and seven (consumer group B).

Let us assume initially that the firm bases its pricing decision upon its market demand curve, D. It can be seen from column five that if the firm levies £5 per unit of output, it will maximise its revenue (with zero production costs), accruing £105. It can be seen that revenue is below this figure at any other price. If it is recognised that the aggregate demand curve is in fact made up of two discernible groups of consumers,

*Table 5.5* Total revenue (consumer expenditure) changes along an
aggregate demand curve made up from the demand curve of
two different groups of consumers

| | Demand | | | Total revenue | | |
|---|---|---|---|---|---|---|
| $P$ | $D$ | $d^A$ | $d^B$ | $TR$ | $tr^A$ | $tr^B$ |
| 12 | 0 | 0 | 0 | 0 | 0 | 0 |
| 11 | 2 | 2 | 0 | 22 | 22 | 0 |
| 10 | 4 | 4 | 0 | 40 | 40 | 0 |
| 9 | 6 | 6 | 0 | 54 | 54 | 0 |
| 8 | 9 | 8 | 1 | 72 | 64 | 8 |
| 7 | 13 | 10 | 3 | 91 | 70 | 21 |
| 6 | 17 | 12 | 5 | 102 | 72 | 30 |
| 5 | 21 | 14 | 7 | 105 | 70 | 35 |
| 4 | 25 | 16 | 9 | 100 | 64 | 36 |
| 3 | 29 | 18 | 11 | 87 | 54 | 33 |
| 2 | 33 | 20 | 13 | 66 | 40 | 26 |
| 1 | 37 | 22 | 15 | 37 | 22 | 15 |
| 0 | 41 | 24 | 17 | 0 | 0 | 0 |

then it is possible to improve upon this level of revenue. Specifically, if
the group of consumers whose demand is more price inelastic (demand
curve $d_A$), are charged a slightly higher price (£6) while individuals with
more price elastic demand (schedule $d_B$) are charged a lower price (£4),
it can be seen from columns six and seven that revenue can be raised
from £105 to £108. As we have already seen, the firm's ability to
discriminate successfully between its consumers in this way rests upon
the ease with which it can prevent 'leakage' between the two groups of
consumers so that people who should be paying £6 are not able to pay
the lower price of £4. The principle behind this policy is depicted in
figure 5.8. Figure 5.8a highlights the overall market demand curve for
a product, calculated by summing the demand curves of two groups of
consumers, A and B, depicted in figures 5.8b and 5.8c respectively. The
advantage of engaging in price discrimination is reflected in the fact that
the revenue rectangle in figure 5.8a is smaller than the sum of the two
corresponding areas in figures 5.8b and 5.8c.

Of course, this is a theoretical example. Segmenting the market and
subsequently requiring consumers to identify the group to which they
belong is not a costless activity and may therefore preclude firms from
adopting such a policy in practice. Nevertheless, such an approach has
been used extensively in such industries as transport, energy and

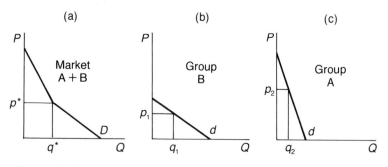

*Figure 5.8* Third-degree price discrimination

telecommunications as well as in leisure and recreation. Thus for example, British Rail charges higher prices to commuters (whose demand is relatively more price inelastic than that of holidaymakers) to travel on 'peak-time' trains, different rates are charged for peak and off-peak electricity and business phone calls from business premises are more expensive than calls from residential lines. The next stage of this analysis will be to consider price discrimination from the point of view of the supply of leisure facilities.

## Price discrimination and the case of leisure provision

Price discrimination is used widely to attract custom to leisure and sport facilities. However, the rationale behind its use varies according to whether the supplier is a private-sector concern or the public sector. In the former situation it could be argued that it is a mechanism by which owners try and encourage demand and thereby increase revenue and profit during off-peak periods. Thus, we can see price discrimination being used primarily to accrue textbook advantages to the facility in question. In contrast, within the public sector, we have already seen that one of the major objectives of local authorities has been to promote consumption by sections of the population who have tended to be low users of sport and leisure facilities, rather than to seek profit explicitly. We have not only seen attempts to discriminate between times of the day but also in terms of the types of consumer who use the facility. Thus many centres operate special pricing schemes for such groups as unemployed people or parents with their children. However, although textbook explanations of discriminatory pricing emphasise the need to pay close attention to the demand curve for the commodity in question, local authority providers have been criticised for not identifying the characteristics which distinguish different user groups from each other. In other words, price discrimination has tended to be used more ineffectively than it might have been.

Concerns about the pricing strategies employed by local authority leisure facilities have now been voiced for a number of years even though they seem largely to have fallen upon deaf ears. In a report produced by the Department of the Environment's Audit Inspectorate (1983) it was noted that:

> In setting prices, most leisure centres make primary reference to the prices at other centres or local facilities. The consequence is to maintain price comparability with other providers of leisure/sports facilities, without specific reference to what the user might be prepared to pay. Even allowing for the effects of social pricing policies, leisure centres tend to generate less income than they might.
>
> (Department of the Environment, Audit Inspectorate, 1983, p. 7)

However, it was recognised that the provision of facilities by local authorities is a recognition that leisure consumption does not simply confer private benefits. Consider the following:

> Greater income, and greater social benefit will be achieved if 20,000 people pay 40p each than if 10,000 pay 70p; but skilled marketing is required to attract the extra 10,000 admissions so that an associated cost will be incurred. This marketing cost could exceed the revenue gain, but the social benefit is still clearly preferable.
>
> (Ibid., p. 38)

With regard to differential pricing, the report argues (pp. 36–7) that although, at the time of writing, attempts had been made to employ third-degree price discrimination at leisure centres, it had not always been successful in promoting using during off-peak periods when demand is more price elastic. Five potential factors were identified:

1   the differential between peak and off-peak may not be large enough to act as an incentive;
2   the location of the centre may not be appropriate for off-peak use;
3   the community's awareness of off-peak discounts may not be adequate;
4   centre staff may not be sufficiently involved in promoting activities to new participants or there may be insufficient provision made for parents with young children;

5    management may not be sufficiently involved in promoting facilities generally.

In other words, varying the price charged to use facilities is only one variable which can affect the level of demand for a facility at any one particular time. In some areas, the time, cost and comfort of travel can be an important consideration, particularly when the visitor is limited to using public transport. This may be a major deterrent for some users, for example parent(s) travelling with children or disabled people.

It is also noticeable that the last three concerns involve the promotion of community awareness of the opportunities which are on offer. Commercial firms frequently use advertising as a means of promoting their goods and services, particularly if they are not yet established on the market, yet local authorities have been willing to build facilities and services 'and then waiting for the community to use them' (Department of the Environment, 1988, p. 21). Although it is noted that there are encouraging signs of intensified promotional activities, there is still the implication that local authorities are not yet doing enough in this respect. However, with facilities now out to competitive tender, managing groups will have every incentive to monitor their success with respect to attracting people to centres, particularly the local authority's target population for the consumption of sport and leisure.

More recent concerns about the use of price discrimination at public leisure facilities has focused upon using price to make a more explicit distinction between different types of potential visitor. In the previous chapter, the rationale for subsidising leisure activities was made, based upon the private and external benefits which active participation can confer. Generally, the response has been in terms of providing 'across-the-board' subsidies to all consumers regardless of their disposable income and willingness to pay. A typical example is the 'Passport to Leisure' which is operated by Nottingham City Council. Under this scheme, city residents are able to purchase a card for a flat fee which entitles them to discounts or even free use of the city's leisure facilities. There are now calls for local authorities to be more imaginative with the pricing policies they adopt in trying to achieve Sport for All. For example, the Department of the Environment notes, with respect to inner city provision, that:

> We recognise the complexities of developing pricing policies for individual facilities which take account of ability to pay but question the cost-effectiveness and benefits of blanket subsidies over which, more often than not, local facility managers have no control.
>
> (Department of the Environment, 1988, p. 21)

In other words, if the majority of sports participants are, by definition, from middle-income groups, then subsidies are effectively being given to consumer groups who are already well-off. Furthermore, without any sort of identification there is the problem, raised in the previous chapter, that one local authority could be subsidising users from another local authority. In either case, there is an inappropriate use of scarce resources. Whitehouse and Gerlach (1991) point to the advantages of using a 'smart-card' as a basis for charging for leisure services. These could be issued to local authority residents, who will pay a lower price for their leisure than non-residents, with further subsidies to target groups activated via the coding held on the magnetic strip on the card. Of course, like any attempt to operate price discriminatory policies, there are the problems of the higher costs for the local authority of servicing the scheme and the possibility that the more innovative members of society will find ways of by-passing the system and paying less than they should. An added advantage of this system is that it can provide information which could be used to judge whether or not identified groups are being targeted effectively. This could then be used as part of an indicator by which performance can be judged, an increasingly important issue given recent government attempts to promote efficiency within many public services, including leisure.

## QUESTIONS FOR DISCUSSION

1    To what extent can price discrimination be used as a basis for pricing leisure facilities in the public sector?
2    Carefully explain what is wrong with the following terms 'elastic demand curve' and 'inelastic demand curve'.

# Chapter 6

# Production and costs

## INTRODUCTION

The analysis to date has been concerned with the economic relationship between buyers and sellers and whether the market which results produces desirable outcomes. Although some discussion has focused upon the firm, it has been conducted at a very general level. The aim of the following two chapters will be to look in more detail at the producer. In Chapter 7 the discussion focuses explicitly upon the importance of market structure as a determinant of producer behaviour. This chapter provides the foundation for such an analysis by looking specifically at the relationship between the different combinations of inputs many firms use, for example labour and capital, and the output which is ultimately generated. Economists encompass this relationship in what is referred to as the production function. To illustrate this concept we shall employ an example drawn directly from the economics of sport literature, specifically, a production function constructed to measure cricketing success. Having identified the basic relationships which may emerge between different input combinations and output, the remainder of the chapter will focus upon the costs associated with production. In particular, we shall consider why costs may differ in the short term and long term for an identical level of output and why it may be advantageous for firms in some industries to produce at a large, rather than at a small scale. Although most research into the relationship between the average unit cost of output and the scale of production has focused upon standard manufacturing operations, we shall consider the advantages of size with special reference to facilities provided at sports centres.

## THE PRODUCTION FUNCTION

Production is a multifaceted transformation process. The most widely perceived definition of production is in terms of the creation of a new commodity, for example the manufacture of a new motor car. However, it should also be seen more generally as a process which adds to existing value, for example a garage respraying a car when its paintwork has been scratched. Production not only refers to final goods, that is, those which are bought and sold in shops, but also intermediate goods. These are outputs which are themselves inputs into another productive process. For example, a firm which makes strings for squash rackets is producing a tangible item in itself but in addition is also going to add to the value of another good, namely the squash racket. Production also refers to the supply of services. However, the output of a service may be more difficult to define. For example, in the case of a fitness gym we may wish to measure output in terms of the number of people who use the facilities over a specific period of time. However, its 'output' cannot be seen as high if the equipment and advice which is available does not enable visitors to make improvements in their general level of physical well-being.

To produce any type of output, firms need access to factors of production (recall that this is a general term to refer to land, labour and capital) together with an array of raw materials and/or intermediate goods. The relationship which defines the maximum output which can be achieved from a given set of inputs over a specific period of time is known as the *production function*. This may be presented in two-dimensional form, for example using a graph measuring output along one axis and the changes in one input along the other (for example labour), or as a more complex mathematical equation, allowing the economists to specify a broader relationship between maximum output and the interaction between different types of input.

It is important to note at this point that production functions are derived under two basic assumptions. The first is that technology is fixed. This means that the relationship between inputs and outputs is established at any given point of time and therefore the production function can be used to highlight the constraints which confront firms on a day-to-day basis. If technology does change, then the relationship between the inputs and output will also change and, by definition, so will the production function. The second assumption states that inputs are used at maximum levels of efficiency. This does not mean that every firm in a particular industry is operating at the frontiers of science using 'state of the art' production techniques. This assumption simply states that the inputs required by the technology currently at the disposal of the firm are put to their best use, thereby maximising output. However, this is a strong assumption to make about the way in which firms operate in practice. Companies may be forced to use factors of production in a suboptimal way because of negotiated work practices. Furthermore, a firm's management may not be aware that a reorganisation of the capital and labour at their disposal can lead to an increase in output.

The customary way of expressing a production function is:

$$Q = f(\text{Land, Labour, Capital}, X_1, \dots X_n, R) \qquad [6.1]$$

where $Q$ denotes maximum output during a given period of time; land, labour and capital are the factors of production used during that period; $X_1, \dots X_n$ denotes any other inputs used per period and $R$ is a returns-to-scale parameter (this term will be explained at a later stage of the chapter). For simplicity, production functions are often written in terms of two variables, capital and labour inputs. This leads to the less daunting expression:

$$Q = f(K,L) \qquad [6.2]$$

where $K$ and $L$ denote the respective quantities of capital and labour used in a given time period. Perhaps the most famous type of production function is one derived by Cobb and Douglas to characterise the US manufacturing industry between 1900 and 1922. It took the form:

$$Q = aL^x K^y \qquad [6.3]$$

Since the parameters estimated by Cobb and Douglas were $a = 1.1$, $x = 0.75$ and $y = 0.25$, a more generalised form of the *Cobb–Douglas production function* is written as:

$$Q = aL^x K^{(1-x)} \qquad [6.4]$$

since the powers $x$ and $y$ in equation [6.3] sum to one. Thus, using the Cobb–Douglas expression [6.3], this would suggest that if 25 units of labour and 50 units of capital were available, output would equal 32.7 whereas if the respective levels of labour and capital were 50 units and 25 units, output would equal 46.2. Obviously, present-day US manufacturing would be characterised by a completely different expression due to the technological changes which have taken place since Cobb and Douglas's pioneering work.

More recent research has seen economists trying to estimate production functions to characterise professional team sports. Initially these studies originated from the US, based upon major league baseball.[1] However, recently the research spotlight has fallen upon professional cricket.[2] It would be inappropriate to use an introductory economics text, albeit a text based upon sport and leisure, as a forum for a line-by-line analysis of undertaking such an exercise. Nevertheless, these studies do highlight some of the more general methodological problems economists face when attempting to derive production functions. To illustrate let us consider a paper by Bairam, Howells and Turner (1990) which focuses upon first-class cricket (not one-day cricket) in the Southern Hemisphere.

The aim of sport-based production function analyses is typically to define the relationship between team success (output) and the team performance inputs required to produce that output. Bairam *et al.* use 'points percentage' as their yardstick for measuring team success (measured as the percentage of the maximum league points achieved by the team) and this is seen as a function of various measures of 'batting input' and 'bowling input':

$$S = f(b_1, b_2, w_1, w_2, w_3) \qquad [6.5]$$

where $S$ measures team success, $b_1$ and $b_2$ measure batting input (runs per completed player innings and runs scored per over respectively) and runs scored per over respectively, $w_1$ denotes bowling average (runs conceded per wicket taken), $w_2$ measures the number of balls bowled per wicket (a reflection of 'attacking bowling') and $w_3$ measures runs scored by the opposition per over (evidence of 'defensive bowling'). The relationship between the variables within the estimated production function showed that in the case of games played in New Zealand, the probability of winning is maximised when teams adopt a strategy of attacking batting and attacking bowling. In contrast, the optimal strategy for Australian teams is to have attacking batsmen and defensive bowling. Thus, from the point of view of selection policy, success in Australia requires team selection to favour specialist players. Thus, at the margin, a specialist bowler should be chosen ahead of cricketer who falls into the 'all-rounder' category[3] since the former is more able to contain the opposition's batting. In New Zealand, all-rounders (in the wider sense) are a more desirable commodity. Ignoring the option of a genuine 'all-rounder', the production function suggests that emphasis should be given to batsmen who can bowl. These differences seem to reflect the playing conditions in the respective countries. In Australia, better batting strips, faster outfields, faster deterioration of the new ball and more consistent light makes it easier for the batsman to dominate the bowler.

Thus, bowlers are more quickly forced from attack into a more containing role. The more variable conditions in New Zealand (and England) not only allow bowlers to attack for longer periods but also give more help to the less skilful bowler.

## PRODUCTION FUNCTIONS IN THE SHORT RUN AND IN THE LONG RUN

To reflect the fact that inputs can be varied at different rates, economists refer to production functions in the short run and in the long run. The standard assumption made by economists is that all inputs can be varied in the long run, whereas in the short run some inputs are assumed fixed. Factors falling into this latter category are machinery, land and factory space. Indeed entrepreneurs may view their workforce as their only variable input in the short term. Over a longer time horizon there are greater opportunities to make multidimensional changes to the relative quantities of the factors of production used to produce a good or service. Thus whereas in the short term we may refer to fixed factors and variable factors, the distinction becomes unnecessary in the long term since all factors are variable.

Having established that the character of the production function is different in the short run and in the long run, the next stage of the analysis will be to consider how we may depict production functions in graphical form. This will not only provide an alternative means of presenting the production function but also to develop the theory needed to derive the cost curves which will be seen to determine a firm's output. For simplicity, the analysis will focus initially upon the short-run production function. We shall then relax the distinction between fixed and variable inputs and utilise a long-term time horizon. Ultimately, we shall see how time plays an important role in determining the relationship between labour and capital and therefore the implications of different levels of output.

### Drawing production functions

*Short-run analysis*

As we have already seen, economists often assume that it is only possible to vary the amount of labour used in production in the short term. This does not mean that the entrepreneur has no capital at his or her disposal, simply that there is a positive but fixed amount of capital alongside which different amounts of labour can be used. Thus, if output is to be increased or decreased, it can only take place by varying the size of the workforce. Rather than using the long-term production function defined in equation [6.2] above, we therefore define the more restricted expression:

$$Q = f(K',L) \qquad\qquad [6.6]$$

where $K'$ denotes the fact that capital is fixed. This may even be written as:

$$Q = f(L) \qquad\qquad [6.7]$$

where $K$ is dropped completely from the expression for convenience.

Let us predict the output effects of adding extra units of labour to a fixed amount of capital. This relationship is expressed in the line $TO$ (denoting total output) in figure 6.1. It can be seen that the $TO$ curve has assumed an elongated S-shape. Let us consider why. Imagine that a firm has two machines which fill up glass bottles with fizzy drink. Assuming that this is a multistage process whereby the bottles have to be loaded on to the conveyor belt, checked for cracks, filled with drink, have their tops put on, be collected into boxes of 24 bottles which are then stacked on a palette and finally driven away to the warehouse. If one person was operating both machines, then he or she would be constantly stopping

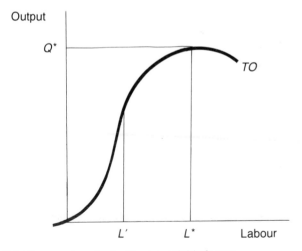

Figure 6.1 Changes in output with one variable factor

and starting the machine in order to keep pace with production. However, as extra workers are employed, each person can be made responsible for fewer stages of production. Initially, this is likely to mean that extra workers allow the rate of production to increase at an increasing rate, or put another way, allow the marginal product to increase. The range of labour inputs to which this applies extends from the origin of the graph to $L'$ in figure 6.1. However, a point will be reached (also known as the point of inflection) such that, although further division of labour enables even higher outputs to be achieved (for example by allowing workers to take staggered tea and meal breaks), the marginal product of successive workers begins to fall; this occurs at $L'$. This is because there are only a fixed number of jobs which can be performed on the machine. Although output may be increased by splitting jobs into two or more tasks, a limit will be reached where the machine cannot produce any more within the given time period. It can be seen that total output is increasing, albeit at a decreasing rate, for labour inputs between $L'$ and $L^*$. $L^*$ will lead to the maximum output for the machinery in question. Beyond $L^*$, output falls as workers get in each others' way. Labour inputs beyond the inflection point are said by economists to lead to diminishing returns. Formally stated, the Law of Diminishing Returns hypothesises that if increasing quantities of a variable factor of production are added to a given quantity of a fixed factor, the marginal product (and average product) of the variable factor will eventually decrease. Diminishing returns are therefore said to exist when the marginal product begins to fall, where output increases at a decreasing rate.

### Long-run analysis

The next stage of the analysis will be to consider how we may graph situations when the producer can change two factors of production simultaneously. Thus, for the purposes of this chapter we will assume that production is mirrored by a production function resembling that depicted in equation [6.2], specifically:

$$Q = f(K,L).$$

This production function can be represented in graphical form by means of a series of *isoquants*. Visually, isoquants resemble indifference curves, though in this case they show the different combinations of capital and labour which can be used to produce a given output, assuming that both inputs are combined optimally. The graph is calibrated such that the quantity of labour inputs is measured on the horizontal axis and the quantity of capital inputs is measured on the vertical axis.

Let us assume for example that we are concerned with a firm engaged in making a number of rugby shirts over a given period. At one extreme, these may be produced using labour-intensive techniques, where workers perform all the major production tasks with minimal amounts of capital (for example, scissors, needles and tape-measures) or, at the other extreme, by capital intensive techniques whereby the rugby shirts are made using computer-guided knitting machines which only require a small complement of workers to oversee production. The firm could also use a combination of labour and capital which falls somewhere in between these two extremes. The alternative combinations of labour and capital which could be used to produce this specific number of rugby shirts can be depicted by an isoquant. The exact shape of the isoquant will be dependent upon the various technologies available to the firm at that given point of time. However, for reasons which will be made clear below, we may not only predict that the isoquant will be negatively sloped but that its basic shape will be convex to the origin.

For simplicity, consider the hypothetical isoquant depicted in figure 6.2 which identifies the combinations of capital and labour which can be used to produce 25 rugby shirts. Five alternative processes are depicted

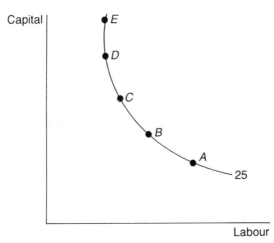

Figure 6.2 Potential capital/labour inputs to produce 25 rugby shirts

along the isoquant, labelled *A* to *E*, where *A* denotes a highly labour-intensive process while shifts to *B*, *C*, *D* and *E* relatively show factor combinations of increasing capital intensity. The negative slope shows that to maintain a given level of production, any reduction in labour input must be met by an increase in the amount of capital used. Had the isoquant been drawn as a straight line, it would have implied a fixed rate of substitution between capital and labour. For example, it may have meant that 25 rugby shirts could have been made using nine units of labour and one unit of capital, eight units of labour and two units of capital, seven units of labour and three units of capital and so on. In this case, a unit reduction in labour must be met by a unit increase in capital. However, it is more likely that the relationship between capital and labour will not be fixed, but instead reflect the impact of diminishing returns. Thus, it is predicted that the greater the amount of labour (capital) used in the production process, the smaller the amount of labour (capital) which needs to be given up to maintain output at the level designated by the isoquant. Any isoquant which is shaped such that it is convex to the origin is said to display a *diminishing marginal rate of technical substitution* (MRTS). This property is identical to that employed in Chapter 2 with respect to the construction of indifference curves.

Isoquants share a number of properties with indifference curves. First, there will be an isoquant passing through every possible combination of capital and labour on the graph. In other words, each combination of capital and labour will be associated with some level of output. Thus, we may draw a whole family of isoquants which reflect increasing levels of output as they move in a north-easterly direction. Second, they cannot cross. This would suggest, somewhat perversely, that two different outputs could lie on exactly the same point, namely where the two isoquants intersect. Finally, as we have already seen, they are likely to be convex to the origin, reflecting a diminishing marginal rate of (technical) substitution. However, isoquants and indifference curves do differ in one important respect. Since output is largely a tangible concept, regardless of the units involved, isoquants can be interpreted as providing a cardinal approach to analysis. It should be recalled that, in contrast, indifference curves are ordinal measures of utility, since it is implausible to attach specific numbers to changes in utility.

It should be highlighted at this stage that the isoquant depicted in figure 6.2 has a nice smooth curve. This suggests that there are an infinite number of capital and labour combinations available to the producer for each given level of output. In reality, there is usually a limited number of viable production techniques available to the entrepreneur. Thus, whereas textbook analysis may suggest that different levels of output can be achieved from a whole multitude of capital/labour combinations, the truth is that there may only be the opportunity to choose between two or three combinations of capital and labour for each given level of output. The resulting isoquants may therefore resemble those depicted in figure 6.3a, with the smooth convexity of previous isoquants replaced by a more jagged shape. Indeed, at the extreme, if there is only one viable capital–labour combination at each level of output, the isoquant will assume an 'L' shape, as depicted in figure 6.3b. In this case, any change in the level of capital or labour, for example a shift from point $P$ to points $Q$ or $R$ has no effect upon the level of output, despite the additional factors of production being used. Only when labour and capital is added in the proportions defined by technology can output actually be increased, for example from $P$ to $S$. However, for the purposes of general explanation, it will be assumed that isoquants are smoothly convex to the origin.

The spacing between isoquants within any diagram can be used to emphasise the capital and labour requirements as output increases in unit terms. This can be seen in figure 6.4 where $K$ and $L$ are used to denote capital and labour respectively (this will be the standard convention used in graphs from now on). In figure 6.4a, the isoquants become progressively closer together as output rises in 100-unit increments. This suggests that the average amount of labour and capital required is falling as output increases. Conversely, if the spacing between isoquants increases, then the average levels of factor inputs would be increasing. This is depicted in figure 6.4b.

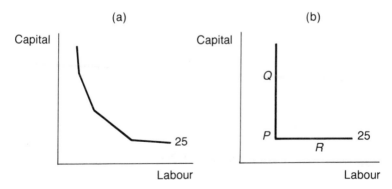

Figure 6.3 Potential shapes for isoquants

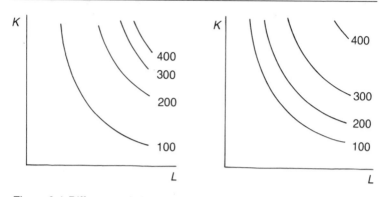

*Figure 6.4* Differences in isoquant spacing

At this point, we are now in a position to provide an explanation of a term introduced at the beginning of the chapter, namely returns to scale. This term refers to changes in output which occur when all inputs are varied in the same proportion. There are three alternative scenarios. First, *increasing returns to scale*; this means that the proportionate change in output exceeds the proportionate change in inputs, for example if the number of inputs are doubled and output trebles in size. Second, there are *decreasing returns to scale*, when the proportionate change in output is less than the proportionate change in inputs. This would arise if all a firm's inputs are trebled but output only doubles as a result. Finally, there are *constant returns to scale* which arise when, for example, a doubling of inputs leads to a doubling of a firm's output. We can clarify the principle of returns to scale by using isoquants. In each of the diagrams within figure 6.5, proportionate changes in capital and labour are represented by the straight line which extends from the origin.

It can be seen in figures 6.5a, 6.5b and 6.5c that the output associated with the arbitrary input combination of $L_1$ and $K_1$ is 20 units (measured with reference to the isoquant passing through point *B*). If the amounts of both capital and labour were doubled to $L_2, K_2$, then increasing returns to scale would be prevailing if, for example, the isoquant passing through point *C* was associated with an output of 60 units (figure 6.5a). It can be seen that the isoquant associated with 40 units of output occurs before point *C* is reached. In contrast, figure 6.5b shows decreasing returns to scale. In this case, the 40-unit isoquant lies beyond point *B*. In this example, output only increases by 50 per cent (to 30 units) despite the doubling of both factor inputs. Finally, in figure 6.5c, the 40-unit

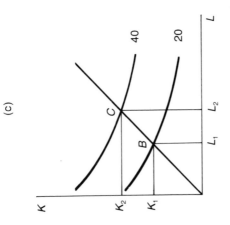

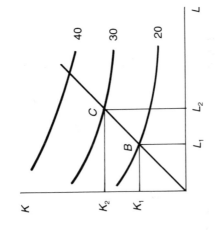

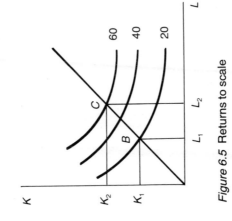

Figure 6.5 Returns to scale

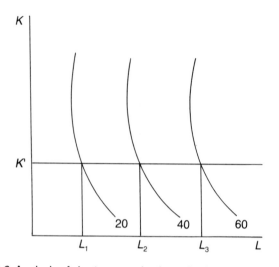

*Figure 6.6* Analysis of short-run production using isoquants

isoquant passes through point $C$. In other words, by using twice as much capital and labour, output has doubled, thereby reflecting constant returns to scale. It should be noted that long-run production functions are not restricted to exhibiting one particular form of returns to scale. They may reflect increasing, decreasing and constant returns to scale as input levels are varied.

To complete this section of analysis, it should be noted that isoquants *can* be used to analyse production functions in the short run. The only modification is for the amount of capital used to be fixed, as is demonstrated in figure 6.6. Thus, by drawing a horizontal line across the graph at $K'$, we can read off the amounts of labour which would be required by the entrepreneur were output to be increased in the short term. For example, to produce 20 units output with $K'$ units of capital, $L_1$ units of labour would be required. If output is to increase to 40 and 60 units, inputs of $L_2$ and $L_3$ would be needed respectively. In the longer term, this constraint could be relaxed, allowing a wider choice of factor combinations to produce each level of output.

## The cost implications of production functions

So far, the discussion has been confined to a consideration of the relationship between output and the factors of production used by the firm. However, factors such as capital and labour are not freely available and must therefore be purchased from other markets. The price of labour over a given period can be defined in terms of the wage which must be paid, for example hourly, weekly, monthly or annually, multiplied by the number of workers employed. For simplicity, it is assumed that all workers are paid the same wage. The cost of capital is, on the other hand, assumed by economists to be an imputed rent paid over its lifetime, even if the firm buys the capital outright. Thus, if a piece of machinery costs £10,000 to buy and it has a productive lifespan of ten years, then the rent paid would be £1,000 per anum (assuming that it has no scrap value).

Let us now consider how we may use this information to derive two cost curves which provide the information needed by an entrepreneur to determine his or her ultimate level of output. The first is the *average total cost curve*, which measures the average unit cost of production at a given level of output, and the second is the *marginal cost curve*, which identifies the cost of producing one extra (or one less) unit of output. As before, the analysis will be conducted initially from the point of view of production in the short run, when only the labour input can be varied, and then in terms of production in the long run, when both factors may be assumed to be variable.

*Costs in the short run*

In the short run, the average total cost curve will be the sum of two other average cost curves: the *average fixed cost curve* and the *average variable cost curve*. The average fixed cost curve can be calculated by multiplying the cost of each unit of capital by the number of units used in production and dividing this figure by the level of output. Since fixed costs are constant, whatever the output, the average fixed cost curve can be represented by the negatively sloped line in figure 6.7, labelled *SRAFC*.

The (short run) average variable cost curve can be calculated in a similar way. Specifically, the prevailing wage rate is multiplied by the number of units of labour used and this figure is then divided by the output produced by that labour input. By comparing the average variable cost curve (labelled *SRAVC* in figure 6.7) with the total output curve in figure 6.1, (which identifies the relationship between the labour inputs used and the output which results) it can be shown that where increasing returns exist, the average variable costs decrease, whereas when diminishing returns set in, average variable costs increase. By adding together the average fixed cost and average variable cost curves, we obtain the total average cost curve for a firm

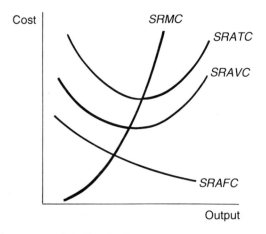

*Figure 6.7* Average costs in the short run

in the short run. This is labelled *SRATC* in figure 6.7.

We may derive the short-run marginal cost curve with reference to the average total cost curve and average variable cost curves. Specifically, if average costs are falling (total or variable), then marginal costs must be below the average and therefore the short-run marginal cost curve (labelled *SRMC*) will lie below both curves. Conversely, if average costs are rising (total or variable), then marginal costs must be greater than the average and therefore the short-run marginal cost curve will lie above the average variable and total cost curves. It therefore follows that the marginal cost curve will cut the average variable cost curve and average total cost curve at their minimum points, as depicted in figure 6.7. For readers who are still unsure about this relationship, consider the case of a cricketer who has amassed 450 runs in ten innings. This suggests a batting average of 45 if we assume that he or she is out on each occasion. If, in the next innings (the marginal innings), a further 45 runs are scored then the batting average remains the same. However, if the cricketer only scores ten runs in the next innings, the aggregate increases to 460 runs and the average falls to 41.8. For the marginal innings to drag down the cricketer's average it must have been less than the existing average. Conversely, had a century been scored in the next innings, the average rises to 50 since the marginal innings exceeds the previous average.

Having derived the four main cost curves as they apply to the firm in the short run, let us now consider the effects of lengthening the producer's time horizon so that both factors of production – capital and labour – can be assumed to be variable.

*Costs in the long run*

With both factors of production now assumed to be variable, there is no need to make a distinction between average variable costs and average fixed costs. Hence we may simply refer to the long-run average cost curve. This may be derived by estimating a budget constraint for the entrepreneur, known as an isocost line, and adding this to the isoquant diagram used earlier.

The isocost line depicts all the combinations of labour and capital which can be afforded with a fixed sum of money. For example, let us assume that for a given time period an entrepreneur has £1,000 to spend on factor inputs. The cost of each unit of labour is £10 while the cost of each unit of capital is £50. If production were to be completely labour intensive (that is, with no capital at all), then the largest number of workers which could be afforded is 100. At the other extreme, 20 units of capital could be afforded if no workers were hired. Of course, both situations are highly implausible since capital ultimately needs someone to operate it and even the most labour-intensive production techniques

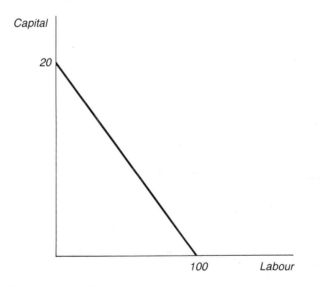

*Figure 6.8* The isocost line

require some capital, however primitive. Thus, it is expected that production will utilise a combination of labour and capital providing that it can be afforded. Mathematically, we may define the constraint facing the producer as:

$$B = wL + rK \tag{6.7}$$

where $w$ and $r$ denote the wage and rent associated with hiring labour ($L$) and capital ($K$) respectively. It can be seen from figure 6.8 that affordable combinations of inputs must lie on, or beneath the isocost line. Any combination lying above it cannot be afforded.

Given a particular budget line, the next stage of the analysis is to determine which combination of affordable inputs should be used by the producer. This can be derived by superimposing a family of isoquants onto the isocost line. Assuming that the producer wishes to maximise output from a given budget, then it is logical to suggest that he or she will select the (attainable) combination of capital and labour where the highest possible isoquant is just tangential to the isocost line. This can be seen in figure 6.9. In this case the highest possible output is 50 units, using the combination of labour and capital $L^*$ and $K^*$ respectively.

Any other affordable combination of labour and capital (either on or inside the isocost line) will produce a smaller output, while the isoquants associated with outputs exceeding 50 units cannot be

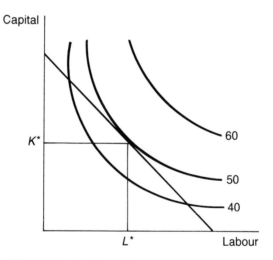

*Figure 6.9* Maximum output for a given cost

afforded. Of course, we could have stated the problem slightly differently and tried to determine the least-cost way in which the entrepreneur could produce 50 units of output. This would be £1,000 using the combination $L^*$ and $K^*$. As long as there is no change in the relative price of the two inputs, capital and labour, or the shape of the isoquant there will be no reason for the optimal output (50 units) or combination of inputs ($L^*$ and $K^*$) to change. It can be seen that the mechanics of this exercise are no different from those employed when indifference curves were used to derive an individual's optimal consumption point.

The next stage of the analysis will be to consider, first, what happens if there is a change in the relative price of one or other of the two inputs (capital or labour) and, second, the implications of an increase in the budget available to the producer (*ceteris paribus*). In either situations, there will be a repositioning of the isocost line. To illustrate, let us assume that there is an increase in the relative price of labour (*ceteris paribus*). In figure 6.10, this is represented by a pivoting of the isocost line from $AA$ to $AB$. The new isocost line shows that the money released from forgoing a unit of capital buys less labour than it did before. This not only reduces the number of affordable factor combinations but ultimately reduces the maximum output which can be produced from a given budget. Thus, before the rise in wages, the isocost line and the

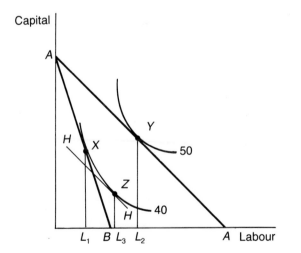

*Figure 6.10* Substitution and output effect from a rise in the wage rate

isoquant were tangential at an output level of 50 units. Now, after the wage increase, maximum output falls to 40 units.

It is also possible to estimate the income effect (which in these circumstances is known as output effect) and the substitution effect which arises from this change by drawing in a hypothetical isocost line *HH*. Using exactly the same principles as those demonstrated in Chapter 2, *HH* is drawn parallel to the new isocost line but tangential to the isoquant associated with 50 units of output. The move from $X$ to $Y$ is the total effect of the change in relative input prices, which can be broken down into the move from $X$ to $Z$ (the substitution effect) and $Z$ to $Y$ (the pure output effect). It can be seen therefore that the increase in wages leads the firm to substitute the relatively cheaper input – capital – for labour. In terms of labour inputs, the total effect is the distance $L_2$ to $L_1$, the substitution effect is $L_3$ to $L_1$ and the output effect is $L_2$ to $L_3$. A similar type of analysis, which isolates the income and output effects, can be undertaken if wages were to fall or the unit price paid for capital were to change in either direction.

The second stage of this analysis will be to consider what happens when the producer has more resources at his or her disposal with which to buy factor inputs. Assuming that the relative prices of the factors do not also change, then we may draw in additional isocost lines, which run parallel to the original, to depict the increase in the budget. This is

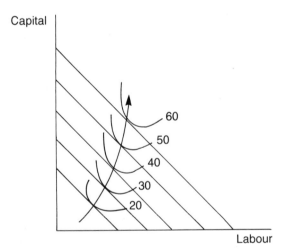

*Figure 6.11*  A long-run expansion path showing increasing capital intensity

shown in figure 6.11. As the relevant isocost line moves outwards from the origin, it is implied that the producer can increase output to the levels associated with the isoquant which is just tangential to it. The line which joins together all these points of tangency is referred to as the *long-run expansion path*. If the long-run expansion path is a straight line extending from the origin of the graph, it indicates that relative factor intensity has remained constant despite the change in output. In contrast, if the long-run expansion path bends towards either the capital or labour axis, then changes in output are also associated with changes in relative factor intensity. For example, the line *AB* indicates that increases in output are associated with increasing capital intensity.

We now have sufficient information to be able to derive a typical average cost curve for a firm in the long run. In order to derive each point on our long run average cost curve (*LRAC*) we simply take each level of output and determine the cheapest combination of factors of production which can be used to produce it; in other words, via the isocost line which is just tangential to the isoquant. We may then divide the appropriate cost by the level of output to determine the average cost. Thus, if the isoquant associated with an output of 100 units is just tangential to the isocost line associated with combinations of capital and labour whose value adds to £150, then the average cost of output is £1.50. Similarly, if the 200 unit isoquant is tangential to the £250 isocost

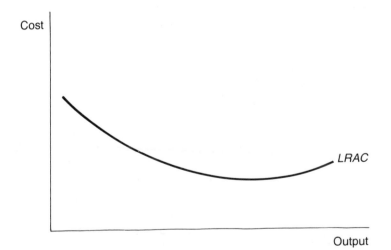

*Figure 6.12* Long-run average costs

line, then the average cost of output has fallen to £1.25. This exercise may be replicated for all levels of output until an average cost curve encompassing a wide range of output levels is derived. It is usually assumed that the long-run average cost curve will assume the shape of a flattened U, implying that as output initially rises, average costs fall. Eventually an output or series of outputs are reached which are associated with the lowest average costs before the average costs start to rise again. This is depicted in figure 6.12.

### Economies of scale and economies of size

When firms enjoy cost advantages from becoming larger, they are said to be exploiting *economies of size*. Similarly, when the average cost of production begins to rise again, *diseconomies of size* are witnessed. Some of the reasons why economies and diseconomies of size emerge will be discussed shortly.

At this point, it is appropriate to clarify a potential area of confusion, particularly for students who have already had some previous exposure to economics. It relates to frequently used terms which are used in a similar context, namely economies of scale and diseconomies of scale. These expressions are also used by commentators to refer to situations when firms experience initial reductions in the average cost of production as output rises and then increases in average cost as output increases beyond a certain point. Strictly speaking however, economies of scale and diseconomies of scale refer to what happens to average cost when the inputs used in production are increased in the same proportion. In other words, following on from earlier analysis, economies of scale emerge when there are increasing returns to scale (such as when doubling all inputs trebles the level of output) and diseconomies of scale refers to situations when there are decreasing returns to scale (such as when the quadrupling of all inputs only doubles output). In either of these situations, relative factor intensity does not actually change and would therefore be reflected by a straight-line long-run expansion path which starts at the origin.[4] Economies and diseconomies of size are less restrictive terms which also encompass changes in relative factor intensity as the level of output changes. Thus, average cost reductions which coincide with increases or decreases in capital intensity are economies of size rather than economies of scale. Thus, if firms were restricted to growth using the same levels of factor intensity, they may find that their average costs may be higher than they would be if they grew at the factor intensity associated with least cost. Of course, in the case of some production processes, the factor combinations associated with economies of size and economies of scale may coincide.

The next stage of the analysis will be to consider why average costs can fall or rise with output in practice. For the most part, the discussion will make reference to economies and diseconomies of size. However, the points made below also apply to the more restricted concepts of economies and diseconomies of scale. The cost advantages of a firm increasing its scale of production can be summarised under four main headings.

*Specialisation*

As the size of industrial operation increases, there is a greater opportunity for firms to utilise specialist staff and specialist machinery which lead to increases in efficiency and therefore reductions in unit cost. The foundations of this principle are deeply rooted in the economics literature. As long ago as 1776, Adam Smith wrote about the benefits of specialisation with reference to a pin factory in which each worker was responsible for one *specific* task within the 18 stages of pin manufacture, rather than all 18. This approach, known as *division of labour*, not only allows workers the opportunity to become experts in the job they undertake but also reduces the amount of time lost when non-specialised workers pass from one task to the next. Examples of division of labour can be seen at all levels of society, ranging from professional sports-persons employing managers to negotiate contracts on their behalf and trained solicitors when they go to court, to firms and governments using specialist advisers to assist in strategic decision-making. Firms are seen to employ specialist accountants and marketing experts, while many individuals choose to employ legal experts rather than represent themselves in a court case. Team sports such as cricket, hockey and soccer provide perfect examples of division of labour in action. In the case of cricket, players usually specialise in batting, bowling or wicket-keeping even though they may be required to perform more than one of these tasks during a game. Similarly, hockey and soccer players typically specialise as goalkeepers, defenders, midfield players or attackers. In all cases, it is more logical for teams to be made up of specialists who are able to support each other rather than to contain 11 'all-rounders' or 11 'utility' players.

*Indivisibilities*

The term 'indivisibilities' refers to the fact that a firm will require a minimum quantity of certain inputs to remain operational and, in turn, these inputs have an optimal level of usage for engineering or social reasons. For example, a squash club will need to have a certain number of courts available if it is to attract custom and these courts need to be of a certain size. A club could not try to double its throughput by dividing each court in two! Optimal usage of these courts will occur if they are in use throughout the time that the club is open to the public. The fewer the number of people using each court, the higher the average cost of supplying them and vice versa. Similarly, clubs will need to employ personnel to co-ordinate court bookings. The more bookings that are handled by that person, the lower the unit cost of running the facility. The indivisibility principle extends all the way down to the smallest items at the club, such as the telephone used for booking courts or the seat being used by the receptionist.

*Purchasing and financial advantages*

Large firms frequently receive preferential treatment when they engage in day-to-day transactions with other economic agents. Since, by definition, large firms will produce their output in much larger quantities than small firms, they will naturally require their inputs in much larger quantites also. The need to buy in bulk often enables larger producers to secure preferential deals, allowing them to purchase raw materials at a lower unit price than their smaller, less economically powerful, counterparts. For similar reasons, smaller firms often find it more difficult to raise external finance. Since smaller firms face a greater risk of bankruptcy, they are a less attractive proposition to financial institutions and are therefore required to pay higher rates of interest on loans. Furthermore, the greater economic uncertainty characterising small firms may also require them to pay back loans over a shorter period than larger firms.

*Law of large numbers*

The law of large numbers features in many textbooks on statistics, though it does have an important application with respect to the production process. The basic principle underlying it can best be demonstrated by a simple example. Let us assume that we toss a coin.

The probability of it landing heads or tails would be 50:50 (assuming it was not loaded!). Thus, if we were to toss a coin 1,000 times, we would expect that it would land approximately 500 times as a head and 500 times as a tail. However, if we were to toss the coin just four times it would not be a surprise if the coin were to fall as heads on three occasions, or even on all four occasions. The more times we toss the coin, the more likely that our expectation of a 50:50 split between heads and tails will occur. The idea behind this basic principle can be applied to the activities of firms.

Let us consider the example of a small firm which owns a particular piece of machinery that is prone to breaking down. Assuming that it is not desirable for production to be delayed for too long, it would be rational for the firm to have a maintenance engineer and a set of spare parts to cover most breakdown contingencies. However, if we turn to a larger company which has five of these machines, it is unlikely that all these machines will break down at exactly the same time nor are they all likely to break down for exactly the same reason. Thus, the larger firm may still only need to have one maintenance engineer and need not have five sets of spares in stock. Thus, the larger company faces lower average costs with respect to the upkeep of its capital. A similar argument can be made with respect to the needs of small and large companies to hold stocks of inputs, finished goods and money in anticipation of fluctuations in demand or receipts (customers may not pay their bills on time during recessions). In general we would expect that the volume of these stocks will vary less than proportionately with the scale of output or receipts.

*Minimum efficient scale*

When a firm is operating at the lowest average cost it is said to be achieving productive efficiency. This may encompass a single output or a wide range of outputs. In either case, it is the point where the *LRAC* curve is at its lowest. The output level at which this occurs is known as the *minimum efficient scale* (mes). In figure 6.13, this occurs at point *A*. Of course, all the outputs between *A* and *B* are also associated with the lowest average cost and therefore the firm is producing efficiently at any of these points.

If a firm is producing beyond output *B*, it can be seen to experience increases in its average costs. In these circumstances diseconomies of size are setting in. The source of these diseconomies is the managerial problems which begin to occur when the firm becomes organisationally more complex. This may arise from the increased bureaucratic structure

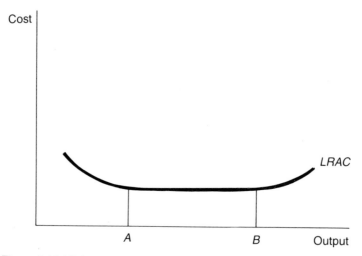

*Figure 6.13* Minimum efficient scale

which often characterises larger firms. Co-ordination problems may be exacerbated further if growth has necessitated the firm to become more geographically spread. We might expect that the first site where a firm chooses to be located is the most desirable with respect to its input, production and distributional requirements. Subsequent sites may be found to be less advantageous, thereby adding to the unit cost of production as output rises.

### External economies and diseconomies of size

The economies and diseconomies of size which have been outlined above are all within the direct control of the firm involved. For example, firms can choose whether or not to use division of labour or whether to spread its operations across a number of geographically disparate sites. For this reason these are known as *internal* (dis)economies of size. However, there is the possibility that a reduction in a firm's unit costs arises because the size of the industry itself is increasing rather than as a result of a change in the output of that particular firm. For example, suppliers of inputs for an expanding industry may themselves be able to exploit internal economies as the demand for their output increases. This reduction in the suppliers' costs may be passed on in part to all the firms who purchase goods from them, thereby reducing the input costs of all

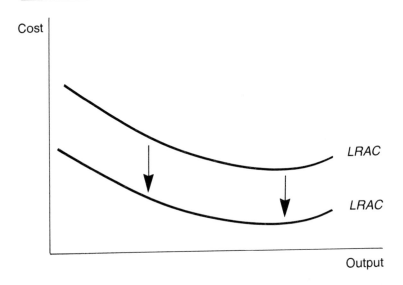

Figure 6.14 External economies of scale

the producers within the expanding industry.

Expanding industries may also receive government help towards the provision of training or in obtaining export licenses. The growth of one or more industries in a particular area may also encourage the construction of a better network of roads to facilitate transportation. The effect of one or all of these initiatives will be to have an impact on the average costs of all firms in the affected industry, not just one or two operators. For this reason, these changes are referred to as *external* (dis)economies of size since they may apply to all firms within an industry. In diagrammatic terms, the effect of external economies, such as those described above, will be to initiate a downward shift in the *LRAC* curve. This is depicted in figure 6.14.

## The relationship between short-run and long-run average costs

Although the preceding discussion has derived short-run and long-run average cost curves as separate entities, it should be stressed that the two are inextricably linked. As we have seen, for firms to be operating along their long-run average cost curve, they need to be using the least-cost combination of resources associated with their level of output. More often than not this will not be the case, since such factors as negotiated

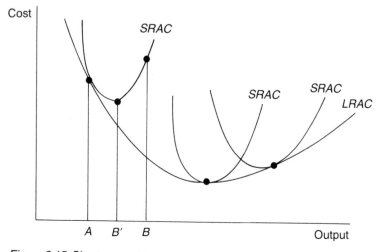

*Figure 6.15* Short-run and long-run average cost

work practices, an inability to access finance or general uncertainty about the industry may preclude them from responding to technological change. However we shall, for the moment, ignore the possibility that firms are not exploiting the most efficient factor combination for the output they produce. Tangential to every point on the long-run average cost curve will lie a short-run average cost curve which indicates the short-run options available to the firm with respect to the relationship between output and costs. Three such cases are highlighted in figure 6.15.

Consider the point labelled *A*. It can be seen that this lies along the section of the long-run average cost curve associated with economies of size. Should the firm's management wish to increase output from *A* to *B* in the long term then it has the option of altering both its capital and labour inputs. However, if the increase in output is only contemplated in the short term then the producer cannot change the amount of capital employed, only the amount of labour. Thus, in this case, the increase in output results in an increase in average cost in the short term since the producer can only add more labour to the existing stock of capital. Had the increase in output only been to point *B'*, average costs would have fallen, but not by as much as they would in the longer term. It can also be seen in figure 6.15 that if the firm is operating at the lowest point on its long-run average cost curve, then any change in output, either in the long run or the short run, will increase average costs. However, the limited opportunities in the short term will magnify the increase. A similar argument can be employed with respect to production where diseconomies of size exist.

Having established the shape and relationship between average cost curves in the short and long run, the next stage of the analysis will consider the problems economists face when they try to estimate cost curves in practice. Particular reference will be made to the problems of determining (dis)economies of size and the problems leisure economists face when they try to apply the principle to sports facilities such as leisure centres.

**Estimating costs in practice**

As we have seen, economic theory suggests that long-run average cost curves are U-shaped. However, empirical studies tend to imply that they are more likely to be L-shaped, in other words, average costs tend to remain constant beyond a certain point. The aim of this section is to introduce briefly the techniques economists have used to try and estimate production costs and hence to determine the prevalence of size economies in various industries, and then to consider their viability with respect to estimating the costs associated with supplying sports facilities.

Economists have adopted three basic approaches to gain an insight into the degree to which firms can exploit scale economies. The first is known as *statistical cost analysis*. Essentially, this involves a comparison of one or more firms as their level of output changes over time (time-series analysis) or by comparing the costs of different sized firms (cross-sectional analysis). However, there is a need to take account of such parameters as differences in the age of capital stock, differences in input prices and the degree to which firms are diversified into other industries. Attempts to standardise for such differences abound in the literature, so that estimates are likely to be sensitive to the conventions adopted by individual researchers. A more detailed analysis of the problems of utilising this approach will be considered shortly when we look specifically at the possibility of estimating cost curves for sports centres.

The second technique adopted by economists is known as the *engineering approach*. Engineers who plan new production units and plants will accumulate significant amounts of information with respect to alternative production technologies/plant layout and their associated operating costs. Since this approach derives cost functions directly from the underlying technological relationships, it can provide good theoretical estimates, though these may differ from the costs that firms are experiencing in reality. An added problem is that respondents may not be aware of the average costs of producing at levels which they do not actually operate and that the approach is concerned with technical relationships. It does not yield estimates for the administrative and research costs which are also being incurred.

The final technique which has been used in the literature is one which tried to circumvent the problems encountered in the previous two approaches, namely valuation and informational difficulties respectively. It is known as the *survivor technique* and rests on the principle that firms whose share of an industry's output grows over time are efficient, while firms whose share diminishes over time are either too large or too small. The main problem with this approach is that it is not just identifying a simple relationship between size and cost. It is embracing a whole matrix of interrelationships which determine the long-term performance of firms. Hence researchers have found that firms' 'survival' can be somewhat arbitrary. For example, survival may ultimately depend upon restrictive agreements or barriers preventing new firms from entering the market.

## Scale economies and leisure centres

Any attempt to estimate the cost advantages (or disadvantages) of increasing the scale of production requires us to be able to define an appropriate unit of output. For manufactured goods, this is relatively easy, since we can talk about the production of tennis rackets, sweatshirts or mountain bikes. However, in the case of many leisure services, output is often defined in terms of the number of customers who are served over a given period of time. However, this is demand rather than supply. Put another way, a study attempting to calculate size economies within the car industry would refer to the output of cars by individual factories, not how many of these cars are demanded. In the case of many leisure services, output must therefore be defined in terms of capacity within a given time period, or if combined with demand, capacity utilisation.

However, the definition of capacity is not necessarily an exact science in the same way as defining manufactured output. In the case of a squash court, the basic conventions of a normal game suggest that two, rather than three or four, players should be present at any one time. However, there is disparity between sports centres with respect to the length of time each pair of consumers is allowed to play for the appropriate court fee. Thus, although two squash clubs may have exactly the same number of courts available for its customers and operate the same opening hours, the maximum usage of those facilities will depend ultimately upon management policy with respect to what constitutes an appropriate playing time for the court fee levied. Taking a further example, there is a difference between the number of people who could safely be admitted to a swimming pool at one particular time and the number which pool users would deem to be acceptable so that their swim is enjoyable and relatively unrestricted. An added problem emerges with respect to multipurpose facilities frequently seen at leisure centres. For example, the floor space used for badminton courts can also be used for volleyball, basketball, keepfit or aerobics. Thus, the capacity of that floor space will depend upon the mix of activities which are available at that centre. In the public sector, this will depend upon the range of activities offered at other centres within the locality.

We have already discussed three possible ways of deriving a cost curve capable of identifying whether there are size economies. The first was statistical analysis, based upon evidence from existing producers; the second was by the use of information from engineering blueprints; and the third involved the survivor technique, which identifies the long-term growth (contraction) of low (high) cost producers. From the point of view of carrying out analysis based upon public leisure centres, neither of the last two approaches is applicable. In the case of the survivor technique, we are dealing with centres which are not exposed to the full forces of competition, where cost recovery frequently reflects political rather than economic decision-making. Furthermore, the markets in which sports centres operate are extremely localised where travel cost rather than activity price is likely to play a significant role in determining which centres consumers ultimately visit. The use of the engineering approach would demand information beyond that which is routinely available at local or national level and, as we have already seen, the use of activity areas will be extremely dependent upon local management decisions, for example, the weekly phasing of activities from a given area of floor space. Thus, from the point of view of carrying out a suitable analysis, we would have to use some form of statistical cost analysis with the following conditions:

1    all facilities in the sample must be operating at, or close to, full capacity;
2    facilities in the sample are of a similar technological vintage;

3    input prices must be the same for all facilities in the sample;
4    each facility in the sample must be offering the same (or similar) range of activities.

However, as a 1979 Scottish Sports Council study discovered, it is extremely difficult to achieve simultaneously all four of the above criteria. For example, 'dry' sports centres (centres without swimming pools) tended to fall foul of the last two criteria whereas analysis using pools and wet/dry centres explicitly encountered all but the second condition.

Although the previous analysis suggests policy-makers' interest in the relationship between the supply of leisure facilities and average cost, it should be understood that it is the size of the market which will be the key factor in determining the size of any productive unit. For example, in a classic British study embracing a whole range of manufacturing processes, Pratten (1971) found that the minimum efficient scale as a percentage of the UK market can exceed 100 per cent (for example for dyes, aircraft and machine tools), thereby stressing the need for firms to export if they wish to exploit fully any potential scale economies which exist. However, sports facility planners rarely have this option. For most activities, markets are extremely localised, often reflecting travel cost (money and time), with little realistic opportunity to market facilities outside of their immediate catchment area. Thus, for local authorities, with infinite claims on their scarce resources, there is very little point in building or expanding a sports centre capable of reducing average costs to the minimum if there is insufficient demand to justify a facility of that size. The problems which would arise can be demonstrated using an example which draws upon some of the theory introduced in the previous section of this chapter.

Let us assume that at the planning stage of a leisure centre a local authority decides to build a facility with a given array of activity areas. The actual blend of facilities will depend in part upon the perceived demand factors associated with the new centre's catchment population as well as the mix of facilities already on offer at nearby centres (in both the public and private sectors). However, there remains a question of what size of facility to construct. Let us also assume that there is evidence from existing centres which indicates that it is possible to achieve economies of size. It should be recalled that the points on the long-run average cost curve assume that the facilities in question are operating at full capacity. If there is insufficient demand in the new location to sustain the facility, then it may prove more expensive to

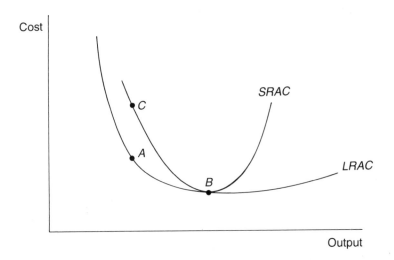

*Figure 6.16* Average costs and the leisure centre – the implications of the catchment population

operate the larger facility at below full capacity than the smaller facility at full capacity, as is demonstrated in figure 6.16.

It can be seen that the average costs of running the smaller facility at full capacity (or near full capacity) are smaller than they are to operate a larger facility with a suboptimal input of variable factors. An expansion from *A* to *B* will only reduce average costs if the catchment population is sufficiently large to be able to utilise the facilities on offer. If this is not possible, costs associated with point *C* will be incurred. This analysis reinforces points made in previous chapters which emphasise the need for planners to be fully aware of the characteristics of demand for the product they wish to supply.

## QUESTIONS FOR DISCUSSION

1   In terms of a leisure facility such as a sports centre, explain the difference between *economies of scale* and *economies of size*.
2   What are the problems associated with estimating the cost curves appertaining to a leisure facility?

# Chapter 7

# Business objectives

## INTRODUCTION

The analysis in Chapter 6, identified the distinction economists make between costs in the short run and costs in the long run and examined the reasons why we might expect average costs to fall as a firm increases its scale of production. However, the level of output produced ultimately by a firm is not simply a function of producing at the lowest possible average cost. It will be seen in the discussion to follow that there are a whole plethora of factors which will determine the level of output of a firm ranging from the objectives of its managers to the actions of other firms operating in the industry. The standard assumption made by economists is that firms will select an output which will maximise their profits. The aim of this chapter is to look at the general implications of this strategy, in terms of the level of output which will be generated, and compare this with other strategies which the firm could employ.

Although the manufacture and retailing of many leisure goods and services tends to be the preserve of commercial operators (for example, clothing, equipment, restaurants, public houses, professional sports teams, private sports clubs and so on), and therefore might be expected to base their output decisions on pure commercial criteria, it should already be very evident that the public and voluntary sectors play a very important role in the provision of leisure and recreation facilities. As we have already seen, the emphasis of local authorities with respect to the facilities they provide is not on profit *per se* but to increase throughput, particularly of targeted social groups. Similarly, the sport-related arm of voluntary organisations such as local cricket or football clubs usually need constant cross-subsidisation from bar sales, raffle tickets and other fund-raising exercises. In both cases, we are witnessing the continued existence of many organisations for which shortfalls of income in relation to expenditure is a regular occurrence.

The aim of this chapter is to look specifically at how economists have perceived the way in which organisations respond to their economic environment, with respect to their pricing and output decisions. This will necessitate consideration of a variety of alternatives, ranging from the frequently used assumption of profit maximisation to strategies which embrace such variables as output, sales revenue or long-term company growth. It will be seen that some economists have retained maximisation as a basic principle, even if profit is not the major goal. Other practitioners have broken away from the very idea of maximisation and looked at how firms are forced to make compromises during the everyday running of their operations. This analysis will move from the general to the specific, focusing initially upon the economics literature as it relates to economists' theories of firm behaviour, before moving on to consider such objectives as they apply to professional team sports. Finally the chapter will consider how non-commercial suppliers of sport and leisure can monitor their performance over time.

## PROFIT MAXIMISATION

In many respects, profit maximisation is a natural extension of the principle of utility maximisation that is used to underpin much consumer theory. The ability to maximise utility is justified whenever individuals are in charge of their own destiny (rather than having other people's preferences imposed upon them) and, more importantly, when consumers *want* to maximise their own utility. This does not rule out the possibility of altruism since benevolent actions do not only generate utility for the recipient but also for the donor. Analogously, the assumption of profit maximisation not only requires the owner of an enterprise to be in direct control of its day-to-day running but also for the owner actually to desire higher profits (which enter his or her utility stream). However, it is the doubt concerning the justification for both of these requirements, particularly in situations where the firm is so large that it is owned by a significant number of shareholders, which has led economists to seek alternative explanations as to why firms behave in the way they do.

Most shareholders do not have time to participate directly in the daily business of the firm(s) they have invested in. Thus, they elect a group of directors to look after their interests. They in turn appoint managers to take responsibility for the decisions made at 'ground level'. By definition, this process will drive a wedge between the owners of the firm and those people who are in day-to-day control. If the firm is performing badly, then shareholders may sell their shares (because they expect higher returns elsewhere). If sufficient individuals feel the same way, there will be an oversupply of that company's shares on the stock market. This will drive down their price and possibly make the company vulnerable to a take-over bid by another company which believes it can run the firm more efficiently than the existing managment. Since this restructuring may well lead to a new management team being installed, there is an incentive for the present team to perform well. Alternatively, the shareholders may sack the current directors and appoint a new board. If individual shareholders each have a small number of shares and there are consequently many of them, this latter option will depend upon their ability to organise a significant and cohesive pressure group. Thus, the security of the jobs of existing managers will in part depend upon the size and structure of a company's shareholders. If there are only a small number of people holding a particular company's shares, then it is easier for them to be co-ordinated and/or have sufficient holdings to exert group or even individual influence upon a firm's activities. In contrast, if the group of shareholders is large and their holdings are evenly spread then the actions of small groups of individuals will have little impact on either the share price or the stability of the current directorship. This will be further exacerbated if the shareholders are not fully informed about the expected performance of their investment. Thus, small shareholders simply become disparate rentiers who lend money to firms (in return for a dividend) but play no direct role in determining company policy. In such circumstances this wedge between a firm's owners and those directly in control provides the opportunity for managers to pursue their own objectives (discussed below) while keeping enough shareholders happy to prevent pressure groups emerging.

Over the past three decades, however, we have witnessed an increase in the number of shares whose ownership is not characterised by asymmetrical information about a given company's economic well being. Financial institutions and pension funds are owning an increasing proportion of shares in public companies in the UK. Indeed, since 1957, their holdings have risen from 17.9 per cent to over 40 per cent. With their bulk holdings, specialist knowledge of current and expected business conditions and their own need to maximise the returns on their holdings, such institutions are able to exert a powerful and continuing influence upon the activities of a firm's management team.[1]

## MARKET STRUCTURE

Many economics textbooks identify a number of potential market structures, each characterised by a unique set of assumptions which will exert an influence on price and output decisions. Being theoretical generalisations, it is very difficult to find industries which fit neatly into any one definition. Nevertheless, they provide a valuable set of insights into how businesses will behave in response to the market structure within which they belong.

To begin, let us consider the two most extreme forms of market organisation, perfect competition and pure monopoly. They can then be used as a focus for comparison of three other structures which conform more readily to 'real world' situations: monopolistic competition, oligopoly and duopoly.

### Perfect competition

Models based upon the scenario of perfect competition make the following assumptions:

1   there are a large number of firms (sellers) – referred to as an *atomistic* structure;
2   there are a large number of buyers;
3   the quantities bought and sold by buyers and firms respectively are so small, relative to the total amount traded, that the market price is completely unaffected;
4   the goods or services traded on the market are completely identical – products are said to be homogeneous;
5   buyers and sellers are assumed to be endowed with perfect information about the market;
6   there is complete freedom of entry to and exit from the industry, both in terms of it being a costless activity and that there are no entry restrictions (for example, the need to get a specific qualification).

In perfect competition, neither the buyers nor the sellers are sufficiently large to be able to influence the market price. They are both said to be price takers. Thus, should a customer increase his or her demand for the product in question, it will have no effect upon the market price. Similarly, should a firm set its price above that of the market, it will lose all its customers to its competitors which by definition are offering an identical product. Conversely, should a firm hold its price below the market price, it will attract custom, thereby forcing other firms to reduce their price or to leave the industry. The previous assumptions also imply that in the long term, firms in the industry can only accrue what is known as *normal profit*. This is the level of profit which is just sufficient to encourage the entrepreneur to remain in the industry and not to switch to an alternative activity. Thus, if profits are below the normal profit, the entrepreneur can costlessly leave the industry and move into an alternative, more profitable, activity. Conversely, if firms in the industry are earning more than normal profit, referred to as *supernormal profit*, other entrepreneurs will be attracted to this line of business and gradually supernormal profits will be eroded away to the point when all the firms in the industry will be earning normal profit only.

## Pure monopoly

At the other end of the spectrum there is pure monopoly. Unlike perfect competition, there is only one seller of a given output and hence pure monopoly is the most extreme form of market concentration. Strictly speaking, the product in question is assumed to have no close substitutes, though this criterion depends upon the definition of substitute one wants to use. Demand is characterised by a large number of competing buyers which therefore have no market power. Monopolists are not price takers in the sense of the perfectly competitive firm and hence face a standard downward sloping demand curve which defines their price and output choices. Either the firm chooses to restrict output and charges a high price or it reduces output and charges a relatively lower price. Since buyers cannot be coerced into purchasing the product in question, the monopolist can only exert control over one of the two variables, either the price or the quantity, rather than both. Unlike firms operating in a perfectly competitive industry, it is possible for the monopolist to make long-term supernormal profits (profits in excess of normal profit). Much will depend upon the degree to which the monopolist can prevent other firms entering the industry. This may be because the product in question would involve high start-up costs, is protected by patent or is an extremely well-established brand name. However, if the monopolist believes that there is the potential for entry to take place, he or she may hold down prices below their profit maximising level in order to provide an extra deterrent.

It is very difficult to find real world examples which conform exactly to either of these polar forms of market organisation. For example, it may be seen that an open-air fruit and vegetable market fulfils some of the criteria of perfect competition. However, variations in the quality and price of produce, even at adjoining stalls, is common. Furthermore, the ability of an individual to set up a (legal) stall will depend upon a whole series of planning regulations and ground rents. In other words, entry into the industry is not costless. Similarly, although private health and fitness clubs now abound in most major cities, they differ widely in terms of the facilities they offer. In contrast, the ability of a firm to be a pure monopolist and exert total control over the market will depend upon whether there are substitutes for its product. For example, Leicester City offers the only opportunity to watch professional soccer within the city. However, it cannot be viewed as a monopoly supplier of soccer. There are other football league clubs a short distance away, for example Notts County and Nottingham Forest, a whole range of local football clubs outside the Football League, as well as the competing attractions of a successful rugby union side and, at the beginning and end of the season, the opportunity to watch Leicestershire County Cricket Club.

Having considered the two most extreme forms of market organisation, let us now turn to the three cases which fall somewhere in between perfect competition and pure monopoly, and in addition, can provide a stream of real world examples. As already noted, these are referred to by economists as duopoly, oligopoly and monopolistic competition. Given that duopoly is a special case of oligopoly, we may consider the main characteristics of both within the same basic discussion.

**Oligopoly and duopoly**

Oligopolistic markets are highly concentrated, with a small number of firms accounting for a large proportion of output. In the case of duopoly, this is limited to two firms. An example of an oligopolistic market in the UK is the confectionery industry (Cadbury, Mars and Rowntree Mackintosh) while the market for soap powders is effectively duopolistic (Lever Brothers and Procter & Gamble), despite an apparently large number of branded powders. The result of all this is that firms are highly dependent upon one another so that one producer's decisions will have a knock-on effect upon the activities of its competitors.

In the case of consumer goods, there is much emphasis given to product differentiation and advertising in order to protect and enhance existing market shares. Thus, the economics literature often portrays oligopolistic (and duopolistic) behaviour in terms of a type of game where firms attempt to combat their uncertainties by adopting particular strategies based upon the expected outcome of different price, output and advertising decisions. For example, we frequently see price and advertising wars emerging between the three main supermarket chains (Asda, Sainsbury and Tesco) which between them take around 40 per cent of total sales while rivalry between confectionery firms has often manifested itself in non-price competition by adding to the weight of chocolate bars (at no extra cost to the consumer).

Firms may choose to collude in an attempt to reduce the costs of outguessing rivals (since this will reduce profits) by establishing a cartel which may have the objective of maximising joint profits and/or preventing new entrants. However, cartels are illegal in most countries since they reduce competition and hence are detrimental to the consumer. The most famous example of a cartel is the agreement made between some of the major oil producing countries (OPEC). However, cartels are notoriously unstable since participants have an incentive to cheat on negotiated prices and outputs in order to gain short-term economic advantage. Thus, cartels rely on the ability of certain members to police agreements. The dominance of Saudi Arabia within OPEC allows it to fulfil this role, despite brief hiccups during the last two decades. Furthermore, cartels can only work successfully if all the major players are parties to the agreement. Again, citing the case of OPEC, there is considerable uncertainty about the future actions of major oil producers within the former Soviet Union, such as Kazakhstan.

The difficulties which face firms in oligopolistic industries can be seen by referring to an example frequently used in the economics literature known as the *Prisoners' Dilemma*.[2] A simplified version of the problem is given in table 7.1. Assume that there are two firms deciding whether to adopt a high-advertising or a low-advertising strategy. The matrix in table 7.1 sets out the profits (in millions of pounds) which will accrue to each firm from its own and its competitor's advertising campaign. Based upon the information in this *pay-off matrix*, let us consider the options facing each firm. If firm B opts for a high-advertising strategy, A would be better off doing the same thing since it would only receive a profit of £5 million if it followed the low-advertising strategy. If B followed the low-advertising strategy, firm A would still be better off following the high-output strategy since it would make a profit of £30 million instead of £20 million. Thus, in either case, the dominant strategy for A is to advertise heavily. By a similar line of argument, the same can be said of firm B. The net result is that they both receive profits of £15 million. Clearly, it would be advantageous for each firm to follow a low-advertising strategy since profits of £20 million would then accrue to both. Clearly, tensions would exist even if the firms agreed to follow the optimal strategy since there is always the

*Table 7.1* The Prisoners' Dilemma

|  |  | *Firm B* | |
|---|---|---|---|
|  |  | *Low* | *High* |
| *Firm A* | *Low* | 20,20 | 5,30 |
|  | *High* | 30,5 | 15,15 |

opportunity to get a higher pay-off in the short term by engaging in increased advertising.

## Monopolistic competition

Monopolistic competition is said to emerge when there are a large number of firms operating within a market but they each offer a similar, but not identical, product. This may be because the commodities they produce are differentiated and/or because firms are located in different geographical areas. Although there are a lot of these firms, they face a downward-sloping rather than a horizontal demand curve. Thus unlike perfect competition, a firm has the option to increase its price without losing all its customers. This will depend upon the degree to which products differ from each other (have different attributes) and are protected by their geographical location.

An everyday example of monopolistic competition is between pubs within a locality. In terms of the basic commodity they offer, they usually sell similar products, specifically a selection of beers, wines, spirits and soft drinks together with the opportunity to consume a snack or meal. However, they will differ in terms of the brands of drink on sale, consistency of beer quality, the general atmosphere of the bars (for example, the type of decor and whether there are slot-machines, pool tables and juke-boxes), the range and quality of bar food on offer and so on. The fact that people display significant differences in preference means that one pub can charge higher prices than an establishment located close by without having a detrimental effect on sales, provided it offers an attractive product to its customers. Readers will probably have already experienced the fact that the pub which offers the cheapest drink is not necessarily the one with the most customers!

Fitness gyms are another example of monopolistic competition. Numerous outlets co-exist in the same geographical area and offer potential clients broadly similar facilities, for example, sunbeds, weight training facilities, rowing machines, exercise cycles, aerobics sessions, fitness advice and so on. However, the price or membership arrangements will depend, amongst other things, upon the quantity and quality of facilities, the location of the gym and the quality of post-activity refreshment areas which are available. It should not be forgotten that private gyms/fitness centres, together with such outlets as squash and badminton clubs, also compete with provision from local authorities and the voluntary sector as well as facilities provided by large employers. These latter examples all reflect the merit good status of sporting activity and are therefore likely to be characterised by objectives which include maximising throughput and the promotion of sport and leisure to all socio-economic groups. In contrast, private clubs are more likely to target higher income groups and to follow a business strategy more in keeping with the principle of profit maximisation.

Having considered the five main types of market structure, the next stage of the analysis will be to consider the different price/output strategies firms may adopt. It was noted earlier that the standard assumption economists make is that of profit maximisation. For this reason this strategy will be considered first, using as its example the case of pure monopoly. Given the aims of this text, it would be inappropriate to devote space to profit maximisation in terms of how it would affect firms operating within the other four market structures. The example used provides the opportunity to draw out the main economic implications of this assumption. Readers interested in this dimension should consult a standard introductory text. Having considered the economic implications of profit maximisation, the discussion will consider other maximisation strategies that a firm may adopt, such as sales revenue, as well as the reasons why firms may not maximise anything. All these principles will then be applied to the specific example of professional sports leagues and the clubs which compete within them.

## PROFIT MAXIMISATION: THE CASE OF PURE MONOPOLY

It has already been argued that the profit maximisation assumption does not simply require the owner(s) of a firm to desire profits to be maximised but also for them to be in day-to-day control of the firm's activities. If this is the case, the basic rule to follow is for the firm to equate its marginal revenue with its marginal costs. This principle is analogous to the consumer choosing his or her optimal consumption point by equating the marginal cost of consumption with the marginal benefits derived from a product. In the case of the firm, in this case a pure monopoly, we need to define the concept of marginal revenue and then derive the marginal revenue curve. It should be recalled that the derivation of the marginal cost curve was undertaken in the previous chapter.

Specifically, marginal revenue refers to the change in the total revenue of a producer after a unit increase or decrease in output. Thus, if an extra unit of production increases total revenue from £20 to £25, marginal revenue equals £5. Recall, marginal cost is the increase in a firm's costs brought about by a unit increase or decrease in output. If the marginal revenue from a unit increase in output exceeds the marginal cost, it is rational to produce it. Conversely, if the marginal cost of an extra unit of output is greater than its marginal revenue, then it would be inappropriate for it to be produced, since the cost of that unit exceeds the revenue which would be derived from it. It therefore follows that production should stop at the level of output where marginal revenue and marginal cost are exactly equal.

Before we can demonstrate this principle on a diagram, we need to derive the firm's marginal revenue curve. In relation to the demand curve drawn in figure 7.1, it can be seen that the marginal revenue curve (labelled *MR*) is not only downward-sloping but also twice as steep, such that it intersects the *x* axis at half the output of the intersection point of the demand curve (*D*) and the *x* axis. Let us consider why.

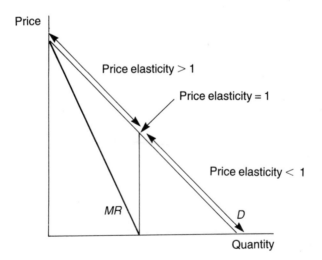

*Figure 7.1* The marginal revenue curve

The negative slope of the demand curve tells us that if a firm charges a single price for its product (and does not engage in some form of price discrimination) and it wishes to sell an extra unit of output, then it must charge a lower price for all the previous units of output as well. For some price–output combinations (where demand is price elastic) the reduction in price will increase total revenue, hence marginal revenue will be positive. For price–output combinations on the price inelastic section of the demand curve, a reduction in price will reduce total revenue, hence marginal revenue will be negative. Marginal revenue will therefore be zero at the point where total revenue is maximised, which in the case of a straight-line demand curve, will coincide with the mid-point of the demand curve.

Let us now isolate the marginal revenue curve derived above and superimpose it on a marginal cost curve to illustrate the basic principles of profit maximisation. Recalling the rule that marginal revenue and marginal cost should be equated if profits are to be maximised, it can be seen in figure 7.2 that intersection points occur at two levels of output, $q_1$ and $q_2$. It can be shown that only one of these outputs, $q_2$, is the rational level of production for the producer. Let us see why. For each unit of output below $q_1$, marginal cost exceeds marginal revenue. Thus by producing at $q_1$, the firm would be incurring a loss equal to the cumulative difference between marginal revenue and marginal cost. This

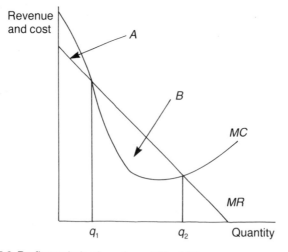

Figure 7.2 Profit maximisation where $MC = MR$

is represented by the area $A$. Beyond $q_1$, it can be seen that marginal revenue exceeds marginal cost. Thus if output continues to increase, the firm is making a profit on these additional units. So, by a similar argument, output should continue to increase up to the point $q_2$. Area $B$ therefore denotes the profit which will be made by producing between $q_1$ and $q_2$. It would be irrational to produce beyond $q_2$ because marginal costs again begin to exceed marginal revenue and the firm would therefore be incurring losses on each unit of output again. Overall, the total profit made by the firm is the difference between the two areas. If area $B$ exceeds area $A$, then the firm is making an overall profit. Conversely, if area $A$ is greater than area $B$, the firm is making a loss, though at the output level $q_2$ this loss is minimised. This therefore suggests that we need a slightly redefined version of our previous profit maximisation rule. Specifically, we should say that profit is maximised (or the loss minimised) at the output where marginal revenue equals marginal cost but also where the marginal cost curve cuts the marginal revenue curve *from below*.

Let us now develop the preceding analysis and apply it directly to the case of a monopolist. It can be seen in figure 7.3 that we have added the monopolist's average total cost curve (derived in Chapter 6) since this can be used to determine the monopolist's profit. According to the basic rule of profit maximisation, the monopolist's optimal output will occur

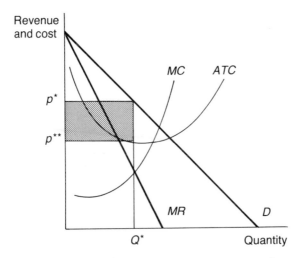

*Figure 7.3* Profit maximisation in the case of a pure monopoly

where marginal costs are equal to marginal revenue,[3] specifically $Q*$. Our demand curve tells us that these $Q*$ units of output can each be sold at a price of $P*$. It can also be seen that the average total cost incurred by the producer equals $P**$. The difference between the average revenue received by the firm ($P*$) and the average cost which is incurred during production ($P**$) represents the profit which is earned on each unit of output. Thus, total profit will be equal to area $A$ in figure 7.3. Assuming that there is no change in the demand for the commodity produced by the monopolist or the level of costs he or she faces, then this profit will be earned in every period. If, on the other hand, the average total cost curve lies above the demand curve at the ouput where marginal revenue and marginal costs are equated, then the average cost of producing each unit is exceeding the price which is being received for each unit. Should these losses persist, the firm will cease to produce. Readers should draw this scenario for themselves, based upon the previous diagram. Care should be taken to ensure that the average cost curve is cut by the marginal cost curve at its minimum point.

The aim of this section has been to show briefly the implications of adopting a profit maximising strategy. Although we have only considered one type of producer, namely the monopolist, the basic rationale behind the approach can be applied to any other market structure, ranging from perfect competition through to duopoly. The next section of this chapter considers some of the alternative strategies to profit maximisation which producers may choose to adopt.

## ALTERNATIVES TO THE PROFIT MAXIMISATION ASSUMPTION

Alternative assumptions about a firm's behaviour reflect, to varying degrees, the likelihood that its manager(s) can pursue objectives more in keeping with their own personal utility function than that of the owner. Economists often refer to this situation as the *principal–agent* problem. The 'principal' is the person who wants a particular job done, for example a firm's owner(s), while the 'agent' is the person who is employed to do it, for example the manager. This relationship also exists further down a firm's hierarchy, such as the manager (the principal) and the personnel to whom he or she delegates work (the agents). The principal–agent problem arises when the interests of the principal are different from the interests of the agent. Thus, if shareholders expect a good return on their investment while managers are pursuing high salaries and prestige, there is a strong likelihood that these objectives will conflict to some degree, hence the principal–agent problem.

Alternatives to the profit maximising assumption can be placed into two general categories: those which continue to stress some form of maximisation behaviour, albeit another variable under the control of the manager, and those which do not. The former examples fall into a body of literature known as *managerial theories* whereas the latter are referred to as *behavioural theories*. Common to both sets of literature is the prediction that firms, especially those in non-competitive industries, will not produce at minimum cost due to the existence of *organisational slack*. This arises because payments need to be made to different groups combining within a firm in order to contain any conflict which may arise from the principal–agent relationship. These payments may be in pure cash or in-kind (such as time off). However, top managers will not know exactly the minimum payments required by workers lower down the hierarchy. The difference between what labour is willing to work for and the amount they actually receive is known as organisational slack. Organisational slack should not be confused with the term *x-inefficiency*, a concept also used in the industrial economics literature. X-inefficiency refers to technical or organisational inefficiencies which exist in the firm and prevent profits being maximised. Thus the degree to which a firm's costs exceed the minimum will not only reflect x-inefficiency that exists but also any additional side payments which are being made to keep certain coalitions stable.

## Managerial theories

### Sales revenue maximisation

Under this scenario, the salaries (and perks) of managers, particularly in oligopolistic industries, are related more to sales revenue than to profit. This is seen to reflect the disadvantages of declining sales, which would detract from the status of the firm's management. It may result in a loss of distributors, a decline in the demand for the firm's product (if customers perceive it to be losing its popularity), less-favourable treatment from banks and less scope to compete against rivals. However, managers do not have complete autonomy in their actions and will ultimately be required to account for their performance by the share-holders. Thus, it is more likely that sales revenue maximisation will be constrained by the sum level of profit which must be earned before the pursuit of sales revenue can override profits. This would offer an 'acceptable' return to the firm's owners. The implications of this strategy

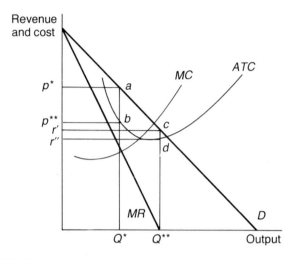

*Figure 7.4* Sales revenue maximisation

can be seen by referring to figure 7.4. As we have already seen, profit maximisation will take place at the output where marginal cost equals marginal revenue, namely $Q^*$. Analysis in Chapter 5 demonstrated that a producer's revenue will be maximised at the half-way point along a straight-line demand curve. Thus, by this analysis, sales revenue will be maximised at $Q^{**}$, a point where marginal revenue equals zero. It can be seen that sales revenue maximisation implies a greater level of output than profit maximisation. If a policy of constrained sales revenue maximisation is followed, such that a minimum profit is required (assumed to be greater than $r'r''dc$) then output will fall to some point between $Q^*$ and $Q^{**}$. Although this explanation seems highly plausible, research has not produced unambiguous empirical evidence to suggest that managerial salaries are strongly correlated with sales revenue in practice.

*Managerial utility*

A closely related analytical framework sees managers desiring to exploit any day-to-day autonomy and therefore to pursue personal objectives at work. For example, managers are seen to desire high salaries, job security and professional status subject to a minimum level of profit. Their personal utility was increased by having a larger than necessary

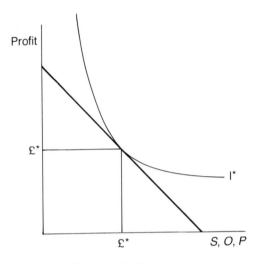

*Figure 7.5* Managerial utility maximisation

pool of high-quality staff under their control (*S*), spending additional money on high-quality office accommodation (*O*) and by diverting funds to pursue 'pet projects' (*P*). The degree to which a manager deviates from profit maximising behaviour depends upon the degree to which this discretionary expenditure (made up of *S,O* and *P*) exceeds zero. The flavour of the approach can be seen in figure 7.5 which utilises indifference curve analysis.

It can be seen that reported profits are measured on the vertical axis. It will be assumed that this variable is maximised if *S*, *O* and *P* sum to zero. On the horizontal axis, the sum total of *S*, *O* and *P* is measured under the assumption that it can be monetised. This is maximised if reported profits are zero. By drawing a straight line between these two points, it is possible to define the constraint within which the manager can operate. The optimal combination of reported profit and discretionary expenditure is that which is just tangential to the highest (managerial) indifference curve, whose shape is determined by the manager's own utility function. If the optimal point on the constraint reflects a level of reported profit below that which is deemed 'acceptable' then the manager will be forced to operate at a point below that which maximises utility.

*Company growth*

The pursuit of company growth is one objective to which both owners and managers are likely to subscribe. For managers, expanding firms are more likely to enhance their personal utility through being able to pay higher salaries and by providing an environment more capable of promoting job security and professional status. Similarly, many of a firm's owners (shareholders) do not desire short-term gain but instead long-term wealth. Thus, their concern is to maximise the present value of future expected dividends and the value of their shareholdings when they are realised.

The analysis hinges upon the concept of the *retention ratio* which is the ratio of retained profits to distributed profits. Essentially, managers have a choice. They could distribute most of the profits to shareholders (a low retention ratio). This will keep shareholders happy and keep the share price high enough to deter any threat of takeover (likely to lead to reduced job security). Alternatively, they could follow a strategy which incorporates a high retention ratio strategy in order to stimulate investment and hence company growth (assumed to be through product diversification rather than through increased revenue from existing production lines). However, this may lead to disgruntled shareholders if pursued over a long period of time. Thus, managers need to find the right balance between company growth and an acceptable retention ratio which also coincides with shareholders' long-term desire to maximise wealth.

## Non-maximising theories

At this point, some readers may be thinking that the very idea of a firm maximising a given variable (such as profit) is an abstract representation of reality. Even if decision-makers are aware of the concept of marginal analysis, the information at their disposal is unlikely to be sufficiently accurate to implement it. In a changing business environment, data need to be collected and processed rapidly if they are to be of use and this may impose prohibitive costs upon a firm. Furthermore, maximising theories tend to concentrate upon one variable, whereas in practice business organisations may be forced into simultaneously taking account of a whole range of variables which influence their day-to-day activities. However, these comments should not be perceived as a criticism of economic theory. By employing marginal analysis, economists are able to determine expected values for such variables as price and output and therefore use their model to compare these outcomes with a firm's stated aims and subsequent performance.

Thus, economics does not purport to provide a detailed insight into what actually occurs within the 'black box'. This is an area of study for behavioural theorists. They emphasise the interaction between the various groups operating within an organisation, for example shareholders, managers and trade unions. All the way down the firm's hierarchy, there will be examples of the principal–agent problem which necessitate compromises in everyday decisions. Much will depend upon the relative power of each group within the organisation. For example, during the 1960s and 1970s, trade unions were better able to exert control over the share of a firm's revenue that was directed towards their members' wages than they are today, due to the impact of government legislation and high mass unemployment. Acknowledgement of the bargaining process between groups within a firm encourages the formation of minimum levels of acceptable achievement. Since these are minimum levels, there is no unique value for such variables as output or profit to take. In this situation, firms are said to be *satisficing*. A more detailed analysis of the behavioural theory literature is beyond the scope of this book. The main problem with the approach is that it does not provide concrete predictions about how a firm will behave in given situations. Nevertheless, it does recognise the internal complexities which can prevent firms from behaving in the manner some textbooks would suggest.

## THE ECONOMICS OF PROFESSIONAL SPORTS LEAGUES

In many respects, an analysis of teams within professional sports leagues is no different from an analysis of any other type of firm. As we have already seen, it will reflect a complex interaction between three distinct groups of individuals. First, there are club owners who desire an adequate return on their investment. In many cases this may be a payment in kind, reflecting enhanced personal prestige, rather than the prospect of any long-term financial gain. Second, the club's employees will be seeking financial remuneration, job security and good conditions. In the case of a sports club, this will not only include the most visible employees, namely the players, but also the backroom staff. Finally, there are the consumers, in this case the spectators, who demand to see their team win trophies or contribute to exciting games if not winning on a regular basis.

Usually, teams are organised within a league structure requiring each member to play all the other teams at least once. For example, in the case of professional cricket, there are two separate leagues, made up of the same 18 teams who play each other once per season during weekdays and Saturdays in a series of four-day matches and on a Sunday in a 40-over competition. Entry into the championship is limited so that the most recent entrant, Durham (1992), was admitted over 70 years after the previous county (Northamptonshire, 1921). In contrast, association football in England is organised on a much wider basis: there are 92 clubs divided into four divisions, each team within a division playing each other team twice. Unlike cricket, there is the possibility of promotion and relegation, not only between the divisions themselves but also to and from a part-time 'feeder' league (the GM Vauxhall Conference League). It is this form of organisation which generates the differences between the firms and industries usually found in the economics literature and the professional sports club. Unlike many firms in industry, sports teams actually have a vested interest in the continued success and survival of their competitors – teams not only depend upon the existence of other teams to play against but also teams which can provide opposition that is attractive to spectators on a regular basis. However, as the following analysis will show, sports leagues are extremely unstable cartels, despite the interdependence of clubs which exist within them.

A good starting point for any discussion is a statement by Rottenberg (1956, p. 255) in a now classic analysis of professional baseball in the US:

> Two teams opposed to each other in play are like two firms producing a single product. The product is the game, weighted by the revenues derived from its play. With game admission prices given, the product is the game weighted by the number of paying customers who attend. When 30,000 attend, the output is twice as large as when 15,000 attend. In one sense the teams compete; in another, they combine in a single firm in which the success of each branch requires that it be not 'too much' more efficient than the other. If it is, output falls.

Two observations arise from this quote. First, we should not use the number of games played as an output measure for a sports teams since beyond a certain point on the demand curve, revenues will actually fall. Hence, it is not desirable for clubs to be playing every day of the week. Second, there is a need to maintain an *uncertainty of outcome* for as long as possible during the season. This acts as a shift parameter within the demand function of the spectator such that a game whose outcome is significant with respect to the final outcome of the league is of greater interest than one for which the result is of no consequence. Let us consider the uncertainty of outcome issue further.

Sports leagues exhibit many of the classic problems faced by cartels. They can be viewed primarily from the perspective of the consumer (spectator) as well as of the teams themselves, though it should not be forgotten that non-spectators may also try and free-ride upon the success of a local team. From the point of view of the consumer, it is obvious that all supporters enjoy seeing their team win regularly. A successful season culminating in a championship won not only brings immediate consumption benefits but also pleasure during periods when there are no matches. Regular defeats have the opposite effect. Thus, it is no surprise that most supporters prefer their team to keep winning. If other teams are able to add to the uncertainty of the ultimate outcome, this is an added bonus since it will generate matches which carry additional public interest. However, for supporters of clubs whose performances have increasingly less bearing on the outcome of the league, interest in matches may diminish quickly. Clubs likely to be relegated may attract small attendances for much of the season, but very large crowds if the outcome of matches towards the end of the season are likely to determine whether or not they remain in the higher division. It could be argued that if we focus on benefits at a national level, rather than those of the supporters of any one club, total social benefits are likely to be maximised if, *ceteris paribus*, clubs which naturally attract large attendances (because of their large catchment populations) are successful. Thus, in terms of football, it would be socially desirable for such teams as Manchester United, Liverpool and Leeds United to be contesting the Premiership title throughout the season, rather than Norwich City, Ipswich Town or Swindon Town.

Let us turn to the question of uncertainty of outcome from the point of view of sports club owners. Many of the points made in the previous paragraph apply equally here. If uncertainty of outcome increases attendances and hence club revenue, it is in theory advantageous for winning sides to be able to play other sides who also win on a regular basis. A recurring theme within the literature is that it would be desirable for successful clubs to release 'star' players in order to redistribute success and maintain spectator interest. In the case of soccer, this argument is of limited significance. Owners of clubs which are successful in domestic competitions are given the opportunity to compete against other clubs in one of three European competitions. Thus a large squad containing a large number of high-quality players is necessary if a club is to be successful at both domestic and international level. The large number of games which successful clubs are expected to play during a season means that a small squad of players is impractical, due to injury problems which can beset players at critical times of the season. With international club competitions providing considerable revenue-earning potential for clubs, the retention of star players, which may suppress competition within the domestic league, is helping to promote uncertainty of outcome in European club competitions. The argument that less successful clubs should also purchase 'star' players if they become available on the market will also depend upon their finances. Very few 'unfashionable' clubs have been able to spend heavily in an attempt to 'buy success', the only significant recent example being Blackburn Rovers. It is more common for financial problems to force smaller clubs to sell their most marketable players, even though it reduces their chances of success in the future. A classic example is Norwich City which has brought on a string of high-quality players only to sell them on to bigger clubs.

Szymanski (1993) has attempted to derive a relationship between expenditure on players (measured in terms of transfer fees and salaries) and league position for a sample of 48 soccer clubs in England and Wales for the period 1974–89. He found that 85 per cent of variation in average league position could be accounted for by expenditure on players, such that a 1 per cent increase in wage and transfer spending generates a 1 per cent increase in league position. Thus, taking Szymanski's example, a 1 per cent increase in spending would raise the bottom club by one position, whereas for a club in tenth position, expenditure would have to rise by 10 per cent. Such a relationship therefore suggests that a club desiring success should follow the strategy of Blackburn Rovers and spend money on 'star' players. However, this is only part of the story. The success of such clubs as Liverpool, Arsenal and Manchester United have been long term, not simply limited to the period of the analysis. This success, together with a favourable location with respect to a potentially large catchment population, has enabled such clubs to cultivate a large, expectant and loyal support, thereby providing the impetus to maintain its spending over many years. Thus, although Manchester United were relegated to the old Second Division in the mid 1970s, this failure did not affect their ability to re-establish themselves as a major force within a couple of years. In other words, if Blackburn wish to break into football's elite, their spending must be maintained over a large number of years, rather than make, as Szymanski terms it, a 'short-run dash for growth'.

The controllers of some leagues have adopted a different approach and have tried to promote uncertainty of outcome by controlling the distribution of playing talent between teams. This approach therefore takes us away from individual profit maximisation to joint profit maximisation within an overall cartel. However, if uncertainty of outcome is to be managed, the cartel needs to be sufficiently strong to take account of any imperfections in the market. For example there would be a need to counteract differences in the revenue-raising ability of different teams. This arises because the catchment population of teams can vary widely. One solution to this problem would be for the league to operate a pooling system where all gate monies are redistributed equally between the clubs. Indeed, this system did operate at football league matches in a more diluted form, where away teams were given a certain proportion of gate receipts. However, the larger clubs exerted their greater economic power over the smaller clubs and the league as a whole, and the system was abandoned. To some economists, this outcome is desirable since the idea of cross-subsidisation is inefficient, whatever the circumstances, since it leads to a misallocation of resources.

An alternative way to promote uncertainty of outcome is to regulate the way in which players are sold between teams. This would ensure that the bigger teams cannot absorb all the best players and therefore keep dominating the league. Such a system operated in American baseball between 1879 and 1957 and was known as the 'reserve clause'.[4] Under this system, a player became the exclusive property of the team which owned his registration. If the player found his terms unacceptable with his team, he could not transfer to any other team within the cartel. However, the effect of this system was for wage competition to be suppressed, so that players were not paid their true economic worth. Furthermore, the system did not promote competition. For example, between 1920 and 1968, three teams (St Louis, New York–San Francisco Giants and the Brooklyn–Los Angeles Dodgers) won 33 out of the 48 National League pennants. In the seminal article referred to earlier, Rottenberg (1956) also showed that the distribution of playing talent around the league would have been the same with the reserve clause as it would have been without it.

Much of Rottenberg's argument stems from the fact that if teams are rational profit maximisers, then it will be desirable for talent to be spread around so that uncertainty of outcome is maximised and the league is won by as close a margin as possible. However, American baseball is very insular in that it does not involve international competition as soccer does. The degree to which we can employ Rottenberg's findings therefore depends upon the importance clubs and spectators place upon the international dimension of the game. Although attempts to increase uncertainty of outcome may promote attendances at the domestic game, this may well detract from the ability of domestic teams to compete against clubs in European competition, which itself may have a negative effect upon overall attendances. Taking the argument a stage further, if we argue that the success of international teams depends upon the exposure players get to playing against foreign teams, then it may be better that playing and financial resources are ultimately concentrated amongst a few good teams so that as much international experience as possible is gained.

## DOES PROFIT REALLY MATTER? MEASURING THE PERFORMANCE OF PUBLIC LEISURE CENTRES

Chapters 4 and 5 have already explored some of the reasons why public leisure centres are not run explicitly for profit but, instead, exist to provide local communities with the opportunity to consume a merit good. This suggests that the performance of a public leisure facility should be assessed using different criteria from those that might be used by a producer operating explicitly as a profit-making commercial unit. Thus, whereas some notion of a target profit may be the only objective of many firms, thereby providing a one-dimensional means of assessment, the performance of leisure centres needs to reflect a combination of social and economic criteria. In other words, commercial firms are not concerned about who actually buys their product, provided their primary economic objective is achieved, whether it be a target profit, target share of sales or a stable level of sales revenue. Public-sector leisure suppliers are not only expected to be innovative with respect to reducing any discrepancy between their income and expenditure but also are judged in terms of the degree to which certain groups of the population are encouraged to visit the facility.

If we are to establish a mechanism by which leisure centres can be judged, then any indicator which is used must have certain properties if it is to be informative to decision-makers, though as Gratton and Taylor (1988) point out, it is unlikely that any indicator will possess them all. Nevertheless, performance indicators should:

1   reflect all the objectives associated with the leisure service accurately;

2    be capable of being disaggregated to take account of the fact that different activity areas are likely to have different social objectives (for example squash and swimming);

3    be administratively manageable and easily understood – there is a limit to the amount of information which decision-makers can assimilate effectively;

4    be consistent over time and between service elements or organisations.

Torkildsen (1992) identifies five main categories of indicator by which the performance of a leisure facility should be measured. These embrace the inputs used (e.g. labour costs); the resulting outputs (e.g. number of admissions); the efficiency of production (how well inputs are converted into outputs); the effectiveness of production (how well a facility is meeting its social objectives); and programming (the range of activities available at a centre during a given period of time). Let us consider each of Torkildsen's categories of performance indicator in turn, taking note of the properties they should possess in an ideal world.

## Inputs

Input indicators are intended to monitor the resources absorbed in a given period by each facility. At a relatively aggregated level we may identify overall operating costs as well as such variables as staff costs, energy costs and maintenance costs as ratios of the facility's gross operating expenditure. Costs may also be calculated on an activity-by-activity basis as well as at centre level. By comparing figures over time, it is possible to get an insight into the changing performance of the centre. Furthermore, these figures may be compared with centres offering a similar range of facilities as well as with national averages. However such comparisons must take into account that the inputs used by each sports centre will depend upon the range of facilities on offer at any given point in time and the local authority's social objectives with respect to providing leisure facilities.

## Outputs

Output indicators give emphasis to actual attendances at a given facility. A basic indicator within this category would be a capacity utilisation ratio between actual bookings and total bookings available. This may be disaggregated so as to distinguish between individuals on courses or attending as club or casual users. However, given the emphasis placed upon promoting sport and leisure to specific sections of the population, it is important that indicators emphasise the degree to which these groups are being catered for. This is largely the domain of the effectiveness indicators considered below. Output indicators may also be devised to monitor such variables as basic user fees, bar takings and hire charges as a proportion of total income.

## Efficiency

Efficiency measures are concerned with the relationship between inputs and outputs. They are concerned with how well inputs are converted into outputs. The classic indicator within this category is the ratio between income (from fees and charges) and gross operating costs. This can be disaggregated into different activity areas but it must be remembered that a low level of cost recovery does not necessarily mean that a facility or activity area is being run inefficiently. High levels of subsidy are to be expected for certain types of provision. A commonly used indicator within this category is the ratio between gross operating expenditure and total visits (cost per visit). However, since leisure centre costs are relatively fixed, this measure will tend to fluctuate in response to changes in demand, thereby emphasising throughput rather than financial considerations *per se*. A useful variation can be created by estimating the level of subsidy per visit by taking the ratio of net operating expenditure and total visits. From the point of view of a local authority's social objectives, this measure is particularly useful when disaggregated according to activity areas and different types of user.

## Effectiveness

Effectiveness measures, on the other hand, are concerned with the degree to which a particular facility is meeting its social objectives. This implies a need for constantly monitoring the socio-economic profile of visitors to each centre. Based upon the information gathered during this exercise, indicators can be constructed which provide a numerical indication of the degree to which the facility is being used, particularly by targeted groups within the catchment area. Under this heading we may identify such indicators as the participation rate, and the ratio between a facility's users and the local authority population.

## Programming

Programme indicators are concerned with the wider aspects of a facility's social objectives. This involves continued monitoring of the range of activities and courses on offer, the number of activities available for target groups and the new initiatives used to promote wider use of facilities.

Although these performance measures are not all ratios in the accounting sense, it is clear that they are of great importance if public-sector suppliers, not just of leisure and recreation facilities, are to adjust to the current political climate which places great emphasis on value for money and resource (mis)allocation. As we shall see in Chapter 8, the last 15 years have seen a significant change with respect to the provision of many public services, including the seemingly sacred National Health Service. Since 1988, recreation departments in all local authorities have been preparing for and carrying out a process known as compulsory competitive tendering. This has meant the possibility that private firms can take over the operating of facilities previously run by workers directly employed by the local authority itself. Although local authorities have retained control over such variables as entry prices and opening hours, there is now an even greater need for as much information as possible to be generated with respect to the relationship between the inputs and outputs of their facilities. Some of the reasons why recent governments have tried to expose local authorities to the forces of the market will be explored in the following chapter.

## QUESTIONS FOR DISCUSSION

1   To what extent can a professional sports club (or team) be likened to a commercial business organisation?

2   How would you measure the performance of a public-sector leisure facility?

# Chapter 8

# Privatisation and the leisure industry

## INTRODUCTION

Much of the discussion contained in the first seven chapters of this book has been from a microeconomics perspective, identifying how economics can provide an insight into the actions of consumers of sport and leisure and the suppliers of the goods and services they use. The broad aim of this chapter is to focus upon leisure activity within its wider macroeconomic setting. It will be seen that in common with all individual sectors of the economy, sport and leisure is not only susceptible to the effects of general changes in government policy, such as variations in public expenditure, but also to change in the international economy, such as the general downturn in economic activity which has had such significant ramifications for many Western countries.

It would not be unreasonable to argue that one of the most significant factors to affect public-sector sport and leisure has been the change in government philosophy which has seen it attempt to inject market forces into the public sector via a process known as compulsory competitive tendering. Although current evidence suggests that this exercise has not led to a significant number of private-sector companies taking over the everyday management of local authority leisure facilities, this initiative has stimulated most councils to take an extremely detailed look at the economic characteristics of the facilities they run.

The aim of this chapter is to take a long-term view of the changes in macroeconomic variables which prompted the government to take the approach it has. Two themes will be identified in particular. First, the reason why the control of inflation has superseded the maintenance of a low rate of unemployment as the primary macroeconomic objective of UK governments over the last decade and a half. Second, the analysis will highlight what will be shown as a directly related change in policy:

the desire of recent Conservative governments to reduce government spending and to increase the role of market forces in the activities of nationalised industries, the welfare state and local authority services in general; in particular, leisure and recreation services are examined.

## MACROECONOMIC CHANGE AND LEISURE IN THE UK

### The inter-war and war years

The inter-war years were a period of economic hardship for Britain. This prompted the government to recognise that it had a more significant role (albeit limited, by today's standards) to play in the management of the economy than it had before the First World War. Economic difficulties had emerged from a combination of factors which included an ageing technological base, an over-valued pound and increased international competition. Britain's problems were compounded by the Wall Street Crash in the US (1929), which led the Americans and subsequently the rest of the industrialised world into an era of trade protection. Thus, the average rate of unemployment during the 1920s was 10.6 per cent, while that in the 1930s was even higher, with an average rate of 16.1 per cent. However, this unemployment was not evenly spread across regions or sectors. At its peak (1931–2), 34.5 per cent of coalminers, 36.3 per cent of pottery workers, 43.2 per cent of cotton operatives, 43.8 per cent of pig-iron workers, 47.9 per cent of steelworkers and 62 per cent of shipbuilders were out of work (Hobsbawm, 1978, p. 209). Oases of prosperity did emerge in areas such as the Midlands and South-East which were attracting the newer industries, for example cars, consumer durables and chemicals. As these industries grew during the 1930s, so did the demand for housing and, of course, the demand for associated consumer durables and non-essential goods. For example, increasing real incomes gave more families access to transport and therefore the opportunity to expand their consumption of leisure activities.

In contrast to opinion at the outset of the First World War, it was clear to most people that the government should take responsibility for the general allocation of resources and the regulation of markets from the very outbreak of hostilities. Thus controls were imposed throughout the economy, encompassing domestic production and international trade. However, the problem which faced all governments after the Second World War was how to manage the transition from the restrictions of a wartime economy to the needs of a modern peacetime economy. Politicians were well aware that the period after 1918 was associated with economic dislocation, inflation and, ultimately, high unemployment. On both sides of the political divide there was a determination that history should not repeat itself. The wartime coalition government had committed itself to maintaining a high and stable level of employment and this was embraced by the incoming Attlee Labour government of 1945 as its primary economic objective.

## The immediate post-war years

The approach to unemployment adopted by the incoming Labour government and subsequent post-war administrations was embodied in the work of John Maynard Keynes.[1] His work reflected a desire to provide an explanation for the long-term unemployment which had emerged during the inter-war years. It was particularly distinctive at that time since it argued that the remedy for high unemployment lay directly within the domain of government control. Prior to Keynes, economists had emphasised the self-correcting attributes of the market (see Chapter 2). Thus, any unemployment arising from a downswing in economic activity would be corrected through the downward adjustment of wages. This would be accompanied by a fall in interest rates, ultimately promoting more investment. Eventually, employment would increase, new incomes would be generated and the economy would, as a consequence, expand. However, as we have already seen, evidence suggests that markets were not self-correcting. In contrast, Keynes argued that a general reduction in wages would lower consumption and be detrimental to economic activity. He proposed therefore that if there was a shortfall in aggregate demand which was creating unemployment, there should be government intervention to correct the market failure, for example an expansionary package of public spending. Via a *multiplier effect*, the injection of spending would not only create incomes for workers directly employed by the spending programme (for example road construction), but also generate extra incomes as the demand for goods and services increased. This would have a knock-on effect through the economy, with the rate of income generation being smaller at each stage. The immediate post-war period brought forth a series of governments which were prepared to adopt Keynesian policies in their attempt to fulfil the primary objective of low unemployment.[2]

Concerns about unemployment ran alongside a need to correct Britain's trade imbalance. Policies were geared towards holding down imports and promoting exports. National production targeted export markets at the expense of domestic consumers. This objective precipitated a major devaluation of sterling relative to the dollar in 1949 in order to correct what was seen as an overvalued pound.[3] Unlike today, inflation was not seen as an immediate problem for policy-makers. This reflected fear of a post-war depression and an acceptance that a degree of inflation was inevitable during a period of shortages. In this respect, the bank rate was held at its pre-war level of 2 per cent in order to promote post-war investment. The need to promote economic growth was viewed as being self-evident, given the run-down state which characterised the post-war British economy.

The immediate post-war era also saw the introduction of a major programme of welfare policies (encompassing health, education and social security), together with the nationalisation of certain strategic industries (for example, the railways, gas and coal). Indeed, these initiatives had had significant electoral appeal in 1945, and were able to counteract the significant charisma of the Conservative wartime leader Winston Churchill. State intervention did not simply extend to the immediate need to establish policies capable of getting the economy moving again. Policies were also forward-looking. It was recognised that leisure and recreation were going to play an ever-increasing role in post-war life. Intervention in this sector therefore also increased via the creation of the Arts Council (1947) and the National Parks Commission (1949).[4]

With the benefit of hindsight, it may be argued that the period of reconstruction went extremely smoothly. In 1951 the Conservative Party was re-elected, perhaps reflecting the desire of the electorate to shed some of the restrictions of post-war austerity, even if it did imply greater social inequality. They remained in power for a further 13 years, a period in which the British public 'had never had it so good'. Nevertheless, although the Conservative Party was ideologically committed to private ownership and the advantages of the free market, it only introduced limited denationalisation during 1951–64 (and indeed in its 1970–4 administration). Furthermore, there were no major changes to the welfare state. Consensus between the two major parties on the need to promote full employment continued. Throughout the 1950s, and indeed during the 1960s, the British economy settled into a pattern of activity which is frequently referred to as *stop–go*. This problem reflected a long-standing inability of the British economy to respond quickly to any extra demand for its goods and services. It was this problem, together with the UK's commitment to a system of fixed exchange rates, which effectively forced governments into a trade-off situation.

*Stop–go*

The stop–go cycle would begin when the government saw a need to stimulate the economy in order to counter an increase in unemployment. This led to a Keynesian response, in the form of expansionary fiscal policy. The fact that Britain was part of an expanding international economy which provided an incentive for private investment to take place meant that the government did not actually need to accumulate a large public sector borrowing requirement (PSBR).[5] However, the subsequent expansion in aggregate demand was reflected in a balance of payments deficit on current account. In other words, the increase in domestic demand was met by additional imports of raw materials and finished goods. This was not only detrimental to Britain's balance of payments, but also created pressure on its commitment to maintain a fixed exchange rate.[6] The overriding desire not to devalue the pound, despite mounting speculative pressure upon sterling, forced governments to sacrifice the full-employment objective temporarily.[7] This led to a reversal of the government's expansionary fiscal policy, together with a tightening of monetary policy (through an increase in interest rates and the introduction of a restrictive credit policy). The latter was to reduce the external pressures on the economy. The overall effect of this reversal of policy was to reduce international pressures on the economy but to generate increases in the level of domestic unemployment. Eventually the level of unemployment would rise to a politically unacceptable level and the authorities would again respond by relaxing their fiscal stance and reversing monetary policy (by reducing interest rates and loosening credit restrictions) and the whole process would start all over again.[8] During this period, average levels of unemployment were significantly lower than the 5 per cent envisaged in the original Beveridge Report, ranging between 1.2 per cent and 2.3 per cent during the 1950s. Furthermore, the rate of inflation remained low and reasonably stable, averaging 3 per cent (ignoring the 9 per cent inflation which the Korean War boom had injected into the economy in 1951 and 1952). On the negative side, however, cycles of four to five years' duration characterised the British economy, and Britain's rate of economic growth was poor when compared with those of its international competitors. For example, the average rate of growth for the UK during 1955–60 was 2.8 per cent per annum (high by today's standards) compared to 6.3 per cent in West Germany, 4.6 per cent in France and 9.7 per cent in Japan.

The success of Keynesian policies in maintaining high employment levels gave many young people the means to finance their own leisure activities, however 'distasteful' to their elders.[9] The Wolfenden Report *Sport and the Community* (1960) focused in part upon 'the gap', namely the reduction in sports participation by young people after they leave school.[10] The Report emphasised not only the private and social benefits which sport can generate (see Chapter 4), but also proposed that a Sports Development Council should be established to provide a direct link between the Treasury and sport. The Conservative government responded to this recommendation by appointing Lord Hailsham as the first Minister for Sport in 1963. However, it was the new Labour administration, under the leadership of Harold Wilson, which initially established the Sports Council (1965) to act as an advisory body to provide guidance to the government on issues relating to physical sport and recreation and to define expenditure priorities. A network of nine Regional Sports Councils were also established to identify and co-ordinate developments at a local level. The Sports Council was granted executive status by Royal Charter in 1972.

Policy-making in the 1960s was dominated by balance of payments difficulties and attempts to maintain the fixed value of sterling. The first half of the decade also brought forth attempts by the subsequently outgoing Conservative administration and the incoming Labour government to break the pattern of stop–go and inject growth into the economy. Thus, in 1962 the National Economic Development Council (NEDC) brought together both sides of industry with key government ministers in an attempt to make long-term plans and forecasts which were expected to result in a higher rate of economic growth. However, because the NEDC was not a government department and because there was general suspicion of 'planning' in government and industry, its recommendations were not heeded. The incoming Labour government therefore gave the planning process a governmental outlet, through the newly created Department of Economic Affairs (1964). Although the resulting plans were now incorporated into government policy, the deflationary measures of July 1966, which were prompted by yet another sterling crisis, effectively killed off the (rather optimistic) National Plan and, with it, any chance of breaking the stop–go pattern. Ultimately, the government was forced into a 15 per cent devaluation of sterling in November 1967, a move which initiated a temporary relief from balance of payments difficulties after 1969.

Despite international problems which faced the British economy at this time, the Wilson government was responsible for publishing two important leisure-related White Papers. Both aimed to promote greater equality of opportunity with respect to the consumption of leisure. *A Policy for the Arts: The First Steps* (Department of the Environment, 1965) reflected a desire to facilitate a shift in emphasis away from London so that the arts were more widely available in the provinces. Similarly, the White Paper *Leisure in the Countryside* (Department of the Environment, 1968) saw the Countryside Commission replace the National Parks Commission and this provided a framework for resources to be made available in countryside which lay outside the boundaries of the traditional National Parks. With more countryside areas able to attract funding, the socio-economic profile of visitors could be broadened.

## The breakdown of the Keynesian consensus

Although the need to control inflation had been acknowledged by governments throughout the post-war period, it wasn't until the late 1960s when the inflation began to accelerate noticeably. Indeed in an era when an inverse relationship was perceived to exist between inflation and unemployment, creeping inflation was seen to be a small price to pay for the benefits of full employment.[11] However, attempts by the Labour government to control this increase emerged explicitly with a series of prices and incomes policies (in both voluntary and compulsory forms) in an attempt to place a lid on inflationary pressures from increases in labour costs. Although this approach was discarded by the incoming Conservative government in 1970, a prices and incomes policy was soon reintroduced in the face of continued inflationary pressure. This option seemed more politically viable than the adoption of a series of deflationary policies. Indeed, with unemployment approaching one million, the government felt the need to initiate an expansionary economic policy.[12] However, when trade unions and industry were unable to agree on a further voluntary policy in 1972, a compulsory prices and incomes policy was introduced. This policy was ultimately defeated by the strength of the National Union of Mineworkers and ultimately led to the re-election of a Labour government in 1974. Despite high and rising inflation, the Labour government did little to control wage inflation through the use of incomes policies during their first year of office. This reflected their disinclination to act in a way which would be detrimental to their relationship with the trade unions (which had soured somewhat in the late 1960s). Although the unions argued that such policies were against the spirit of free collective bargaining, a voluntary policy was agreed in mid 1975. Although there were subsequent renewals of the voluntary incomes policy (albeit in slightly different forms), the government was unable to secure union agreeement to an extension of the policy in 1978. This was despite the fact that the policies seemed to be exerting their desired effect.

The 1970s was a particularly important decade, not only with respect to the economic difficulties which the UK was facing but also the change which was taking place within the major political parties. Indeed, many of the factors which have prompted the changes we now see in the present-day leisure and recreation sectors have their origins during this period. It was a decade when much of the Keynesian orthodoxy, with its emphasis upon fine-tuning the economy to counteract variations in the economic cycle, was replaced by a new longer-term framework based upon monetarist concerns about inflation. According to monetarists, increases in prices are related to fluctuations in the money supply, a relationship embodied in the *Quantity Theory of Money*. Put simply, the theory states that if the money supply increases, so will prices, though the degree to which this will occur will depend upon the spending habits of economic agents operating in the economy and the degree to which the economy is operating at full employment levels. Monetarists see the control of the money supply and hence the control of inflation as the primary route to promoting economic stability and ultimately to reducing unemployment. From the statistical evidence which was available, Keynesian policies had failed to provide a remedy for the stagflation (the simultaneous increase of unemployment and inflation) which had emerged by the early 1970s and therefore were falling into disrepute. Furthermore, according to Heald (1983), this change in emphasis which was to characterise government policy from the mid 1970s reflected a change in attitudes towards unemployment and inflation. He notes that 'whereas memories of mass unemployment had faded, experience of inflation was immediate, resulting in a major upwards readjustment in the levels of unemployment which were perceived to be politically and socially tolerable' (Heald, 1983, p. 33). He also suggests that we should not discount the role of Milton Friedman as a respected academic researcher who 'established the intellectual prestige of monetarism and stimulated other work within its theoretical framework' (p. 33).

The inflationary pressures of the 1970s also prompted concern over the growth of the public sector. At that time, public expenditure had been planned in 'volume terms', in other words on a programme-by-programme basis. Thus, in periods of high inflation government departments were committing themselves to ever-increasing levels of expenditure. Concern that the expansion of the public sector was actually detrimental to private-sector activity and therefore detracting from Britain's ability to compete abroad, manifested itself in contributions to what is known as the *crowding out* literature.

There are two basic forms of crowding out. Physical crowding out is said to take place when economic activities undertaken by the public sector pre-empt resources which would have been used by the private sector. In other words, because many services provided by the public sector are not bought and sold in the market place, they have to be financed from taxation levied from the market sector, for example taxes on income and profits. The proponents of this idea, Bacon and Eltis (1976), took evidence from the 1960s through to the early 1970s, a period characterised by rising public spending, a series of balance of payments crises and declining private-sector investment. Although subsequent empirical research casts doubt upon the validity of Bacon and Eltis's work, their hypothesis generated widespread interest, particularly after it was set out in a series of articles in a leading Sunday newspaper.

The second category of crowding out, known as financial or indirect, predates the work of Bacon and Eltis and was developed by leading monetarist writers Brunner and Meltzer during the early 1970s. It is best explained by considering the following chain of events. Assume that a government wishes to raise public expenditure. It can follow one or a combination of two basic strategies. It could increase the supply of money. However, as we shall see shortly, the effect of this will be to increase prices, make manufactured goods and services less competitive abroad and therefore have a detrimental effect on the balance of payments. Furthermore if this inflation is unanticipated, a misallocation of resources may result as economic agents misinterpret market signals.

In addition, the government may choose to increase its level of borrowing. This means that extra securities will be issued by the government for the individuals and institutions who lend money to the government. However, the main problem the government then faces is that there will be a limit to the number of securities that the public wish to hold. Thus, if new government securities are to be attractive to investors, interest rates must rise in order to provide better rates of return on securities. If interest rates increase then two problems may arise. First, interest-sensitive expenditure will be curtailed. This will not only have an adverse effect upon consumer spending, particularly in the case of houses and other consumer durables, but also on business investment decisions. Further problems will arise if the higher interest rates prove attractive to foreign investors, thereby pushing up exchange rates as the demand for sterling increases relative to other currencies.[13] This will make it harder for firms to sell their products abroad and damage firms operating in import-sensitive industries (since imports will be relatively cheaper to buy). The effects may be therefore undesirable with respect to investment and employment.

It is perhaps no surprise that the relationship between the PSBR, money supply and the rate of interest has been referred to as the 'Bermuda triangle of economics' (Robinson, 1986, p. 42). Indeed, as we will see, acceptance of a three-cornered relationship between these three key macroeconomic variables provided part of the rationale for the policies adopted by the incoming 1979 Conservative government.

## From 1979 to the present day

It would not be considered extreme to refer to the election of Margaret Thatcher's Conservative government in 1979 as a significant turning point in the management of the British economy, though some of the seeds were sown during the period of James Callaghan's premiership in the mid 1970s. The increased emphasis given to the relationship between inflation, the money supply and public spending emerged in the government's *medium-term financial strategy*. Other developments can be directly attributed to the Conservative Party's philosophy of promoting economic recovery through the unleashing of previously suppressed market forces upon the economy, known as its *supply side strategy*. This embraced not only a programme of reduced government intervention in the economy but also a set of measures to promote greater incentives within labour markets (such as reduced levels of taxation); to restrict the monopoly power of trade unions; to 'privatise' nationalised industries through the much publicised share flotations (such as British Gas); to de-regulate the transport industry; to introduce competition into the education sector (allowing schools to opt out of the state sector and prompting the recent introduction of 'performance league tables'); to create an internal market for the delivery of health care; and to require local authorities to allow private sector firms to bid for contracts to undertake services previously provided by the council's own departments (such as refuse collection). From the point of view of readers interested in the provision of sport and recreation, it is the latter aspect of Conservative philosophy which is perhaps the most pertinent.

As we have already seen, the provision of sport and recreation is one which has been identified as an important area of market failure. Not only may a market system lead to certain socially desirable facilities being undersupplied, with respect to the perceived 'needs' of population groups (these 'needs' being perceived by others), but where supplied, facilities may be 'over-priced' in terms of the ability to pay of the more disadvantaged groups in society. However, in the 1988 Local Government (Miscellaneous Provisions) Act, local authorities were legally required to put out all their leisure services to competitive tendering by private companies. It was also during the early 1980s that the Sports Council adopted a different approach towards correcting market failure affecting sport and recreation provision in the UK. As we have already seen, in the 1970s the perceived remedy to this problem was supply-led. By the 1980s, it had been recognised that this approach had not always achieved the desired outcomes, with sections of the population continuing to be minor users of public facilities despite their increased accessibility and subsidised prices. Thus, from 1983, the emphasis changed somewhat with the continued growth in public facilities being complemented with a policy to target certain groups within the population. The implications of government attempts to increase market awareness within the leisure sector, in particular with respect to targeting leisure provision to certain socio-economic groups, will be considered shortly.

## The government's medium-term financial strategy

If a government is to manage the rate of growth of the money supply to control inflation, then it must actually be able to define what the money supply is. Although this may seem relatively easy, there exists a whole range of definitions which fall under two main headings: narrow money and broad money. Narrow money definitions to varying degrees use a fairly strict concept of what the money supply is, and include such things as notes and coins in circulation and easily accessed bank deposits. In contrast, broad money definitions reflect potential spending power and include bank deposits which are bound by longer time constraints (these frequently require prior notice of a decision to make a withdrawal) and other types of financial asset, for example holdings of government securities, which can be converted into cash some time in the future.

It was one of the broad money definitions, known as sterling M3 (£M3), which formed the basis of the Conservative government's initial inflation control strategy, since it was seen to provide the 'best' indication of the money supply for policy purposes. Interest rates were increased to reduce the demand for money, thereby requiring a smaller money supply. Indeed, within a few months of coming into office, the minimum lending rate had risen from 12 per cent to 17 per cent. Projections were made for the money supply (as target bands) and the public sector borrowing requirement (PSBR) for a four-year period, from 1980–1 to 1983–4.[14] Over the period, the rate of growth of £M3 was set to fall from a 7–11 per cent band to a 4–8 per cent band. Similarly, the PSBR was set to fall from 3.75 per cent of gross domestic product (GDP) to 1.5 per cent of GDP between 1980–1 and 1983–4.[15] This implied a real reduction in government spending. Unlike the money supply figures, however, the estimates for the PSBR were not hard-and-fast targets since it was recognised that government spending is sensitive to variations in the economic cycle. For example, an increase in unemployment will lead to increased spending on welfare benefits. In the light of economic performance, these targets were modified on an annual basis, maintaining the four-year time horizon.

It soon became clear that the government was having little success targeting its favoured £M3 money supply measure. Indeed, in 1980–1, the projected rate of growth was to fall to between 7 per cent and 11 per cent, yet the actual rate of growth of £M3 was 19.4 per cent. Furthermore PSBR, as a percentage of GDP was 5.6 per cent, as opposed to the projected value of 3.75 per cent. This pattern continued in subsequent years, with £M3 growth and the PSBR exceeding their respective targets. Indeed, by 1982 the government were using three money supply definitions: £M3, plus PSL2 (a very 'broad' definition)[16] and M1 (narrow). The narrow money definition, M1, was subsequently replaced in 1983 by an even 'narrower' definition of money, M0 and this actually performed well with respect to the government's projections. The fact that money supply definitions were being added and discarded during this period tended to detract from the straight-forward message of the medium-term financial strategy. Neverthless, the failure of all but one of the definitions to fall into their prescribed ranges consistently should not obscure the fact that the money supply (whatever definition is adopted) was actually falling, even though respective levels remained above expectation. Indeed, when compared with the rest of Europe at that time, the percentage growth in the money supply was similar to that of France and Italy, though twice as high as West Germany, the country with the lowest rate of inflation.

A similar pattern had emerged with respect to the PSBR. Between 1980 and 1984, the rate of inflation had fallen from 18 per cent to below 5 per cent, suggesting that the government's tight monetary stance had been a success. However, this was also a period of recession, not only in the UK but also worldwide. Britain's ability to ride this international recession was not helped by the high interest rates which had been imposed and the upward pressure North Sea oil imposed on the international value of sterling. Since the government did not try to counter this latter effect, it became increasingly difficult for Britain's exporters to sell their goods abroad. With unemployment rising rapidly, eventually to peak at over three million in 1986, wage negotiations were more subdued, thereby containing any inflationary pressure. Nevertheless, the apparent success of the policy meant that money supply targets were pursued less vigorously. In 1986, £M3 was dropped as a measure of the money supply due to its persistent overshooting, with emphasis given to M0, the government's then preferred narrow money definition and ultimately superseded by a new broad money supply definition, M4.

By the mid 1980s, the government was showing increasing interest in sterling's value on the foreign exchange market. Indeed during 1985–8, when the targeting of the money supply became increasingly less important to the government, the UK money supply grew more rapidly than that of its European neighbours. This change in approach was partly a recognition that sterling's relationship with other currencies, particularly the Deutschmark (DM), had a major influence upon inflation rates at home. By 'shadowing' the Deutschmark, rather than allowing sterling to lose value against it, inflationary pressures would be suppressed (imports would become relatively cheaper). This required a rise in domestic interest rates, which would itself help to bring down the money supply and hence inflation. Such draconian measures would have the effect of imposing discipline on government and industry since the granting of inflationary pay awards would not be compensated for by a reduction in the international exchange value of sterling. With North Sea oil adding to the strength of the pound, interest rates were reduced to prevent speculative pressure from pushing the pound beyond 3DM, the politically sensitive level.

This policy of lower interest rates, when inflationary pressures existed in the economy, together with post-election income tax cuts in 1987, meant that the late 1980s were associated with a major economic upturn. The rise in inflation which followed forced the government to raise interest rates again. Between May 1988 and October 1989, they had doubled from 7.5 per cent to 15 per cent. These rises prompted an appreciation in the value of sterling from around 3DM at the end of 1987 to 3.25DM by the beginning of 1989. This again led to difficulties for British industry, both in terms of investment levels and its ability to compete abroad. By 1990, the pressure from Britain's EC partners to join the Exchange Rate Mechanism (ERM) was having its desired effect and in October of that year, the UK entered at a fixed (± 6 per cent) rate of 2.96DM to the pound. Although high interest rates subsequently led to a reduction in inflation, unemployment rose again as Britain plunged into yet another depression. This in part was due to the government's tight policies but also the emergence of a general worldwide economic downturn. The depth of the depression eventually forced the Chancellor's hand. Britain eventually left the ERM in September 1992 and, in an attempt to 'kick-start' the economy, interest rates were lowered significantly, and sterling was allowed to drop considerably in value. However, this has not yet had the desired results with respect to economic recovery. Although inflation dropped to the historically low level of 1.5 per cent during the latter half of 1993, unemployment has continued to show no signs of falling. At the time of writing the UK, like its European competitors, remains in recession with no immediate prospects for recovery.

## EMPLOYMENT IN THE LEISURE SECTOR SINCE 1979

Four terms of Conservative government have brought about significant change in the way people perceive the role of the state both at national and local levels. The control of inflation has superseded the maintenance of high employment as the primary macroeconomic objective and, as we shall see below, increased emphasis has been given to the need to promote efficiency on the supply side of the economy. Although the number of jobs in all industries has fallen from 22,638,000 in 1979 to 21,217,000 in 1992 (*Employment Gazette*, various years), service employment has risen by almost 15 per cent, from 13,260,000 to 15,238,000. Furthermore, employment in leisure-related activities has grown even more rapidly than this average for the service sector as a whole. This is illustrated in table 8.1. It can be seen that all but one of the five identified categories of leisure-related services have experienced increases in employment beyond that of the general service sector. However, it should be recognised that leisure employment within the service sector only represents 7 per cent of total employment in the UK and that expectations of this sector being a significant employment growth area should not be overstated. In terms of attempts to promote greater efficiency with respect to the supply side of the economy, the introduction of compulsory competitive tendering (CCT) for public-sector leisure services is already having an effect at the interface

*Table 8.1* Employment in selected leisure services ('000s)

| Service | 1979* | 1984* | 1988* | 1992* | Increase (%) |
|---|---|---|---|---|---|
| Restaurants, cafés and snackbars | 186 | 213 | 240 | 296 | 59.1 |
| Public houses and bars | 245 | 252 | 263 | 318 | 29.7 |
| Nightclubs and other licensed clubs | 119 | 138 | 137 | 142 | 19.3 |
| Hotel and other short-stay accommodation | 282 | 266 | 265 | 320 | 13.4 |
| Sport and other recreation activities | 332 | 334 | 375 | 408 | 22.8 |
| Total | 1164 | 1203 | 1280 | 1484 | 27.5 |

*Source*: *Employment Gazette* (various)
*Note*: * Figures relate to June of each year.

between the principle of Sport for All and the quest for greater economic efficiency. It is to these issues that we shall now turn.

## The government's supply-side strategy

As we have already noted, the incoming 1979 Conservative government's commitment to the reduction of inflation was complemented by a series of supply-side measures intended to promote market efficiency. These policies have embraced all sides of the economy: the labour market, the capital market and the goods market. In the case of the labour market the Conservatives have attempted to improve incentives by reducing the real value of welfare benefits and marginal rates of taxation; in the latter case, real increases in basic personal allowances, together with reductions in basic and higher-rate income tax and the creation of a new lower tax band. However, increases in indirect taxation, for example the introduction of VAT on fuel bills, have cast a shadow over the straightforward message that the Conservatives have been articulating: that they are the party of low taxation. In the case of industrial relations, the power of trade unions has been curbed, for example through the abolition of secondary picketing and measures to reduce the ability of unions to enforce closed shops. The well documented 'set-piece' battle between the government and miners in 1983–4 also provided confirmation to the private sector of the government's intentions. In the case of the capital markets, one of the major changes to take place was the decision in 1986 to allow building societies to compete directly with banks.[17] It is the changes which have taken place within goods markets which are of most concern to us here. In particular, government attempts to promote greater competition for the provision of public-sector goods and services has had direct effects on the supply of sport and leisure within all local economies.

The term 'privatisation' is a popular expression used to describe the attempts by post-1979 Conservative goverments to reduce state intervention and to increase competition within the economy. As most readers will be aware, this process has taken a number of different forms. However, it is beyond the scope of this book to look at each in detail. Thus, our analysis will be confined to a brief consideration of the most notable changes from the point of view of the economy as a whole, together with a more detailed examination of the implications of the 'privatisation' process for sport and leisure.

There have been two major changes which have really captured the public's imagination. First, the transfer of some public assets to the private sector. This has been most evident in the growth of 'popular capitalism' where the general public have been given the opportunity to purchase shares in a variety of nationalised industries. For example, when 51 per cent of shares in British Telecom were sold in December 1984, 2.25 million applicants were allocated shares. Other major flotations have included British Gas (1986), British Airways (1987), the regional water authorities (1989) and the electricity supply industry (1990). The promotion of 'popular capitalism' has also been seen through the government's commitment to extend home-ownership as far down the income scale as possible through promoting tenants' 'right to buy' their council houses.

Second, we may also identify attempts to introduce competitive forces into the welfare state, most notably within the National Health Service. The most radical changes to the organisation of health provision in the UK were outlined in the White Paper *Working for Patients* (Department of Health 1989)[18] and formalised in the National Health Service and Community Care Act (1990). Under the new system, a clear distinction is made between purchasers of health care and providers of health care. For example, a hospital (provider) may apply for what is known as 'trust status', which means that it is responsible for its own management, rather than being managed by a District Health Authority. Similarly, general practitioners with more than 9,000 patients can apply for 'fundholder status'. This means that they receive a cash allocation with which they can purchase a specified range of hospital services on behalf of their patients. This therefore allows patients (via their GP) to 'shop-around', thereby forcing the providers of health care to be more responsive to consumer demand. Through such incentives, resource use within the National Health Service will be more efficient. However, this had not been the first attempt by the government to encourage more competition in the National Health Service. Soon after coming into office in 1979, the Conservative government put pressure upon health authorities to use private contractors to undertake such services as cleaning and laundry. This process, known as compulsory competitive tendering, became mandatory for such ancillary services in 1983.

Except for buildings, highways and maintenance (covered by the 1980 Local Government Planning and Land Act), the government was initially sensitive about imposing their preferences upon local authorities with respect to putting work out to tender. It had been hoped that savings made by councils which voluntarily engaged in the exercise (such as Southend-on-Sea, which, by contracting out its refuse and cleaning services, generated savings of £490,000 per annum) would encourage other local authorities to follow suit. However, by early 1985 only 41 out of 456 English and Welsh councils had contracted out any of their main services. Thus, in 1985 the government began to press the issue by bringing forward legislation to force public bodies to put a number of their services out to competition. The provisions of the 1980 Act were therefore extended to such things as waste disposal, cleaning and transport, together with sport and leisure management, through the 1988 Local Government Act. The Department of the Environment were to ensure that the tendering process was not carried out unfairly.

With respect to sport and leisure, government proposals would cover a whole range of services including sports centres, swimming and leisure pools, cycle tracks, artificial and natural ski slopes, skating rinks, golf courses, putting greens, tennis courts, playing pitches, athletics tracks and bowling facilities. The tendering process would embrace all the key management activities, including taking bookings and user-fees (and providing appropriate accounts); supervision and instruction; catering; cleaning and maintenance; equipment hire; heating and lighting; employment and training of staff. Thus, it might be argued that it is through compulsory competitive tendering (CCT) that government policy will have the most explicit impact upon the way in which sport and leisure is delivered in the local community. Thus, the next stage of the analysis will consider in more depth the rationale behind CCT, initially as an economic process and later in terms of its implications for the provision of sport and leisure in the local community.

## COMPULSORY COMPETITIVE TENDERING

One of the main concerns of the incoming 1979 Conservative administration was their belief that local authorities and public organisations such as the National Health Service are highly inefficient in the provision of their services. In this respect, their election manifesto contained such terms as 'waste', 'bureaucracy' and 'over-government'. Although central and local government have a long history of purchasing goods and services from private-sector companies, there is less of a tradition with respect to the supply of goods and services. This latter function has been the preserve of the public organisation's own directly employed labour. Broadly speaking, compulsory competitive tendering gives private-sector companies the opportunity to bid (tender) for the opportunity to supply services previously provided 'in-house' by a public organisation's own directly employed labour, referred to as 'direct service organisations' (DSOs). The DSO may also bid for the contract which, if successful, still requires a clear distinction to be made between the contractor (the service provider) and the client (the public-sector organisation). The key arguments for and against the introduction of CCT are set out below.[19]

### Advantages

1   CCT creates a contestable market situation which encourages suppliers to reduce costs and improve efficiency. In the case of a DSO winning the contract, the exercise may lead to the reform of inappropriate working practices leading to economies in the use of labour and capital.
2   CCT enables the local authority to establish an appropriate set of standards for a given service and control it through penalty clauses and performance bonds. This necessitates the development of a wider statistical base with which to monitor the effectiveness of the contractor, whether an in-house or an outside supplier, than had been in place previously.
3   CCT focuses attention towards the measurement of outputs rather than inputs. In the past, attention tended to focus upon such indicators as the amount invested rather than the quality and

quantity achieved for each pound spent.

4   Suppliers provide services for more than one local authority, thereby allowing them to benefit from economies of scale and specialisation. Previously, the size of in-house suppliers was limited by political rather than economic considerations.

5   Monies are saved by government at local and national levels. In the former case, a given service is expected to cost less to provide, thereby freeing resources for other activities. Furthermore, private-sector contractors which experience increases in their profits will also pay more taxes; this will directly or indirectly benefit taxpayers in general.

## Disadvantages

1   Critics have identified instances where service quality has declined rather than improved. Furthermore, private contractors have defaulted for some reason or other, thereby leaving the council without the service in question. This problem may have arisen because of 'bounded rationality', a term used by economists to suggest that prospective outside contractors may not have been totally aware of the overall implications of their contractual obligations. This problem may diminish as contractors gain experience of putting in appropriate bids.

2   Private-sector contractors may submit low tenders in order to squeeze out the in-house bidder and then renegotiate from a strong position after the DSO is disbanded. This is an example of 'adverse selection', a situation which refers to the 'bad' driving out the 'good' from a particular market and hence can result in market failure. However, this problem can be partly countered within the specification of the basic contract.

3   The CCT process can lead to a deterioration in the payment of labour and in their general working conditions, particularly for the unskilled, as firms seek to promote cost savings. This can affect basic wage rates but has been found to be more likely to manifest itself in lower bonus payments and overtime rates. Added to this, there may be less employee protection (for example less generous sick pay), an increase in redundancies and greater use of casual labour to avoid the payment of National Insurance contributions.

4   Competitive tendering for public service contracts can lead to collusion or even corruption. Parker (1990) refers to the existence of a number of 'rigged' tenders in the road-building industry in

which suppliers have agreed to divide up the market rather than compete against each other.

5   Competitive tendering is not a costless activity. Additional expenditure will arise at all stages of the exercise, for example in specifying, negotiating and awarding contracts, together with the subsequent activities of monitoring contract compliance and re-contracting. Thus, the outcome must be that the 'transactions costs' from the new regime do not exceed those of the old one when changes in such variables as cost, efficiency and accountability are considered.

## Compulsory competitive tendering and the case of public leisure

Predictably, the initial decision to subject council leisure services to the rigours of CCT brought a variety of responses, such as these which appeared in *Leisure Management* (February 1988, p. 38):

I welcome moves by the goverment to test the efficiency of Council management in the leisure operations through competitive tendering – may the best man win!   (Michael Gutherie, Chairman, Mecca Leisure)

The government has no intention of privatising local authority-run sports and leisure facilities, but instead intends to find better ways to use the resources available.   (Colin Moynihan MP, then Minister of Sport)

If profit maximisation becomes the aim of those running the facilities, the likely outcome is that the general public will have to pay much bigger entry fees and maybe even annual membership fees as is already common for private sports centres.   (Councillor Howard Knight, Chair of the Association of Metropolitan Authorities Public Works Committee)

These comments reflect the full spectrum of anticipation and concern which prevailed at the time. The main issues were effectively threefold. First, the degree of private-sector interest which would emerge in the exercise; second, the level of savings which could be generated; and finally, whether the social objectives encompassed in Sport for All would be compromised.

Since Chapter 4, a recurring theme of this text has been the local authorities' response to the positive externalities which leisure activities can generate. Thus, in the case of sport and leisure centres, we would highlight such factors as improvements in health and reduced social deprivation. Thus, the emphasis of most councils has been to encourage participation, for example through price discrimination and the scheduling of special initiatives (such as special mother and toddler swimming sessions). It should be understood at the outset that regardless of which organisation ultimately wins a contract to manage a particular set of facilities (the DSO or a private contractor), the local authority retains control of key decisions which affect its social objectives. Again, in the case of leisure centres this includes when to open particular facilities, the prices it should charge for individual activities, the mix of activities on offer at each venue and the requirement for contractors to promote the facilities to certain socio-economic groups (though there is continued fear that policies which favour low prices and increased access will gradually be eroded). As well as managing the facility, successful contractors will be expected to promote the activities on offer at each location with reference to the council's stated policy requirements. Thus contractors will, on the basis of these constraints, place a tender according to the degree to which it thinks it can supply the appropriate service.

With respect to each council's wider policy objectives for its sport and leisure provision, the Audit Commission (1989, 1990) recommended the undertaking of a 'strategy review', not only in preparation for the first round of CCT, but at regular intervals of at most five years. The aim of this exercise is to 'examine participation, current and future needs and ways of meeting them' (Audit Commission, 1989, p. 19). The strategy review reflects the role economics is now expected to play in highlighting ways in which resources can be allocated to meet a particular community's needs. Many of the issues which the strategy review are intended to raise have already been considered in previous sections of this book, particularly those which relate to aspects of market failure, price discrimination, market structure and business objectives.

Within its strategy review, each local authority is expected to identify groups within a local population to be targeted within their sport and leisure policy. Consideration should not only be given to people who regularly use the authority's facilities but also individuals whose requirements are not specifically catered for at present (for example, there may be suppressed demand from disabled residents) and people who currently have little or no interest in participating in sport. This must be seen in terms of the degree to which sport and leisure facilities are accessible to a given population. Interest should not be restricted to each authority's own provision but to the facilities provided by the private, voluntary and public sectors inside and outside its political boundaries.

In addition, councils should also identify buildings and spaces which are not currently used for sport by the general public but have the potential, for example school and community halls. All such facilities should be monitored with reference to the opinion of actual or potential users (requiring surveys of established clubs and local householders) and its social objectives (see above).

It should of course be recognised that sport and leisure provision is just one service which local authorities provide. As we have already seen, not only has central government placed increased pressure on local government to spend more judiciously, but there are increased expectations from sections of the electorate, who have seen their contribution to local tax rise after the introduction of the (notorious) Community Charge and its replacement, the Council Tax. Thus, any changes in the level of expenditure on sport and leisure has to be seen in its wider context, particularly with respect to updating ageing stock, responding to demographic change and predicting activities of the future. Successful CCT exercises will release scarce resources for other activities. However, this must be viewed alongside the need to monitor each contractor's performance. By setting targets and establishing performance indicators of the kind considered in the previous chapter, councils will be able to assess how well the facilities for which they are ultimately responsible are meeting the needs of the local population. As we have already seen, there are a wide variety of indicators which can be devised to provide information at all levels of aggregation. Targets may therefore revolve around social objectives (for example target participation rates for different consumer groups), facility usage levels, facility accessibility (for example, the proportion of the population within easy reach of a swimming pool) and levels of subsidy. In the long term the strategy review will help to identify a programme of reinvestment, offering different mixes of activities and a means of devising more sophisticated methods of encouraging use by disadvantaged user-groups.

Since the social objectives of local councils override commercial considerations with respect to many leisure facilities, contracts have to be framed so as to ensure contractors can make a profit. Obviously, there is no point in making a bid to manage a particular facility if there is no likelihood of a financial return. One of the major costs of provision are debt charges, external building maintenance and major internal capital costs (for example, air conditioning). These usually remain the responsibility of local authorities. However, other day-to-day costs, such as employees' wages, heating, lighting and general internal maintenance, are assumed by the successful contractor. The Audit Commission (1990, pp. 35–41) lists four main types of financial arrangement which provide contractors with sufficient income to meet their costs and realise a profit.

*Franchises*

This is an option when facilities are profitable on a day-to-day basis (external costs are still met by the local authority), such as golf courses. Under this arrangement, the contractor pays a fee to the council (which may be a fixed sum or be related to profit earned) and retains any subsequent profit.[20] The Audit Commission reports that Romford ice rink is run on the basis that the operator pays a fixed sum to the local council each year, the council takes operating profit up to an agreed limit, with further profits shared out on a predetermined basis.

*Deficit guarantee*

Deficit guarantee schemes are used in situations where the facility in question does not make a profit. There are three variants of this arrangement. Under the most basic approach, the local authority pays a fixed sum to the contractor which, together with income from the facility, is used to meet costs and to provide a profit (if any). The tender for the contract is therefore in terms of the deficit guarantee required by the contractor. Thus, both parties need to be sure about the future income-generating prospects for the facility. If the contractor performs better than expected, then the council will find itself paying out too large a subsidy. Similarly, if the contractor over-estimates the future prospects of the facility, perhaps due to asymmetrical information, it will submit too low a tender and subsequently incur a loss. Whatever the outcome, the contractor has every incentive to promote usage, since it retains the income derived from the facility's operations. Thus, the council will have to be sure that the contractor is operating within the confines of the council's social obligations with respect to sport and leisure provision. Variations of this arrangement may exist if the local authority wishes to protect itself against windfall gains by the contractor. This may revolve around profit sharing or income sharing. However, this will reduce the incentive the contractor has to promote usage of the facility since some of the extra income will accrue to the local authority.

## Risk-sharing

Sometimes, a local authority and an outside commercial agency both make a significant investment in a site. Under a risk-sharing arrangement, both parties share out any income/profit or underwrite any losses incurred. Since the council is only responsible for some of any losses, the contractor has a strong incentive to avoid a deficit.

## 'Open book' management

Under this arrangement, the local authority pays the contractor a fixed fee which is retained regardless of the performance of the facility. The council retains all the income and has to meet all the losses. This type of agreement will be attractive to local authorities if the facility in question is making a profit. However, for loss-making facilities, the council is bearing all the risk and the contractor has no incentive to promote throughput since its fee is fixed.

## Effects of compulsory competitive tendering for leisure services

The timetable for the CCT exercise with respect to leisure and recreation facilities was such that 35 per cent of contracts had to be let by January 1991, 70 per cent by July 1992, with the remainder completed by January 1993, though a number of contracts had been tendered for prior to the main round of competitive tendering. However, with contracts due to run between four and seven years, we are unlikely to get a true picture of the effects of the exercise until the end of the decade. Nevertheless, a recent survey by CDC Research, reported by Jones (1993) in *Leisure Management*, suggests that the private sector has only achieved a market share of 16 per cent, winning only 54 contracts across the country. In other words, the impact of private-sector firms has not been as great as was anticipated. This may in part reflect the fact that the inclusion of leisure services in the 1988 Local Government Act was something of an afterthought.

The short notice implied by the timetable for the CCT exercise meant that private-sector firms were aware that the problem of bounded rationality was going to be significant and this acted as a deterrent. Furthermore, the transaction costs associated with submitting a tender may also have seemed prohibitive. For example, Jones reports the concern of David Bryant, Chair of Contemporary Leisure and ex-Director of Leisure Services for Westminster, who noted the excessive preliminary detail required by some local authorities such that bids had to include menus for canteens and staff rotas. However, Jones suggests that competition from the private sector was muted because many of the savings which could have been made (for example in terms of resource allocation) had already been made by councils and were therefore already included in the specifications of the contract. In other words, the opportunity for private firms to redistribute resources even more efficiently so as to make even more savings, and therefore profits, were therefore restricted.

The announcement that leisure services would be subjected to CCT prompted a whole plethora of literature concerned with the economic advantages and disadvantages of CCT and how the exercise would ultimately affect the provision of services. There is significantly less being written now. In the interim, we are mainly hearing about extremes of performance, either in terms of contractors which have failed to fulfil a contract, where inappropriate contract specifications have led to contradiction of a local authority's social objectives or where major savings have been made due to good quality management. A 1993 survey undertaken by Leisure Futures Limited for ILAM suggests that on average, the quality of service perceived by customers has deteriorated, albeit marginally. Specifically, where private-sector contractors had assumed the running of facilities, standards remained the same. Elsewhere – which we have already seen represents the majority of facilities – such variables as cleanliness and staff attitudes have been seen to deteriorate. Although the survey only encompassed 40 facilities, there is reason to be concerned that such perceptions may ultimately detract from consumers' desire to visit centres.

A target for much recent comment has been the performance of one private-sector firm, Crossland Leisure Enterprises. At the outset of the exercise, Crossland Leisure Enterprises were seen as one of the major players, managing a number of facilities via a profit-sharing deficit guarantee (see above). However, by October 1991, Crossland Leisure Enterprises had been liquidated with 11 contracts. The company had encountered a variety of difficulties which arose when costs and deficits turned out to be higher than expected. In the case of their contract to run The Playground ice rink and swimming pool complex for Basingstoke and Deane Borough Council, problems emerged after energy costs and business rates increased alongside a downturn in the demand for ice skating. Crossland's experience is likely to have put off private-sector companies from submitting tenders for facilities.

With CCT to be extended to local authority arts facility management, concerns have been prompted which are similar to those expressed about the increase in commercial sponsorship. Craig (1992) notes that:

> Whoever wins the contract will be driven to promote the safe, the bland and the popular, at the expense of innovative programming or appealing only to minorities. There would be a retreat from risk taking.

Craig also sees problems with respect to touring productions. The fact that commercial companies are driven by some notion of profit means that they are more likely to extract exacting contracts for these productions. Although this will save money for local authorities, it will increase the need for regional arts boards and the Arts Council to provide larger subsidies. In other words, there is a 'hidden transfer of subsidy' (Craig, 1992, p. 24).

The process of CCT with respect to leisure provision at sports centres has not been easy for many local authorities. However, the fine dividing line between creativity on the one hand and 'safety' on the other will prove to be a more significant test for CCT than the more 'easily' specified activities on offer at sports centres.

## QUESTIONS FOR DISCUSSION

1   To what extent are compulsory competitive tendering and 'Sport for All' incompatible?

2   What factors prompted the government to initiate its policy of 'privatisation' during the 1980s?

# Glossary of economics terms

Many first-time students of economics liken their initial exposure to economics as like learning a foreign language – there are so many new terms with which they must become familiar if the subject is to be understood. Many resort to a dictionary of economics when seeking a quick explanation of key terms while they are revising or producing essays. This glossary is not all-embracing but nevertheless provides brief definitions of over 100 expressions frequently used in this and other introductory economics textbooks. It is organised in alphabetical order, rather than in subject areas, and therefore readers should not expect to have encountered every term on the list until they have read the entire text.

**Affordable set:** A term sometimes used in consumer theory referring to the combination of goods and services which can be purchased with a given amount of income. Combinations that lie on the boundary of this set will completely exhaust this income whereas combinations within it will result in money left over.

**Aggregate demand:** The total demand for goods and services within an economy over a given period.

**Average total cost:** The total cost of producing a number of units of output divided by that number of units. Thus, if it costs £250 to produce 10 units of a commodity, then the average total cost is £25.

**Average revenue:** Total revenue (see below) divided by the total number of goods sold.

**Balance of payments:** A summary of a country's dealings with other countries with respect to imports and exports over a given period. If a country exports more than it imports, it is said to have a surplus balance of payments. When it imports more than it exports, a deficit balance of payments results.

**Behavioural theories of the firm:** A set of theories which reject the idea that firms wish (or are capable) of maximising any given variable, such as profit. The goals of the firm are seen to reflect compromises between the main groups which can exert control over a firm's activities: shareholders, managers, trade unions, etc.

**Capital intensive production:** A process which uses a high proportion of capital inputs relative to those of labour.

**Cardinal measurement:** Measurement when the difference between two figures is numerically significant (see **Ordinal measurement**).

**Cartel:** An agreement between a group of firms which results in them acting as a single seller, rather than as independent sellers. The classic example is the oil producer's cartel, OPEC.

*Ceteris paribus*: A Latin phrase which translates loosely as 'other things remaining equal'. It is often used when economists try to isolate the effects of all but one of the independent variables which can influence quantity demanded or supplied.

**Complements:** Complementary goods are usually consumed together, for example tennis rackets and tennis balls, personal stereos and audio cassettes, or cars and petrol. Thus, we would expect that, to varying degrees, the quantity demanded of one good will be inversely related to the price of its complement.

**Consumer surplus:** The difference between the amount a consumer (or group of consumers) is willing to pay for a commodity and the (lower) price they actually have to pay.

**Cross elasticity of demand:** A measure of the degree of responsiveness of the quantity demanded of one commodity to changes in the price of another. In the case of substitute commodities (see **Substitutes**), a cross elasticity calculation will produce a positive figure whereas for complements (see above), a negative figure will result.

**Crowding out:** Takes place when intervention in the economy by the state leads to a reduction in private-sector activity. Two basic forms of crowding out have been hypothesised. Physical crowding out arises when an expansion in state activity actually usurps resources from the private sector (see Bacon and Eltis, 1976). Financial crowding out occurs when an increase in government borrowing leads to an increase in interest rates and therefore adversely affects industries whose activities are particularly sensitive to changes in interest rates, for example the construction industry and firms who rely on export markets (higher interest rates lead to an appreciation of a country's international currency value and therefore makes exports more expensive in foreign markets).

**Demand:** The relationship between the amount of a commodity that consumers are willing and able to buy per unit of time and the price of that commodity.

**Demand curve:** The graphical relationship between the amount of a commodity consumers are willing and able to buy per unit of time and the price of that commodity, *ceteris paribus*. Price is measured along the vertical ($y$) axis of the graph and quantity demanded is measured along the horizontal ($x$) axis.

**Demand function:** An expression which identifies the relationship between quantity demanded and the variables which can affect it (such as price, income, etc.). Although this can be specified mathematically, introductory economics texts place more stress on identifying the key variables rather than their exact relationship.

**Dependent variable:** A variable whose value is determined by the value(s) taken by other variables. Thus, in the case of a demand function, 'quantity demanded' is the dependent variable whose value is determined by such variables as own price, income, taste, etc.

**Derived demand:** A term which refers to the fact that the demand for factors of production by firms, for example capital and labour, is derived from their desire to produce output rather than to hire labour/rent capital for its own sake. A similar case can be put forward for such commodities as petrol, a good which is not desired for its own intrinsic value but because of our desire to travel by car, bus, etc.

**Division of labour:** When a productive process is divided up into individual tasks which are undertaken by different workers. Through repetition, workers become 'expert' in their designated task, increasing output over and above what it would be if each worker had to master all the individual components of the productive process.

**Duopoly:** An industry which contains only two firms.

**Economic growth:** The increase in the total output of a nation over time. If output falls, economic growth is said to be negative.

**Economies of scale:** When an increase in the scale of production, with factor inputs increased in the same proportion, generates a reduction in the average unit cost of production. Economies of scale are a more specific version of economies of size (see below).

**Economies of size:** When an increase in the scale of production, regardless of the relative combination of factor inputs, generates a reduction in the average unit cost of production.

**Elasticity of demand:** see **Cross elasticity of demand**, **Income elasticity of demand** and **Price elasticity of demand**.

**Elasticity of supply:** see **Price elasticity of supply**.

**Engel curve:** The graphical relationship between the quantity demanded of a particular commodity and income. For normal goods (see below) this will slope upwards whereas for inferior goods (see below) it will slope downwards.

**Engel expenditure curve:** The graphical relationship between the amount spent on a particular group of commodities (e.g. food or leisure goods) and income. Assuming that normal goods (see below) are likely to outweigh inferior goods (see below) within most commodity groups, we should expect the Engel Expenditure Curve to slope upwards.

**Equilibrium:** A situation when opposing forces are in balance such that there is no tendency for change.

**Equilibrium price:** The price at which quantity demanded exactly equals quantity supplied.

**Equilibrium quantity:** The amount that is bought and sold at the equilibrium price.

**Exchange rate:** The amount of one currency which is needed to buy a unit of another foreign currency. If exchange rates are allowed to move freely in response to the interaction between supply and demand for the respective currencies, we say that the exchange rate is 'floating'. If, on the other hand, governments agree to maintain a given rate of exchange between currencies (or within a narrow range of values), the exchange rate is said to be 'fixed'.

**Externality situations:** These arise when the actions of one economic agent have a direct effect upon the welfare of others without them actually playing a role in the market mechanism. Externalities can be desirable or undesirable and apply to consumers or firms. Thus, a person choosing to be inoculated against influenza also reduces the chances of others catching it, even though they have not been involved in the original decision. An opposite case can be made for a person playing their radio too loud in public. Similar examples can be identified for the activities of firms.

**Factors of production:** Resources used to produce goods and services. There are three main factors: land, labour and capital (factories, machinery, etc.), though microeconomic analysis frequently utilises a two-dimensional framework containing labour and capital for simplicity.

**Fixed factor:** A factor of production whose input is assumed to be fixed in the short term. Usually this is assumed to be capital. In the long term, there is no need to make such a distinction since all factors of production can be assumed to vary (see **Variable factor**).

**Free-rider problem:** Arises when some consumers of public goods (see below) do not reveal the full extent of their preference in the hope that others will pay for them.

**Gross domestic product:** The value of total output within an economy over a given time period. Output may be by foreign-owned producers as well as domestic ones.

**Identification problem:** A problem which arises when trying to derive a single demand and/or supply curve (under the *ceteris paribus* assumption) using time-series data, when in reality the demand/supply curves are shifting around with time.

**Income effect:** The change in quantity demanded brought about by a change in real income (see below).

**Income elasticity of demand:** The measure of responsiveness of quantity demanded to changes in consumers' income. Normal goods (see below) will be associated with positive income elasticities whereas inferior goods (see below) lead to negative income elasticities.

**Independent variable:** A variable whose value determines the value taken by another (dependent) variable.

**Indifference curve:** A line which shows all the combinations of goods and services which provide equal levels of satisfaction (utility) to the consumer. Although they can be drawn three dimensionally to depict three goods, they are typically drawn with reference to two goods.

**Inferior good:** A good or service which consumers buy less of as their income rises (opposite to a normal good).

**Inflation:** An increase in the general price level which results in a reduction in the purchasing power of a given amount of money.

**Intermediate goods:** Goods and services which are themselves inputs into further productive processes.

**Isocost line:** A line which depicts all the factor combinations which can be bought by a firm for the same level of total expenditure.

**Isoquant:** A line which identifies the minimum factor combinations (usually capital and labour) which can be used to produce a given quantity of output. In theory, isoquants are drawn smooth and convex to the origin, implying that there are a wide range of efficient factor combinations which can be used to produce a given output. In reality, technological constraints may mean that only a handful of efficient combinations exist. The optimal factor combination on the isoquant may be determined with reference to the firm's isocost line (see above).

**Labour intensive production:** A process which uses large quantities of labour relative to capital inputs.

**Macroeconomics:** The study of economic aggregates such as the price level, unemployment, economic growth, balance of payments and so on.

**Managerial theories of the firm:** A set of theories which emphasise the willingness and ability of managers (as opposed to owners) to play a role in determining the values of other variables under their control rather than specifically aiming to maximise profit. Examples include sales revenue or their own personal utility functions.

**Marginal benefit:** The increase in total benefits enjoyed by an individual after consuming one extra unit of a particular commodity.

**Marginal cost:** The increase in a firm's total costs brought about by increasing production by one extra unit or the cost incurred by an individual from consuming an extra unit of a product.

**Marginal revenue:** The increase in a firm's total revenue brought about by increasing production by one extra unit.

**Market:** Markets are formed when buyers and sellers meet in order to trade. The location need not be defined in a geographical sense and may simply take place over the telephone or through the post.

**Merit bad:** A good or service which, although not necessarily banned, a 'paternalist' society deems to be undesirable and therefore discourages consumption through prohibitive taxation, restriction and advisory programmes. An example would be tobacco.

**Merit good:** A good or service which a 'paternalist' society deems to be desirable and therefore encourages its consumption through subsidy and or promotional programmes. An example would be keeping fit.

**Microeconomics:** The study of individual decision-making units, for example consumers, households or firms.

**Minimum efficient scale:** The lowest level of output at which long-run average costs are minimised.

**Model:** A theoretical set of relationships (usually simplified) which attempts to capture the key features of real world economic processes.

**Monetarism:** An economic doctrine which stresses the importance of monetary phenomena in determining economic activity in an economy.

**Money supply:** The total amount of money available in an economy. In recent years, governments have used both 'narrow' and 'broad' measures of the money supply which reflect the degree to which financial securities can be readily converted into money.

**Monopolistic competition:** A market structure in which there are many firms but the products each produces are slightly differentiated enabling each firm to exert some control over price. A similar situation arises if each firm enjoys a degree of geographical isolation from its competitors.

**Monopoly:** In theory, this arises when an industry is in control of a single producer. In practice, references to monopoly are more pragmatic and embrace both duopolistic and oligopolistic market structures.

**Multiplier effect:** When an injection of expenditure into an economy leads to an increase in national income in excess of the original injection.

**Normal good:** A good or service which consumers buy more of as their income rises (opposite to an inferior good).

**Normal profit:** That level of profit which just induces an entrepreneur to remain in his or her present activity.

**Normative economics:** Economic statements based on value judgements, for example, what ought to happen.

**Oligopoly:** An industry which contains a small number of firms.

**Ordinal measurement:** Measurement which emphasises the ranking of items rather than the numerical difference between them. Thus we would say that '*A* is greater than *B*' rather than by how much. This principle underpins the derivation of indifference curves.

**Organisational slack:** Payments made by firms in order to contain potential conflict which may arise from the existence of different interest groups existing within a firm.

**Perfect competition:** A market structure containing numerous small firms (atomistic). Their size necessitates them to be price-takers and there is freedom of entry and exit into the industry.

**Positive economics:** Economics which is concerned with developing empirically testable hypotheses (which can be accepted or refuted using appropriate evidence).

**Price discrimination:** When a firm sells different units of a product at different prices for reasons other than cost differences. For example, a leisure centre charging different prices for peak and off-peak facility use.

**Price elasticity of demand:** The measure of responsiveness of quantity demanded to changes in the own price of a good or service. Technically, price elasticity calculations should almost always produce a negative figure since the relationship between quantity demanded and own price is invariably negative. Readers should be aware that some economists 'drop' the negative sign when reporting price elasticity of demand figures.

**Price elasticity of supply:** The measure of responsiveness of quantity supplied to changes in the own price of a good or service.

**Price-taker:** An economic agent which is in no position to influence the price of a commodity. In the case of perfect competition (see above), firms can change their level of output without affecting market price.

**Principal–agent problem:** Arises when a firm's manager(s) are able to pursue objectives in line with their own personal utility function rather than that of the firm's owner(s).

**Private benefit:** A benefit which accrues to an individual.

**Private cost:** A cost incurred by an individual.

**Private good:** A commodity which, if consumed by one person, cannot be subsequently consumed by another.

**Producer surplus:** The difference between the price at which a producer is willing and able to supply a unit of good or service and the price he or she actually receives.

**Production function:** Mathematically, it is an expression which identifies the maximum output which can be achieved from alternative input combinations. In introductory texts, production functions may simply identify the key variables within the equation without specifying their exact relationship.

**Public good:** A commodity which, if consumed by one person, can still be consumed by others (e.g. streetlighting). When all consumers can consume identical amounts of such a good, we say that it is a pure public good. Usually however, public goods fall into the category of quasi-public goods (see below).

**Public sector borrowing requirement:** The amount by which public expenditure exceeds revenue.

**Quasi-public good:** A commodity which has the main attributes of a public good (see above) but of which individuals do not necessarily receive the same quantity. For example, everyone is protected by their local fire or ambulance services but will receive different levels of service according to geographical location.

**Rationality:** An assumption often used in economic theory which assumes that decision-makers are fully informed about the consequences of their actions.

**Real income:** Income measured in terms of the goods and services it can be used to purchase.

**Returns to scale:** Term which refers to what happens to output when all inputs are changed by the same proportion. Returns to scale can be increasing, decreasing or constant. Thus, if a doubling of a firm's inputs leads to a trebling of output, then returns to scale are said to be increasing.

**Shadow price:** A price which economists ascribe to commodities which are not traded in markets. An example would be attempts to place a value on leisure time.

**Short run:** A time period in which certain factors of production cannot be varied, usually assumed to be capital.

**Social benefit:** Benefits which accrue to society as a whole, as well as the original decision-taker(s).

**Social cost:** Costs which are imposed on society as a whole as well as on the original decision-taker(s).

**Substitutes:** Substitute goods are those which are perceived as alternatives for each other, for example tea and coffee or bus travel and rail travel. To varying degrees we would expect the demand for one good to be positively related to price changes in a substitute good. For example, an increase in the price of coffee is likely to induce an increase in the demand for tea (*ceteris paribus*).

**Substitution effect:** The change in quantity demanded brought about by a change in a commodity's relative price when resulting changes in real income are supressed.

**Supernormal profit:** Profit over and above normal profit (see above).

**Supply curve:** The graphical relationship between what producers are willing and able to supply in a given period of time and the price of the commodity in question, *ceteris paribus*. As with the demand curve (see above), it is usual to measure price along the vertical (*y*) axis and quantity along the horizontal (*x*) axis.

**Supply function:** An expression which specifies the relationship between quantity supplied and the variables which can affect it (such as price, technology, etc.). Supply functions can be expressed as a mathematical relationship but introductory textbooks place more emphasis upon the identification of appropriate variables rather than the exact relationship between them.

**Total revenue:** The total amount of money that a firm receives from the sale of its output (price multiplied by quantity).

**Unaffordable set:** A term sometimes used in consumer theory referring to combinations of goods and services which an individual cannot afford with his or her present income.

**Unemployment:** There is no single satisfactory definition of unemployment. Distinctions are sometimes made between those people who wish to work and cannot get a job (involuntary unemployment) and those people who prefer leisure to working (voluntary unemployment).

**Utility:** The satisfaction or pleasure that an individual derives from consuming a good or service.

**Utility function:** An expression which contains all the information needed to estimate the utility an individual will derive from consuming one or more commodities. Utility functions can be specified mathematically but in introductory economics it is common to simply list the relevant variables in the function rather than define the exact relationship between them.

**Variable factor:** A factor of production whose level can vary in the short run. Usually, this is assumed to be labour. In the longer term, the distinction between fixed (see above) and variable factors is irrelevant.

**X-inefficiency:** Organisational and technical inefficiencies which prevent a firm maximising profit.

# Notes

## 1 ECONOMICS AND THE LEISURE ENVIRONMENT

1   These terms are used in a 1986 report produced for the Sports Council by the Henley Centre for Forecasting, *The Economic Impact and Importance of Sport in the UK*, pp. 29–30. Reference will be made to this publication later on in this chapter.

2   The Standard Industrial Classification (SIC) was introduced in 1948 to promote uniformity in official industrial statistics. Establishments are classified according to the type of economic activity in which they are engaged. However, revisions in the classification of headings has been made periodically in response to changes in the nature and emphasis of production. The 1992 revision is the fourth change which has taken place (previous revisions were in 1958, 1968 and 1980). Readers using statistics which incorporate the SIC system should ensure therefore that they are comparing like with like if data sets embrace two or more SIC periods. The main advantage of the new system, which will not be seen in publications until 1995 (due to the lead time which exists between the collection and publication of statistics), has almost 600 activity headings, as opposed to the 344 of the old 1980 SIC system.

3   The OPCS is a separate government department. As well as being responsible for undertaking the national census and overseeing the registration of births, deaths and marriages, it conducts surveys for other government departments and public bodies.

4   Other years include 1977, 1980, 1983, 1986, 1987 and 1990.

5   The 1987 *GHS* section on leisure is distinctive because it appears in a separate volume. This outlines the key differences between the methodology underlying pre-1987 and post-1987 surveys. Readers should consult this document if they intend to undertake a comparison which cuts across this watershed.

6   A new Leisure Day Visits Survey is now being compiled covering the period April 1991 to March 1992.

## 2 THE DEMAND FOR LEISURE

1   The term *ceteris paribus* is taken from Latin and means 'other things being equal'.

2   Some textbooks refer to the total effect as the *price effect*, reflecting the fact that we are analysing the effects of changes in relative prices.

3   This outcome is consistent with the results derived previously when a fall in the price of one good not only makes it possible for more of that good to be bought, but also increases a consumer's general purchasing power with respect to other goods (assuming incomes remain fixed).

4   Although correct, this statement seems to contradict the 'rules' offered in many introductory texts with respect to the direction of income and substitution effects. This simply reflects the type of example being used here.

## 3   ESTIMATING DEMAND AND THE MARKET FOR LEISURE ACTIVITIES

1   The technique was originally recommended by Harold Hotelling in a letter to the United States Park Service in 1949 though it gained its popularity through the work of Marion Clawson.

2   It can be argued that this is a very strong assumption to employ. Strict homogeneity between catchment populations will rarely, if ever, be encountered. Thus, if the results from a travel cost exercise are to be meaningful, the researcher will need to be satisfied that zonal populations do not differ significantly with respect to their tastes and preferences.

3   As most readers will have learned through bitter experience, they are more likely to make an 'irrational' decision when purchasing from adverts. Although mail-order catalogues carry money-back guarantees, there are the additional personal costs associated with returning unwanted items.

## 4   MARKET FAILURE IN LEISURE

1   Although the term was first coined by the Council of Europe in 1966, the basic concept was already established, particularly in Nordic countries.

2   One of the pioneering studies to establish a link between exercise and health was undertaken by Morris *et al.* (1953, 1965). It was found that highly active conductors on London buses stood less risk of a heart attack than drivers, who were sitting regularly at the wheel.

3   Indeed, we could argue that these costs are also imposed upon people throughout society since sports injuries divert medical resources away from other specialties within the health service, thereby contributing to waiting lists which exist for other, non-sport-related, medical treatment.

4   Although there are individuals who do not agree with the way in which their nation is defended from external attack, such as whether or not to have nuclear weapons, the population will receive broadly the same amounts of protection from the chosen system of national defence.

5   The Countryside Commission replaced the National Parks Commission which had been established in 1949.

6   In 1978 the Sports Council had revised its original targets downwards to take account of lower than expected population increases.

## 5    ELASTICITY AND THE PRICING OF LEISURE FACILITIES

1    For example, 10 per cent divided by 2 per cent equals 5 not 5 per cent.

2    If the demand curve is not a straight line, for example if the equation contains an additional squared term, then we would need the specific gradient of the demand curve as it applies to the point at which the analysis is being undertaken. Students familiar with calculus will recognise the need to take the general equation and calculate the differential of $Q$ with respect to $P$ in order to derive the gradient. However, for the purposes of this text we shall ignore such situations.

3    On some occasions, researchers discover that a given set of data is more suited to a non-linear demand curve. If this takes the form of a *rectangular hyperbola*, which has a convex-to-the-origin shape akin to an indifference curve, it can be shown that price elasticity of demand remains constant throughout its entire length. The result is that regardless of the price charged for the product in question, the level of consumer expenditure will remain constant.

4    For the equation $Q = 50 - P$, the price elasticity calculation is $-2 \times 8/34 = -16/34 = -0.47$ whereas for the equation $Q = 20 - 2P$ the appropriate figures are $-2 \times 8/4 = -16/4 = -4$.

5    Many of the issues which relate to how market structure and the cost structure of a firm affects price and output will be addressed more precisely in Chapter 7. The points made in this context so far reflect intuitive rather than technical understanding.

## 6    PRODUCTION AND COSTS

1    Early North American examples include G. Scully (1974) 'Pay and Performance in Major League Baseball', *American Economic Review*, vol. 64, pp. 915–30, and C. Zech (1981) 'An Empirical Estimation of a Production Function: the Case of Major League Baseball', *American Economist*, vol. 25, pp. 19–33.

2    Research based upon the English game can be seen in J. Scofield (1988), 'Production Functions in the Sport Industry: an Empirical Analysis of Professional Cricket', *Applied Economics*, vol. 20, pp. 177–93.

3    Genuine 'all rounders' are cricketers who are capable of meriting a team place on the basis of their batting *or* their bowling. A recent example would be Ian Botham who, despite being the third leading test wicket taker of all time, is probably best remembered for his batting exploits (with over 5,000 test runs to his name). Other examples include Sir Garfield Sobers (West Indies) and Keith Miller (Australia). Since the advent of the one-day game, the term 'all rounder' is applied more loosely, extending to batsmen who can bowl and bowlers who can bat.

4    Readers should also be clear about the distinction between the terms *economies of scale* and *returns to scale*. Returns to scale refers to changes in *physical output* as factor inputs are increased proportionately. In contrast, economies of scale refers to changes in the *money cost* of production. As noted earlier, the two are directly related such that a firm experiencing increasing returns to scale will be simultaneously enjoying economies of scale.

## 7  BUSINESS OBJECTIVES

1    The pioneering empirical work on the subject was undertaken by Berle and Means (1934) who argued that 44 per cent of large firms in the US were 'manager controlled'. However, their assumption that owner control can only be exerted with 20 per cent or more of shares has been deemed too high in the subsequent literature. A reduced figure of 10 per cent was adopted by Larner (1966) while Nyman and Silberstone used a figure of 5 per cent. In the case of Larner's study, it was argued that 85 per cent of US firms were subject to managerial control, while in a UK study Nyman and Silberstone suggested 56 per cent of firms were owner controlled. A more detailed insight into these studies can be found in Griffiths and Wall (1993).

2    The term Prisoners' Dilemma has its origins in the choices facing two prisoners sitting in separate interview rooms at a police station deciding whether or not to plead guilty to an offence of which they are accused (and guilty). If both stay silent, a minor sentence will follow. If one person implicates the other, he or she can walk free while the co-accused faces a heavy prison sentence. If both are implicated, both receive heavy prison sentences. Overall, the best outcome is for both to remain silent. However, the temptation for each suspect to incriminate the other is high (since prison is avoided), leading to mutual distrust and a heavy sentence for both.

3    In the case of the diagram, this position is explicit since the marginal revenue and marginal cost curves only intersect at one point. As noted earlier in this chapter, had they intersected twice, then we would take that level of output where the marginal cost curve cut the marginal revenue curve from below.

4    A clear and detailed explanation of the 'rise and fall' of the reserve clause can be found in Leftwich and Ekert (1985, pp. 507–17).

## 8  PRIVATISATION AND THE LEISURE INDUSTRY

1    Which had culminated in his now famous book of 1936 *General Theory of Employment, Interest and Money*, London: Macmillan.

2    The advent of Keynesian economics saw the 'involuntary' unemployed (who may be defined as people who want jobs) divided into two categories: labour which could be brought into employment by policies designed to raise aggregate demand and labour which could not. This latter category includes workers who are structurally unemployed (due to a decline in demand for products of a specific industry, such as coal), the seasonally unemployed, the frictionally unemployed (individuals in the process of changing jobs) and the unemployable (for example the most severely handicapped). The remainder, often referred to as the cyclically unemployed, is the labour force which is targeted by Keynesian policy since their unemployment arises from a general downswing in the economy.

3    An over-valued pound was partly to blame for the economic difficulties faced by the UK during the 1920s.

4    State intervention in the leisure sector extends back to Victorian times, for example, the Public Baths and Washrooms Act (1846). However, the motive behind this legislation reflected a desire to contain disease amongst the

working class (encouraging them to bathe in disinfected water) rather than to promote swimming *per se*. The early twentieth century saw recreational open space defined as a distinct category of land in the Town Planning Act of 1909. More explicit leisure-related intervention can be seen in the establishment of the Forestry Commission (1919), the first governmental body to be given a statutory duty to provide for recreation, and the Physical Training and Recreation Act (1937). The latter, though a response to the potentially destablising effects of unemployment and the growth of Fascism, led to a sum of £2 million being made available for recreation based initiatives. We should also not forget the establishment of the British Broadcasting Corporation (BBC) which was to play a major role in the way in which people spent their leisure time.

5    The degree to which government expenditure exceeds its income.

6    An excess of imports over exports will place a downward pressure on the value of a nation's currency. In a system of freely floating exchange rates, the value of the currency may reach a new (lower) value against other currencies. When exchange rates are fixed, governments of countries with weak (strong) currencies are obliged to intervene in the market and buy (sell) their own currency, thereby countering the pressures placed upon it within the international money markets.

7    If foreign speculators believed that sterling would be devalued and therefore be of less value against other currencies, they would sell some or all of their holdings of sterling and buy other currencies instead. This would place further pressure on sterling since there would be an excess supply of it in world currency markets. Government desire not to devalue it and therefore to protect sterling at all costs reflected sterling's role as a reserve currency for international trade and a belief in government circles that a devaluation was a sign of economic failure.

8    Indeed, having been constant at 2 per cent between 1932 and 1951, the bank rate was changed 24 times between 1951 and 1964 with a peak of 7 per cent in 1957. Such changes are highly detrimental to industry since they can lead to a high degree of uncertainty.

9    For example rock and roll.

10    The Report was also commissioned to consider reasons for the UK's poor Olympic record.

11    This relation is referred to by economists as the 'Phillips Curve'. The statistical inverse relationship between inflation and unemployment was, as its name suggests, identified by Professor A.W. Phillips in 1958 and implied that low unemployment could only be achieved at the cost of higher rates of inflation. Towards the end of the 1960s, this inverse relationship began to break down as inflation and unemployment began to rise simultaneously. The precise relationship between inflation and unemployment is one which continues to interest economists throughout the world.

12    Subsequently known as the 'Barber Boom' after the then Chancellor of the Exchequer, Anthony Barber.

13    By 1972, the fixed system of exchange rates which had constrained policy-makers throughout the 1950s and 1960s had collapsed and was replaced by a system of freely floating exchange rates.

14    It was hoped that economic agents would attach more credibility to the

policy if it was backed by statements of intention.

15   Gross domestic product (GDP) is a measure of the value of economic activity taking place in a country. Variables, such as government spending and the PSBR, are often expressed as a percentage of GDP to provide a means of comparison between years or between countries.

16   PSL stands for 'public sector liquidity'.

17   The non-inclusion of building society deposits within money supply definitions prior to 1986 was part of the reason why the government found it so difficult to keep to its money supply targets. When the new aggregate M4 was introduced, which included building society deposits, the fluctuations caused by economic agents switching between banks and building societies was removed.

18   Also in a series of working papers.

19   This taxonomy follows that contained in Parker (1990).

20   Some readers may already be aware of franchise operations in the supply of many brands of take-away food, for example McDonalds.

# References

Anthony, D. (1980), *A Strategy for British Sport*, London: C. Hurst.

Audit Commission (1989), *Sport For Whom?*, London: HMSO.

Audit Commission (1990), *Local Authority Support for Sport*, London: HMSO.

Bacon, R. and Eltis, W. (1976), *Britain's Economic Problems: Too Few Producers*, London: Macmillan.

Bairam, E., Howells, J. and Turner, G. (1990), 'Production Functions in Cricket: the Australian and New Zealand Experience', *Applied Economics*, vol. 22, pp. 871–9.

Baty, S. and Richards, S. (1991), 'Results from the Leisure Day Visits Survey 1988–89', *Employment Gazette*, May, pp. 257–68.

Bird, P. (1982), 'The Demand for League Football', *Applied Economics*, vol. 14, pp. 637–49.

Bishop, R. and Heberlein, T. (1979), 'Measuring Values of Extra Market Goods: Are Indirect Measures Biased?', *American Journal of Agricultural Economics*, vol. 61, pp. 926–30.

Burgess, J. (1991), 'Economics of CCT: Part II', *Leisure Management*, April, pp. 58–9.

Butson, P. (1983) *The Financing of Sport in the UK*, Sports Council Information Services no. 8, London: Sports Council.

Cairns, J., Jennett, N. and Sloane, P. (1986), 'The Economics of Professional Team Sports: a Survey of Theory and Evidence', *Journal of Economic Studies*, vol. 13, pp. 3–80.

Central Statistical Office (1992), *Standard Industrial Classification of Economic Activities 1992*, London: HMSO.

Central Statistical Office (1993), *Social Trends 1993*, London: HMSO.

Cesario, F. and Knetsch (1976), 'A Recreation Site and Benefit Estimation Model', *Regional Studies*, vol. 10, pp. 97–104.

Chapman, D., Tyrell, T. and Mount, T. (1972), 'Electricity Demand Growth and the Energy Crisis', *Science*, 17 November, p. 705.

Chartered Institute of Public Finance and Accountancy (1993), *Charges for Leisure Services Statistics*, London: CIPFA.

Chartered Institute of Public Finance and Accountancy (1993), *Leisure and Recreation Statistics*, London: CIPFA.

Chartered Institute of Public Finance and Accountancy (1993), *Leisure Usage Statistics*, London: CIPFA.

Clawson, M. (1959), *Methods of Measuring the Demand for and Value of Outdoor Recreation*, Washington: Resources for the Future Inc.

Clawson, M. and Knetsch, J. (1966), *The Economics of Outdoor Recreation*, Baltimore: Johns Hopkins University Press.

Cooke, A. (1993), 'Deriving Leisure Time Values for Visitors to Urban Sports Centres', *Leisure Studies*, vol. 12, pp. 2221–31.

Craig, S. (1992), 'Competition versus Quality', *Leisure Management*, July, pp. 24–5.

Deaton, A. (1975), *Models and Projections of Demand in Postwar Britain*, London: Chapman & Hall.

Department of the Environment (1965), *A Policy for the Arts: The First Steps*, London: HMSO.

Department of the Environment (1968), *Leisure in the Countryside*, London: HMSO.

Department of the Environment (1975), *Sport and Recreation*, London: HMSO.

Department of the Environment (1977), *Policy for Inner Cities*, London: HMSO.

Department of the Environment (1988), *Sport and Active Recreation Provision in the Inner Cities*, London: HMSO.

Department of the Environment, Audit Inspectorate (1983), *Development and Operation of Leisure Centres*, London: HMSO.

Department of Health (1989), *Working for Patients*, London: HMSO.

Department of Health and Social Security (1977), *Prevention and Health*, London: HMSO.

Department of National Heritage (1993), *Annual Report 1993, the Government's Expenditure Plans 1993–94 to 1995–96*, London: HMSO.

Department of Transport (1987), *Values for Journey Time Saving*, London: HMSO.

Dobson, S. and Goddard, J. (1992), 'The Demand for Standing and Seated Viewing Accommodation in the English League', *Applied Economics*, vol. 24, pp. 1155–64.

Fentem, P. and Bassey, E. (1978), *The Case For Exercise*, London: Sports Council.

Football Trust (1992), *Digest of Football Statistics*, London: Football Trust.

Gratton, C. and Taylor, P. (1985), *Sport and Recreation: An Economic Analysis*, London: E. & F.N. Spon.

Gratton, C. and Taylor, P. (1988), *Economics of Leisure Services Management*, Essex: Longman.

Gratton, C. and Taylor, P. (1991), 'Economics of CCT: Part I', *Leisure Management*, April, pp. 54–6.

Griffiths, A. and Wall, S. (1993), *Applied Economics: An Introductory Course*, 5th edn, London: Longman.

Haywood, L., Kew, F. and Bramham, P. (1989), *Understanding Leisure*, London: Hutchinson.

Heald, D. (1983), *Public Expenditure*, Oxford: Martin Robertson.

Henry, I. (ed.) (1990), *Management and Planning in the Leisure Industries*, London: Macmillan.

Hobsbawm, E.J. (1978), *Industry and Empire*, Harmondsworth, Middx: Penguin.

Hoggett, P. and Bishop, J. (1986), *The Social Organisation of Leisure: A Study of Groups in Their Voluntary Context*, London: Sports Council/ESRC.

Holmes, E. (1991), 'Fit to Win?', *Leisure Management*, April, pp. 60–1.

Johnson, C. (1990), 'Pool Resources', *Leisure Management*, Sept., pp. 22–4.

Jones, T. (1993), 'Dissecting CCT', *Leisure Management*, May, pp. 24–5.

Leftwich, R. and Ekert, R. (1985), *The Price System and Resource Allocation*, New York: Dryden Press.

Leisure Futures Ltd (1993), *Has CCT Led to Better Services?*, London: Institute of Leisure and Amenity Management (ILAM).

*Leisure Management* (1992), 'CCT: The Story So Far', *Leisure Management*, May, pp. 26–7.

Marchand, J. (1990), *Sport for All in Europe*, London: HMSO.

Matheson, J. (1987), *Participation in Sport*, supplement to the *1987 General Household Survey*, London: HMSO.

McGuirk, T. (1991), 'In-house or Out-of-house?', *Leisure Management*, June, pp. 42–4.

McLatchie, G. (1986), *Essentials of Sports Medicine*, London: Churchill Livingstone.

Milne, R. and McGee, M. (1992), 'Compulsory Competitive Tendering in the NHS: a New Look at Some Old Estimates', *Fiscal Studies*, vol. 13 no. 3, pp. 96–111.

Mintel (1991), 'Business of Playing Golf in the UK', in *Leisure Intelligence*, vol. 2, London: Mintel International Group Ltd.

Mintel (1992), 'Leisure Centres', in *Leisure Intelligence*, vol. 2, London: Mintel International Group Ltd.

Morris, J., Heady, J., Raffle, P., Roberts, C. and Parks, J. (1953), 'Coronary Heart Disease and Physical Activity of Work', *Lancet*, vol. 2, pp. 1053–7 and 1111–20.

Morris, J., Kagan, A., Pattison, D., Gardner, M. and Raffle, P. (1965), 'Incidence and Prediction of Ischaemic Heart Disease in London Busmen', *Lancet*, vol. 2, pp. 553–9.

Office of Population Censuses and Surveys (various years), *General Household Survey*, London: HMSO.

Parker, D. (1990), 'The 1988 Local Government Act and Compulsory Competitive Tendering', *Urban Studies*, vol. 27, no. 5, pp. 653–68.

Prais, S. and Houthakker, H. (1955), *The Analysis of Family Budgets*, Cambridge: Cambridge University Press.

Pratten, C. (1971), *Economies of Scale in Manufacturing Industry*, Cambridge: Cambridge University Press.

Ravenscroft, N. (1993), 'Public Leisure Provision and the Good Citizen', *Leisure Studies*, vol. 12, pp. 33–44.

Robinson, D. (1986), *Monetarism and the Labour Market*, Oxford: Clarendon Press.

Rottenberg, S. (1956), 'The Baseball Players' Labour Market', *Journal of Political Economy*, vol. 64, pp. 243–58.

Scarman, Lord (1981), *The British Disorders, 10–12 April 1981*, London: HMSO.

Scottish Sports Council (1979), *A Question of Balance*, Edinburgh: Scottish Sports Council.

Smith, T. (1989), 'Competition in the Sports Field', *Public Finance and Accountancy*, 6 October, pp. 11–12.

Sports Council (1982), *Sport in the Community: The Next Ten Years*, London: Sports Council.

Sports Council (1986), *The Economic Impact and Importance of Sport in the UK*, London: Sports Council.

Sports Council (1988), *Sport in the Community: Into the 1990s*, London: Sports Council.

Sports Council (1991), *A Digest of Sports Statistics for the UK*, London: Sports Council.

Sports Council/Henley Centre for Forecasting (1992), *The Economic Impact of Sport in the United Kingdom in 1990*, London: Sports Council.

Szymanski, S. (1993), 'The Economics of Footballing Success', *Economic Review*, April, pp. 14–18.

Tatem, H. (1988), 'Is There a Case for the Injured Sportsperson?', unpublished report, Nottingham: Nottingham School of Nursing.

Thomas, K. (1991), 'CCT: Round One', *Leisure Management*, March, pp. 46–7.

Torkildsen, G. (1992), *Leisure and Recreation Management*, 3rd edn, London: E. & F.N. Spon.

Whitehouse, J. and Gerlach, R. (1991), 'What Price Leisure?', *Public Finance and Accountancy*, 29 March, pp. 9–11.

Wolfenden Committee on Sport (1960), *Sport and the Community*, London: Central Council for Physical Recreation.

# Index